FAILURES OF THE PRESIDENTS

FAILURES OF THE PRESIDENTS

FROM THE WHISKEY REBELLION AND WAR OF 1812 TO THE BAY OF PIGS AND WAR IN IRAQ

THOMAS J. CRAUGHWELL
WITH M. WILLIAM PHELPS

FAIR WINDS
PRESS
BEVERLY, MASSACHUSETTS

Text © 2008 Thomas J. Craughwell

First published in the USA in 2008 by
Fair Winds Press, a member of
Quayside Publishing Group
100 Cummings Center
Suite 406-L
Beverly, MA 01915-6101
www.fairwindspress.com

12 11 10 09 08   1 2 3 4 5

ISBN-13: 978-1-59233-299-1
ISBN-10: 1-59233-299-4

Library of Congress Cataloging-in-Publication Data
Craughwell, Thomas J., 1956-
  Failures of the presidents : from the Whiskey Rebellion to the War of 1812 to the Bay of Pigs to the Iran-Contra Affair / Thomas J. Craughwell with M. William Phelps.
     p. cm.
  Includes bibliographical references and index.
  ISBN-13: 978-1-59233-299-1
  ISBN-10: 1-59233-299-4
  1. Presidents--United States--History. 2. Presidents--United States--Decision making--Case studies. 3. United States--Politics and government--Case studies. 4. United States--Foreign relations--Case studies. 5. Political leadership--United States--Case studies. 6. Executive power--United States--Case studies. I. Phelps, M. William. II. Title.
  E176.1.C88 2008
  973.09'9--dc22
                                         2008012637

Contributing writers: Thomas J. Craughwell (Introduction, Washington, Adams, Jefferson, Madison, Jackson, Pierce, Grant, Hoover, Kennedy), Kevin Dwyer (Nixon [Cambodia], Carter), Edwin Kiester (McKinley, Bush), Mark LaFlaur (Roosevelt, Reagan), M. William Phelps (Cleveland, Wilson, Johnson, Nixon [Watergate])

Cover and book design: Peter Long

Printed and bound in Singapore

CONTENTS

INTRODUCTION

CHANGING VIEWS

OF PRESIDENTIAL SUCCESS AND FAILURE

UNTIL RECENTLY, THE ROMAN CATHOLIC CHURCH WAITED FIFTY YEARS AFTER THE death of a candidate for sainthood before beginning the investigation into his or her life and merits. Centuries of experience had taught the Vatican that when someone with a reputation for holiness dies, a great emotional outburst naturally follows, as happened with the death of Pope John Paul II. But wait fifty years, and all the hysteria as well as the hyperbole will have settled down, and the men whose job it is to examine the lives of potential saints can go about their business like scholars—in a judicious, methodical, and rational manner.

Something similar happens when an American president leaves office, or leaves this world. Washington correspondents, political pundits, and cable news commentators vie with one another to make the most sweeping statements—and quotable sound bites—about the success or failure of the former president's administration. It can't be helped; the format of twenty-four-hour news coverage demands on-the-spot assessments, and then assessments of the assessments.

But as with sorting out saints, weighing the successes and failures of a presidency takes time. History will always have its say, but many years may pass before it speaks. Harry S. Truman is a classic case. He left the White House in 1953 in near disgrace with an approval rating down around 22 percent. Even president-elect Dwight D. Eisenhower snubbed Truman, at first refusing his

invitation to a pre-inaugural luncheon at the White House, then failing even to make the customary courtesy call on the outgoing president and first lady. Instead, the general sat in his car outside the White House, waiting for President Truman to come to him.

Twenty years later, Truman's reputation was reborn thanks to Merle Miller's popular book *Plain Speaking: An Oral Biography of Harry S. Truman*, published in 1974, followed the next year by the one-man show *Give 'em Hell, Harry!* Truman, once derided as Franklin D. Roosevelt's hapless successor, a man entirely out of his depth in post–World War II politics, was now hailed as a feisty, straight-talking man of the people who fought for his principles, and perhaps was ahead of his time. He urged Congress to pass a national health insurance program, saying, "The health of American children, like their education, should be recognized as a definite public responsibility." (Sadly, Truman's proposal was rejected, thanks in part to the American Medical Association, which campaigned against the program, claiming it was "socialized medicine" and calling the Truman administration "followers of the Moscow party line.")

Even Richard Nixon's reputation has been refurbished a bit. At the time of his resignation in August 1974, Nixon was one of the most intensely despised men in America. He was airlifted by helicopter off the White House lawn into

FOR MANY AMERICANS THE IMAGE OF THE SCORCHED WRECKAGE OF AN AMERICAN C-130, WHICH COLLIDED WITH A U.S. HELICOPTER DURING A FAILED MISSION TO RESCUE HOSTAGES IN IRAN IN 1980, REMAINS A BRUTAL REMINDER OF THIS JIMMY CARTER FOREIGN POLICY FAILURE.

political exile; by and large he kept out of the public spotlight, although he was a prolific writer of memoirs and many books on foreign policy (*The Memoirs of Richard Nixon, Beyond Peace, In the Arena*, etc.). In recent years, however, historians have reminded us of Nixon's support for environmental protection (he founded the Environmental Protection Agency in 1970) and his call for universal health care. It's not enough to obliterate the stigma of the Watergate debacle, but after the passage of decades, some of his accomplishments mitigate the well-worn impression of Nixon as a complete ogre.

Readers who scan this book's table of contents may wonder what happened to the chapter about Bill Clinton's impeachment and his scandalous relations with Monica Lewinsky and other women.

The Clinton sex scandals and the charges of perjury and obstruction of justice were tawdry, they were a national embarrassment, and they were a major distraction from the nation's business, but my coauthors and I, along with our editors, could not agree definitively that the Clinton scandals, for all the "sound and fury" that came with them, actually inflicted serious damage on the United States at the time. It could be argued that had he not been distracted by the scandals and the impeachment, Clinton might have been able to broker a peace treaty between Israel and the Palestinians that could have prevented the Second Intifada of 2000. The suggestion makes for an interesting discussion, but in the end, such discussions are hypothetical.

GROVER CLEVELAND'S DECISION TO SEND IN MILITARY FORCES TO QUELL THE PULLMAN LABOR STRIKE IN 1894 SPARKED RIOTS AND ULTIMATELY STAINED HIS LEGACY WITH AMERICAN BLOOD.

Finally, a word about our method. We are not out to "bash" any president, nor do we seek to canonize any saints. Our goal has been to "get inside their heads," to review the circumstances they faced, consider their options, and understand their motives for acting as they did. Some of their motivations may make us cringe, but it is important nonetheless to try to understand a president's rationale for sending the U.S. Army against rebellious backwoodsmen in Pennsylvania, for example, or rounding up southeastern Indian tribes who had tried to assimilate into American society and marching them off to Oklahoma.

Our hope is that readers will come away from this book with a finer appreciation of some of the most formative, consequential predicaments that have faced American presidents since the nation's founding. We hope, too, that readers will feel some of the sympathetic understanding that historians owe to their subjects. In each chapter we have tried to be fair in presenting a human being in a set of circumstances where he has to make a choice based on the facts as he understands them, and upon the often conflicting views of advisers. His choice will very likely nudge history in one direction or another, but ultimately he cannot know what the consequences of his decision will be.

ALTHOUGH THE POLITICAL CONSEQUENCES OF INTERNING 120,000 JAPANESE AMERICANS AFTER THE BOMBING OF PEARL HARBOR IN 1941 WERE SLIGHT TO NIL FOR FRANKLIN D. ROOSEVELT, THE DECISION IS AN INDELIBLE STAIN ON THE UNITED STATES' REPUTATION FOR PROTECTING CIVIL RIGHTS.

CHAPTER I

THE WHISKEY REBELLION

GEORGE WASHINGTON

AT DAWN ON JULY 16, 1794, JOHN NEVILLE, SIXTY-THREE YEARS OLD, CLIMBED out of bed and began to dress. His preparations for a new day, however, were interrupted by the noise of a large crowd gathering outside his house. A veteran of the American Revolution in which he had risen to the rank of brigadier general, Neville was one of the wealthiest men in the western counties of Pennsylvania. His estate, Bower Hill, in the Chartier Valley outside of Pittsburgh, extended over more than a thousand acres. In addition, Neville owned eighteen slaves, ten horses, sixteen head of cattle, and twenty-three sheep. He also drew a salary as the region's inspector for the collection of a federal tax on whiskey and all other distilled spirits.

The men who stood outside General Neville's door were not wealthy. Few, if any, in the crowd owned more than a hundred acres of farmland. Most had little or no cash; they used the whiskey they distilled on their farms to barter for the necessities they could not produce themselves. The government's new ten-cent tax on every gallon of whiskey hit these men hard, and so they refused to pay it.

The day before, Neville had acted as guide for a federal marshal, David Lenox, who had come into the country to serve writs on backwoodsmen who were delinquent in paying the whiskey tax. Some of the men outside Neville's house had been served, and they were angry about it. Standing at his threshold, Neville demanded to know what the crowd wanted. They said they wanted

Lenox to come to them. They said Lenox's life was in danger, and they had come to protect him. Neville didn't believe a word of it, and besides, Marshal Lenox was not there. The general ordered the crowd off his property, and when they refused to go, he grabbed his gun and fired into the mob. A musket ball struck and killed one of the crowd's leaders, Oliver Miller. As Miller fell, the mob raised their own muskets and fired on the house. Neville slammed the door shut and bolted it, then seized a signal horn and gave a long, strong blast. Suddenly, the crowd's flank was raked by repeated shotgun blasts from the slave quarters. Neville's slaves had armed themselves and were fighting for their master. The mob stood their ground for another twenty-five minutes, firing at the main house and the slave quarters, but after six of their men lay wounded on the ground, the backwoodsmen lifted their injured companions, picked up Miller's body, and retreated.

The clapboards of Neville's house were pockmarked with bullet holes, but no one inside had been injured. Nonetheless, the general expected the mob would be back and with a larger force. He sent a note to his son, Presley Neville, in Pittsburgh with instructions to bring the militia immediately to help defend Bower Hill.

A LITTLE HORSE TRADING At the end of the American Revolution in

1783, the thirteen states and the Congress owed money to foreign governments, such as France, that had helped finance the war, as well as to a host of Americans who had sold horses, provisions, and other supplies to the Continental Army. Initially, each state struggled to meet its financial obligations on its own, but by 1790 it was evident that servicing the debt was crippling local economies. Treasury Secretary Alexander Hamilton proposed that the federal government make itself responsible for the states' debts. If consolidated with the national debt, they would total $80 million (approximately $1.820 billion in modern money).

To pay off the enormous liability, Hamilton insisted that taxes would have to rise. Hamilton's political adversary, Thomas Jefferson, was an inveterate opponent of taxes, but he agreed to support the proposal because he recognized the need to generate income that would retire the national debt. But as a good politician, Jefferson also indulged in a little horse trading: In return for his support for Hamilton's tax plan, Jefferson wanted Hamilton to support a proposal to relocate the national capital from Philadelphia to one of the southern states. Hamilton agreed, and they had a deal.

In December 1790, Hamilton released his report on the finances of the national government. He projected that given current levels of income and expenditures—particularly now that the national government had assumed responsibility of the states' debts—the federal budget in 1791 would see a short-fall of $826,624.73. In other words, the federal government would be more deeply in debt in 1791 than it was in 1790. If the government placed an excise tax on domestically produced spirits, however, Hamilton projected that in 1791 the government would take in $975,000, thus keeping it safely in the black.

The kind of tax Hamilton had in mind is called an excise. The word comes from an archaic term meaning *inland* or *interior* because it refers to taxes levied on goods produced within the country as opposed to taxes levied on imported foreign goods. An excise tax is collected either at the point where the product is manufactured, when it is sold to a distributor, or when it is sold to a consumer. Excise taxes had a long history in both Great Britain and America, and consumers and shopkeepers had always loathed them. In 1643, when the English Parliament placed an excise on beer and beef, mobs led by outraged butchers rioted in the streets. After the adoption of the U.S. Constitution in 1787, a group known as Anti-Federalists, political watchdogs who feared the new federal government would overwhelm state and local governments and infringe on the liberties of the people, predicted that American voters would regret the day they had ratified a Constitution that gave the national government the power to assess and collect excise taxes.

The idea of taxing whiskey made President George Washington uneasy. He did not argue against the fundamental premise that the federal government must find ways to generate more revenue, but he worried that the independent, often volatile, people of the backcountry might refuse to pay an excise on whiskey. In order to get a sense of how the ordinary American voter would receive the tax, in the spring of 1791, Washington made a tour through western Virginia and western Pennsylvania, areas with large populations of frontiersmen. Unfortunately, the president did not penetrate very deeply into the backwoods, and the local government officials he met, naturally wanting to please the great war hero, assured the former general that once the necessity of the excise was explained to the people, they would pay it. Once Washington was back in Philadelphia, he went to Congress and persuaded the members to modify the excise legislation so that whiskey distillers could pay their tax in monthly installments rather than in one lump sum. Congress passed the legislation in 1791.

PRESIDENTIAL BRIEFING
(1732-1799)

• FIRST PRESIDENT OF THE
UNITED STATES OF AMERICA
(1789-97)

• BORN FEBRUARY 22, 1732,
IN WESTMORELAND COUNTY,
VIRGINIA

• DIED DECEMBER 14, 1799,
IN MOUNT VERNON, VIRGINIA

• MEMBER OF 1ST AND 2ND
CONTINENTAL CONGRESS
(1774, 1775)

• PRESIDED OVER
CONSTITUTIONAL
CONVENTION IN
PHILADELPHIA (1787)

• COMMANDER IN CHIEF
OF CONTINENTAL ARMY
(1775-83)

• ELECTED PRESIDENT 1789:
FIRST ACT WAS TO URGE
ADOPTION OF BILL OF RIGHTS;
FEDERALIZED MILITIA TO
QUELL WHISKEY REBELLION
(1794)

AS SECRETARY OF THE
TREASURY, ALEXANDER
HAMILTON WAS DETERMINED
TO PUT THE UNITED STATES
ON A SOUND FINANCIAL
BASIS. AS A STAUNCH
FEDERALIST, HE INSISTED
THAT THE FEDERAL
GOVERNMENT HAD THE
POWER TO COMPEL UNRULY
BACKWOODSMEN TO PAY
THEIR TAXES.

"UTOPIAN SCHEMES" In the summer of 1791, Robert Johnson had taken the job as the federal government's collector of the whiskey excise in Allegheny and Washington counties in western Pennsylvania. Johnson probably expected that he would not be a welcome visitor at many backcountry cabins, yet because he did not expect any serious trouble, when he went out to collect the tax money he rode alone.

On September 11, 1791, Johnson was at Pigeon Creek near Canonsburg in Washington County when eleven men dressed as women stepped out of the woods and surrounded him. It took all of the tax collector's courage not to panic when he saw the cauldron of hot tar and the sack of feathers. The men stripped Johnson naked, hacked off his hair, then tarred and feathered him. This grotesque form of mob justice involved pouring or painting hot tar on the victim's body, then dumping or rolling him in chicken feathers. The tar burned the skin, and it took days to peel it all off. When the men were finished, they took Johnson's horse and left him in the woods.

In spite of the mens' disguises, Johnson recognized two of his attackers. Once Johnson had recovered, he swore out complaints before a judge who issued arrest warrants for the suspects. In light of what had happened to Johnson, the deputy marshal was reluctant to serve the warrants himself; instead, he hired a cattle drover named John Connor to deliver the warrants. The gang that had attacked Johnson ambushed Connor, stripped him, flogged him, and tarred and feathered him. After pocketing Connor's money and taking his horse, the culprits left him tied to a tree in the forest where he passed five long hours screaming for help before some passerby wandered within earshot and came to his rescue.

That was enough for Johnson. He published a notice in the Pittsburgh *Gazette* that read, "Finding the opposition to the revenue law more violent than I expected … I think it my duty and do resign my commission."

Many settlers in the backcountry regarded the tax on whiskey as the last straw. For a century, they had petitioned the colonial and then the state legislatures for garrisons to protect them from the Indians and for surveyors to establish clear, legal boundaries on their land. The settlers had asked for fair play so that all of the best land would not go to land speculators back East, and they had asked for construction of roads and canals so they could get their produce to market. Invariably their petitions were ignored or rejected. During the Revolution, the frontiersmen tried a new tack, petitioning for independence, reasoning that as separate states they could form a government that would respond to their needs. The Continental Congress rejected this appeal, too, as the work of troublemakers and anarchists. John Adams dismissed such a petition from settlers in Kentucky as so many "utopian schemes."

Against this backdrop, the hostile reaction of the farmers in western Pennsylvania becomes comprehensible. Most of them were scraping by on farms of a hundred acres or less. Very few of these farms were anywhere near roads or navigable rivers that could take their grain crops to the markets of Philadelphia. Those farms that were near roads or rivers could not afford the freight charges that ranged from $5 to $10 per hundred pounds of grain. The farmers had found, however, that by distilling their grain into whiskey, they could load two eight-gallon kegs on a horse and walk to Philadelphia, where backcountry liquor sold for $1 a gallon. Now the federal government wanted them to pay a tax of ten cents on each gallon of whiskey they distilled.

Yet large distillers were taxed at a lower rate, and they could pass the cost of the excise tax on to their customers. The backwoods distillers could not easily push the added cost onto their neighboring customers, however, for they, too, were mostly cash-poor farmers and laborers. Because the frontier farmers kept a large percentage of the whiskey they distilled for their own consumption and used the surplus to barter for other goods, they felt that a disproportionate share of the tax burden was falling upon them.

They had a point. In New Hampshire, for example, where scarcely anyone had a still, the whiskey tax would have virtually no impact. But in western Pennsylvania, at least one farmer in five distilled his own whiskey. In 1783, when the Pennsylvania state legislature had tried to place a tax on whiskey, the westerners had forced the legislators to repeal the tax. Why should they not enjoy the same success against the federal government?

A FIRE AT BOWER HILL By the evening of July 16, the people of the backwoods were already describing the death of Miller outside the Neville house as murder. The men who had confronted Neville that morning were joined by many others in a nighttime meeting to discuss what they ought to do next. Someone, whose name was not recorded, proposed that "a sum of money [should] be raised and given to some ordinary persons to lie in wait and privately take the life of General Neville." This was voted down, but there was agreement to march on Neville's house again the next day and avenge Miller's death. Exactly how they would take their revenge was not specified.

Neville's appeal for men from the local militia to come help him defend his home was declined, but Major James Kirkpatrick and ten soldiers from nearby Fort Pitt volunteered to help defend Bower Hill. The troops were joined there by the general's son, Presley Neville, who, as expected, would fight for his home.

At 5 P.M the next day, July 17, between 500 and 700 frontiersmen, marching to the sound of drums, assembled before Bower Hill. John Neville was not there to see it because Major Kirkpatrick had already smuggled him out of the house and told him to lie low in a heavily forested ravine. The frontiersmen's new captain was James McFarlane, a former lieutenant in the American Revolution. Stepping forward under a flag of truce, McFarlane commanded Neville to come out and surrender the tax records. Kirkpatrick replied that Neville was not at home, but said he would permit six of McFarlane's men to search the house and confiscate whatever official documents they liked.

That was not good enough for McFarlane. He insisted that Kirkpatrick and the soldiers from Fort Pitt come out and lay down their arms. Kirkpatrick refused, saying he could see plainly that McFarlane and his men planned to destroy the Neville family's property. After this exchange, the frontiersmen surrounded the house, then set fire to a barn and one of the slave cabins. McFarlane made one final offer: He would give safe conduct to Mrs. Neville "and any other female part of the family" who wished to leave the house. Kirkpatrick accepted this offer, and the women of the house evacuated. Once the women were a safe distance from Bower Hill, the frontiersmen opened fire.

For more than an hour, the defenders and the frontiersmen blasted away at one another. Then McFarlane believed he heard someone inside the house call to him. He ordered his men to hold their fire, and, expecting that Major Kirkpatrick or Presley Neville was ready to agree to terms, he stepped out from behind the tree where he had taken cover during the gun battle. Several shots rang out from the house, and McFarlane fell dead.

To the frontiersmen, it appeared to have been a cowardly trick, and they avenged their captain by setting fire to the other barns and outbuildings of the Neville estate. The men inside Bower Hill fought on, but when the frontiersmen set fire to the kitchen beside the house, Kirkpatrick and Presley Neville knew the house was doomed. They surrendered.

No precise casualty list exists for the fight at Bower Hill. Three or four of Kirkpatrick's soldiers were wounded, and one of them may have died later. One or two frontiersmen, along with McFarlane, died, but there is no record of how many were wounded, nor if any of these wounded died of their injuries. Kirkpatrick and Presley Neville were manhandled by their captors, but they were not injured. Meanwhile, Bower Hill, General Neville's estate, burned to the ground.

As for McFarlane, his friends gave him a martyr's funeral. The headstone erected over his grave read: "He departed this life July 17, 1794, aged forty-five. He served through the war, with undaunted courage in defense of American independence, against the lawless and despotic encroachments of Great Britain. He fell at last by the hands of an unprincipled villain in support of what he supposed to be the rights of his country, much lamented by a numerous and respectable circle of acquaintances."

HOW WHISKEY SAVED PITTSBURGH

Five days after the burning of General Neville's estate, a large, motley group of men assembled at the Mingo Creek Meetinghouse, the log church of the region's Presbyterian congregation. Many in the crowd had fought at Bower Hill and numbered themselves among McFarlane's friends, but there was a new kind of man present at this meeting— wealthy land owners, lawyers, politicians. Prominent among them were Hugh Henry Brackenridge, an attorney and author; Albert Gallatin, a Swiss aristocrat who had fought in the American Revolution and was a close friend and political ally of Thomas Jefferson; and David Bradford, who in spite of being

THIS CARTOON SHOWS A LARGER-THAN-LIFE TAX COLLECTOR RUNNING OFF WITH TWO BARRELS OF WHISKEY WHILE TWO ANGRY FARMERS GIVE CHASE, CARRYING THE EQUIPMENT THEY NEED TO TAR AND FEATHER HIM.

one of the richest men in Washington County was popular with his back-country neighbors. Some of these men, particularly Gallatin and Bradford, were fervently anti-Federalist and sympathetic to the rebels. Many other well-to-do gentlemen in the meetinghouse that day had come because they were afraid to oppose the frontiersmen after what had happened to General Neville.

Brackenridge warned his neighbors that after the attack on the Neville house there was a good chance that President Washington would send the militia against them. This assessment did not go over well with the crowd, and as the grumbling grew louder and angrier, Brackenridge thought it prudent to leave the meeting. Bradford, on the other hand, whipped up the assembly to a state of near frenzy as he launched into a stinging attack on the federal government. Nonetheless, the Mingo Creek meeting came to no firm conclusion about what to do next, except the plan to meet again in three weeks' time.

Bradford, however, began instigating trouble on his own. With a small band of followers as reckless as himself, Bradford ambushed the mail carrier who traveled between Pittsburgh and Philadelphia. In the mailbag, they found several letters written by residents of Pittsburgh condemning the attack on the Neville place and other acts of violence perpetrated by the rebels. Using these purloined letters as an excuse, Bradford called on the frontiersmen to arm themselves and prepare to attack Pittsburgh.

WHEN A CROWD OF 7,000 SHOWED UP, IT BECAME OBVIOUS THAT BRADFORD WOULD NOT BE ABLE TO CONTROL THEM. MANY IN THE CROWD WERE REFERRING TO PITTSBURGH AS "SODOM," AND THEY WERE OBVIOUSLY LOOKING FORWARD TO DESCENDING ON THE TOWN LIKE THE WRATH OF GOD.

The people of Pittsburgh responded as if they were about to be attacked by Indian warriors. They banished the three letter writers who had gotten them into this mess. Then they elected a committee of delegates to meet the rebels, report that the troublemakers had been driven out of Pittsburgh, and assure them that the rest of the population sided with the frontiersmen against this unjust tax on whiskey. While the frightened delegation tried to calm the angry rebels, the women of Pittsburgh quickly hid their valuables.

Bradford had set August 1 as the date for the frontiersmen to assemble for the attack on Pittsburgh. When a crowd of 7,000 showed up, it became obvious that Bradford would not be able to control them. Many in the crowd were referring to Pittsburgh as "Sodom," and they were obviously looking forward to descending on the town like the wrath of God. Men and women in the crowd spoke openly about the guns, clothes, furniture, silver, and other luxuries they expected to carry off. It looked bad for Pittsburgh, but the residents would not abandon hope. The delegation's report that the rebels' critics had been banished was well received, as were the barrels of whiskey sent from the town. The gift of whiskey was a calculated risk: It could have inflamed the passions of such a huge crowd, yet happily it had the opposite effect. By the end of the day, almost everyone was drunk, and they had lost interest in sacking Pittsburgh. Staggering, the 7,000 rebels dispersed to their farms in the woods.

THE FORCES OF ANARCHY AND CONFUSION
The next day, August 2, while nearly 7,000 men and women in western Pennsylvania nursed their hangovers, President Washington met with his cabinet in Philadelphia to discuss unrest in the backcountry of the United States. The trouble was spreading. In Georgia, settlers were moving into the territory of the Creek Indians, intent upon founding a new state. In Kentucky, frontiersmen frustrated that the Spanish colonial government in Louisiana had closed the Mississippi River to American navigation, thus barring them from shipping any of their trade goods south, were threatening to assemble an army of 2,000 and march on New Orleans. After summarizing these disturbing developments, Washington said that such acts of defiance in the western country struck "at the root of all law and order."

Treasury Secretary Hamilton, ever watchful for an opportunity to exert the authority of the federal government, declared that in such a crisis "an immediate resort to military force" was a necessity, and he recommended that the military target the whiskey rebels in Pennsylvania. Both Hamilton and Washington remembered Shays' Rebellion in western Massachusetts only a few years before, in 1786 and 1787, an uprising against taxes that had shown the need for a strong central government if the new nation were to enforce its federal laws. Washington conceded that "anarchy and confusion" had the upper hand in western Pennsylvania, but still he held back from calling out the militia to suppress the rebellion. Instead, Washington decided to send three peace commissioners to reason with the rebels in Pennsylvania.

Five days after the cabinet meeting, Attorney General William Bradford (no relation to rabble-rouser David Bradford), Pennsylvania Supreme Court Justice Jasper Yeates, and Senator James Ross set out on their mission. They were authorized to grant amnesty to everyone who had interfered with the collection of the whiskey tax and attacked government officials, but Washington instructed them not to promise that the whiskey tax would be repealed. In return for amnesty, Washington demanded that the rebels promise to make no further attempts to obstruct the lawful collection of the whiskey tax, nor to harm or threaten any government officials.

DURING THE AMERICAN REVOLUTION, HENRY "LIGHT HORSE HARRY" LEE PROVED HIMSELF TO BE A BRILLIANT CAVALRYMAN. WASHINGTON PUT HIM IN COMMAND OF THE MILITIA WITH ORDERS TO SUPPRESS THE WHISKEY REBELLION.

To greet the peace commissioners, a band of rebels raised a liberty pole. In the years before the American Revolution, liberty poles—tall flagstaffs with a liberty cap perched on the top, or flying a flag—had been a favorite emblem of the Sons of Liberty, who erected them in town squares to show their defiance of British authority. The message was perfectly clear to Washington's delegates: The western Pennsylvania rebels were equating themselves with the Sons of Liberty, and the federal government with the British Crown that had once run roughshod over American liberties. Every day Bradford, Yeates, and Ross encountered angry, violent bands of rebels who cried out for the overthrow of the federal government.

Hoping to appease these men, the peace commissioners exceeded their authority. They promised, on the government's behalf—contrary to President Washington's instructions—to make "beneficial arrangements" for those who were delinquent in paying their taxes. But nothing could satisfy the rebels. On August 23, Bradford wrote to Hamilton that the rebels were beyond the reach of reason. The commissioners concluded that the president must send a large force of militia to western Pennsylvania "to overawe the disaffected individuals." Within a day or two of receiving Bradford's letter, Washington and Hamilton began planning a military expedition to crush the Whiskey Rebellion.

NO ONE TO FIGHT
On September 29, dragoons from Washington's army raced through the countryside outside Carlisle, Pennsylvania, hunting for the rebels who had erected liberty poles in the town. In Myerstown, they dragged a young man from his sickbed, charging him with rebellion against the federal government. The young man insisted he was no rebel, and besides, he had been too ill to help set up a liberty pole. The dragoons did not believe him, and they forced him outside. Unable to stand, and desperate to get back to his bed, the young man turned back to his house. One of the dragoons cocked his pistol and ordered him to stop. The dragoon said that if the prisoner could not stand, then he would be permitted to sit or even lie on the ground. As the young man started to lie down, the dragoon tried to uncock his pistol. Instead the pistol went off, and the bullet struck the young man in the groin. It was an agonizing wound, and it was mortal. The young man bled to death.

With nearly 13,000 militiamen in the country, tragedies such as the accidental killing of the sick young man from Myerstown were unavoidable. Nearly as damaging to the reputation of the militia was the bad behavior of troops who stole provisions from farmers, trampled down fields of ripe grain, and generally made themselves obnoxious. Nonetheless, when President Washington arrived at the militia's camp outside Carlisle on October 4, the officers of the militia put on a grand show of military pomp and discipline. The man who had led the fledgling United States to victory against Great Britain, then the greatest military power in the world, was back in uniform and among his troops. One anonymous but well-read militiaman plainly was dazzled by the occasion. Drawing upon Homer's *Iliad* for inspiration, the trooper said that as Washington inspected the army he bore "a mien intrepid as that of Hector, yet graceful as that of Paris."

Five days later, on October 9, two representatives from the western counties called upon Washington. Order was returning to their part of Pennsylvania, they claimed, and there was no need to march an army into the country. The president was polite but firm. Before Washington could disband the militia, he required "unequivocal proof of [the rebels'] absolute submission." This the delegates could not supply, and so they went home anxious and distressed. Once they were gone, Washington confided to an aide, "I believe they are scared." Fear would work to the government's advantage, and Washington gave it time to spread across the west country. Washington didn't order the militia to move out until October 20, eleven days after his meeting with the rebels' delegates. Then he handed over command to another veteran of the American Revolution, General Henry Lee, and returned to Philadelphia.

In the army's march westward, it met angry men and women who stood alongside the road railing at the troops, but there were no acts of violence. No rebel army came out to meet the militia, and no sharpshooters fired at them from the cover of the forest. Frustrated at having marched all this way only to find no enemy to fight, cavalry officers sent units into the countryside to arrest suspected rebels. The prisoners seized in these roundups became the targets of their captors' pent-up aggression. One officer, Andrew White, seized forty suspects. He had them tied in pairs, back to back, then thrown into an unfinished cellar, where they were kept for two days without food or a fire, in spite of the winter weather that struck western Pennsylvania early that year. Another 150 suspects were rounded up on the night of November 13 and forced out into a storm of snow and sleet in their nightshirts. These prisoners were locked in a pen with no protection from the foul weather, and no fire. But at least they were fed—raw meat and raw dough.

None of these prisoners, however, were the instigators of the whiskey rebellion. The chief rebels and their followers—perhaps as many as 2,000 of them—had fled into the mountains, beyond the reach of the militia. It was a great disappointment to Hamilton, who had hoped to bring rebel leaders such as David Bradford to trial in Philadelphia—and possibly see them hung for treason. Instead, when the militia at last turned back, out of all the suspects they had seized a mere twenty were selected to serve as examples. They were at worst bit players in the uprising, but they were better than nothing.

The militia and its prisoners arrived in Philadelphia on Christmas Day. As artillery boomed out and the bells of Christ Church pealed, a huge throng lined Broad Street to cheer the troops and mock the rebels. Present in the crowd that day was Presley Neville, whose father's house had been burned by the rebels a few months earlier. Watching the humiliated, bedraggled, half-starved prisoners hobble down the street, Neville said he "could not help feeling sorry for them." As the parade passed the president's house, Washington stepped outside to watch the prisoners go by. Then, without saying a word, he went back inside his house.

THE END OF THE FEDERALISTS It was six months before all of the accused rebels were tried. In the end, of the twenty prisoners hauled to Philadelphia, only two were found guilty of treasonous activity. The rest were acquitted for a variety of reasons—unreliable testimony, lack of witnesses, and even mistaken identity. The two men convicted were John Mitchell, a farmer so poor he could not afford a still, and Philip Wigle (or Vigol), a man who owned no land at all and was entirely penniless. In all likelihood they would have been acquitted, too, but for Pennsylvania Supreme Court Justice William Paterson's instructions to the jury to find the men guilty of treason.

Justice Paterson must have been frantic. After three years of lawlessness in the backwoods, culminating with 13,000 militiamen marching into western Pennsylvania to put down the Whiskey Rebellion, the federal government would look foolish if in the end no one was convicted of treason. The jury did as the justice commanded and found Mitchell and Wigle guilty of treason. The penalty in such a case was death, yet Mitchell and Wigle did not hang; President Washington pardoned them.

As for the tax on whiskey, it remained as difficult as ever to collect. It stayed on the law books for the duration of Washington's presidency and through the four years John Adams served as president. But in 1802, after Jefferson moved into the White House, the whiskey tax was abolished. By the 1830s, when the French political observer Alexis de Tocqueville toured the United States, he reported that it had become commonly accepted among ordinary Americans that any attempt by the federal government to tax liquor—except in a grave emergency, such as wartime, when the nation required additional sources of income—would lead to armed insurrection.

Although Jefferson served as Washington's secretary of state from 1789 to 1794, he had never been comfortable with the idea of a powerful federal government. Jefferson's ideal America was a nation of self-sufficient farmers, shopkeepers, craftsmen, and small manufacturers who governed themselves with minimal interference from the national government. Had Jefferson's views found a following only among aggrieved frontiersmen, his party probably would have remained in the minority, but it also attracted support in the South from wealthy landowners who also opposed the Federalist model of government that gave the greatest share of power to the national government, at the expense of state and local governments. Led by Jefferson and then his protégés, James Madison and James Monroe, this unlikely alliance of southern plantation aristocrats, common farmers, and dirt-poor frontiersmen drove the Federalists from power and in short order finished the Federalist Party.

The Federalists enjoyed one last hurrah in 1796 with the election of John Adams to the presidency, but after that the party went into free-fall. Many Americans came to regard the whiskey tax as unfair and the federal government's use of force against poor farmers of the back country as heavy-handed. Voters began to view the Federalists as power-hungry absolutists, ready to trample underfoot the rights of the states and the rights of individuals. And so voters turned away from the party of Washington and threw their support behind the party of Jefferson. The Democratic-Republicans, as the followers of Jefferson called themselves, held on to the White House from 1800 to 1825. Meanwhile the Federalists dwindled away, becoming so insignificant in American politics that in the election of 1820 they did not even put up a candidate. This was a stunning reversal of political fortunes. The Federalists, the party of the great, almost universally beloved George Washington, was dead.

The elimination of the Federalists from the American political scene hamstrung the national government for sixty years. States' rights, and eventually regional rights such as the people of western Pennsylvania, Georgia, and Kentucky had asserted in the eighteenth century, dominated the national scene until the outbreak of the Civil War in 1861. With the Union victory over the Confederacy in 1865, the national government became the primary power broker in American politics, and the authority of the states slipped into second place. Neither the whiskey rebels nor President Washington could have foreseen such a result, and yet that is how it played out, and it all began with a tax revolt in the backwoods of Pennsylvania.

CHAPTER 2

THE ALIEN AND SEDITION ACTS

JOHN ADAMS

ONE MORNING IN MAY 1798, PRESIDENT JOHN ADAMS GLANCED OUT A WINDOW OF his house on Market Street in Philadelphia and saw a strange sight: About forty men were loitering around the perimeter of his property. That forty strangers should suddenly dawdle before the president's house was odd; the fact that all forty wore in their hats the cockade of the French Revolution made their appearance ominous. A year earlier in an address to Congress, Adams had warned of French plots to subvert the government of the United States. New legislation to control foreigners whom the government considered dangerous, the Alien and Sedition Acts, was being debated in Congress and would be passed in a few weeks. Yet at that very moment, it seemed to Adams that all of his fears regarding French saboteurs were about to be played out on his doorstep.

As Adams wondered what, if anything, he ought to do, some of his neighbors came out of their houses to ask the strangers what business they had at the president's house. The loiterers refused to answer questions. As the conversation between the two groups grew heated, someone ordered the men with the cockades to disperse. They refused. America is "a land of liberty," they said, and they would stand about wherever they pleased. At that a fight broke out between the defenders of the president and the cockade wearers.

Passersby joined in on the side of Adams's neighbors, and soon the scuffle escalated into an enormous, violent street brawl. Adams and his servants were

THE TREATY JOHN JAY NEGOTIATED WITH GREAT BRITAIN OUTRAGED FRANCE'S NEW REVOLUTIONARY GOVERNMENT, LEADING TO FEARS AMONG THE FEDERALISTS THAT FRENCH SABOTEURS WERE PLOTTING A COUP AGAINST THE GOVERNMENT OF THE UNITED STATES.

convinced that the men in cockades were agents of France intent on storming the house and assassinating the president. As the servants barricaded the doors, Adams sent an urgent message to the War Office nearby, ordering a supply of arms and ammunition to be brought immediately by back streets and alleys to his house to defend the president and the government of the United States. Meanwhile more Adams supporters rushed to the battle, bearing their own pistols, muskets, and swords. As this large body of angry armed men bore down on them, the men in cockades thought better of their *coup d'etat* and fled.

For the rest of the day, thousands of loyal Philadelphians stood guard in a protective ring around Adams's house, while a troop of cavalry rode back and forth on Market Street. After dark, groups of citizens took to the streets. They patrolled the entire city from dusk to dawn, watching for suspicious characters—especially strangers wearing the French cockade.

A GUILLOTINE IN PHILADELPHIA? The identity of the loiterers has never

been established. Even if they had not come to assassinate Adams, their presence outside his house was clearly intended as a form of intimidation.

Ironically, though, twenty years earlier the appearance of forty men wearing an emblem of France would have been a cause for rejoicing in Philadelphia. In 1778, France became the first nation to recognize American independence and form an alliance with the United States. French money, arms, and troops had been decisive factors in America's victory over the British. But the France of 1798 was not the France Americans had known during the heady days of the War for Independence. In 1789, when the French people rose up against their king, Louis XVI, Americans cheered—and Thomas Jefferson was one of the most vocal among them. In the years that followed, however, the French Revolution careened out of control.

IT DID NOT SEEM FARFETCHED TO AMERICAN LEADERS SUCH AS GEORGE WASHINGTON, PRESIDENT ADAMS, ALEXANDER HAMILTON, AND THEIR FELLOW FEDERALISTS THAT ONE DAY SOON A GUILLOTINE MIGHT BE SET UP IN FRONT OF PHILADELPHIA'S INDEPENDENCE HALL.

The stories of noblemen and noblewomen being torn apart in the streets by furious mobs and the stories of thousands of "counter-revolutionaries" being murdered outright or dragged to the guillotine were horrible enough. Even more distressing was the French radicals' promise that they would export their revolution around the world. As one of their foremost spokesmen, Jacques-Pierre Brissot, put it, they were ready to launch "a crusade for universal liberty." As the Netherlands, Switzerland, and Venice (all republics, like France) fell to the revolutionary forces, it did not seem farfetched to American leaders such as

George Washington, President Adams, Alexander Hamilton, and their fellow Federalists that one day soon a guillotine might be set up in front of Philadelphia's Independence Hall.

The 1790s had seen a surge of French immigration to the United States. Most of the émigrés were plantation owners fleeing the slave uprising on the island of Santo Domingo in the Caribbean, members of the French aristocracy, or Catholic priests—the latter two were prime targets during the Reign of Terror. Federalist members of Congress and President Adams feared that among the French immigrants was a clandestine group who espoused the radical ideas of the French Revolution and had come to America to lead a violent insurgency against the government. Adams said as much in a speech before Congress on May 16, 1797, when he warned that agents of France were at work in America stirring up "aggressions so dangerous to the Constitution, union, and even independence of the nation." This was the rhetoric of fearmongering; there was no sign that French émigrés were plotting against America.

Just as worrisome to the Federalists was the latest influx of Irish immigrants. Unlike the unskilled, ignorant peasants who would later stream into the United States during the Potato Famine of the 1840s, the Irish immigrants of the 1790s tended to be educated, sophisticated political radicals. Many of them were members of the United Irishmen, a group of political activists who had invited France's revolutionary government to invade Ireland, help drive out the English, and establish an Irish republic. A French fleet carrying 15,000 troops did enter Bantry Bay in Ireland in December 1796, but winter storms kept the French army from landing, and the fleet turned back. Nonetheless, in spring 1798, Irish rebels, this time without a French army to back them up, made a desperate attempt to overthrow English rule in Ireland. The British Army crushed the uprising in a matter of weeks. As British troops marched from town to town rounding up rebels, many of Ireland's most outspoken political activists abandoned their homeland for the safety of the United States. In the United States, the Irish may have been safe, but they were not welcome.

To the Federalists, it seemed that in every coffeehouse and tavern one heard Irish voices spouting inflammatory political rhetoric. Almost all of these rants were directed against the British, but that was enough to make Federalists uneasy. In the war between England and France, the Federalists' sympathies were with England, where law and order still prevailed. The Irish sided with France, which put them in the camp of the Jeffersonian Republicans who also supported the French Revolution. Congressman Harrison Gray Otis of Massachusetts spoke for many Federalists when he deplored the arrival of "hordes of wild Irishmen ... [who] come with a view to disturb our tranquility."

PRESIDENTIAL BRIEFING

(1735-1826)

• SECOND PRESIDENT OF THE UNITED STATES (1797-1801), DIPLOMAT, AND MEMBER OF THE CONTINENTAL CONGRESS

• BORN IN BRAINTREE (NOW QUINCY), MASSACHUSETTS

• DIED JULY 4, 1826, IN QUINCY, MASSACHUSETTS (THE SAME DAY THOMAS JEFFERSON DIED)

• AT THE CONTINENTAL CONGRESS IN 1775, ADAMS NOMINATED GEORGE WASHINGTON FOR COMMANDER IN CHIEF.

• UNDER WASHINGTON, WAS THE NATION'S FIRST VICE PRESIDENT (1789-97) AND WAS ELECTED PRESIDENT IN 1796 AS A FEDERALIST (1797-1801)

• HIS REFUSAL TO DECLARE WAR ON FRANCE AND HIS SIGNING OF THE ALIEN AND SEDITION ACTS IN 1790 TURNED THE FEDERALIST PARTY AGAINST "HIS ROTUNDITY."

JAY'S TREATY

Tensions between the United States and the revolutionary government of France had remained bubbling below the surface until 1794. In that year, President Washington sent John Jay, chief justice of the U.S. Supreme Court and a man known for his pro-British sympathies, to London to resolve four problems that had plagued American-British relations since the end of the American Revolution.

Jay's mission was largely successful, from the American perspective. The British agreed to evacuate six forts they held in American territory; they pledged to pay more than $10 million in compensation to American ship owners whose cargo had been seized by the Royal Navy; and they agreed to send the matter regarding the Maine-Canada border to arbitration.

President Washington and the Federalists were delighted with what has come to be known as Jay's Treaty. The Jeffersonian Republicans, however, denounced the treaty as a pact with aristocrats and monarchists that undermined the American commitment to democratic principles. The Jeffersonian Republicans, led by the example of the founder of their party, Thomas Jefferson, were enthusiastic supporters of the French Revolution. The Federalists, led by Hamilton, recoiled at the violence, destruction, and social and political chaos into which France had descended. In the war that was now raging between France and England, the Federalists' sympathies were entirely with the English. For the Federalists, Britain represented political stability. For the Jeffersonian Republicans, however, the most important political goal was the overthrow of monarchy, which is what the French were trying to do all across Europe. Washington's government never openly repudiated the treaty the United States made with France in 1778, yet the Jeffersonian Republicans interpreted Jay's Treaty as a shift in American policy. So did the French.

Once Jay's Treaty was ratified, the government in Paris recalled its minister to the United States, Pierre Adet. They also refused to receive America's new minister to France, Charles Pinckney, and expelled him from the country. Then France began seizing American ships and cargo on the high seas.

When President Washington left office on March 4, 1797, the animosity between France and the United States was unresolved. The first crisis of President Adams's administration would be finding a way to stay friends with the English, mollify the French, and keep America out of the war raging in Europe.

WITH PASSAGE OF THE ALIEN ACT, CONGRESS GAVE THE PRESIDENT AUTHORITY TO DEPORT ANY FOREIGNER HE BELIEVED WAS A DANGER TO THE PEACE AND SECURITY OF THE UNITED STATES.

PAYING THROUGH THE NOSE

As a nobleman and a bishop, Charles-Maurice de Talleyrand-Périgord initially opposed the French Revolution, but when he understood that the forces of revolution were gaining the upper hand in France, he switched sides. By 1796, he had given up the Church and accepted

FIFTH *CONGRESS* OF THE UNITED STATES:

At the Second Session.

Begun and held at the city of *Philadelphia*, in the state of PENNSYLVANIA, on *Monday*, the thirteenth of *November*, one thousand seven hundred and ninety-seven.

An ACT *concerning aliens.*

BE it enacted by the Senate and House of Representatives of the United States of America, in Congress assembled, That it shall be lawful for the President of the United States at any time during the continuance of this act, to order all such aliens as he shall judge dangerous to the peace and safety of the United States, or shall have reasonable grounds to suspect are concerned in any treasonable or secret machinations against the government thereof, to depart out of the territory of the United States, within such time as shall be expressed in such order, which order shall be served on such alien by delivering him a copy thereof, or leaving the same at his usual abode, and returned to the office of the Secretary of State, by the Marshal or other person to whom the same shall be directed. And in case any alien so ordered to depart, shall be found at large within the United States after the time limited in such order for his departure, and not having obtained a licence from the President to reside therein, or having obtained such licence shall not have conformed thereto, every such alien shall on conviction thereof, be imprisoned for a term not exceeding three years and shall never after be admitted to become a citizen of the United States. Provided always, and be it further enacted, That if any alien so ordered to depart shall prove to the satisfaction of the President, by evidence to be taken before such person or persons as the President shall direct, who are for that purpose hereby authorized to administer oaths, that no injury or danger to the United States will arise from suffering such alien to reside therein, the President may grant a licence to such alien to remain within the United States for such time as he shall judge proper, and at such place as he may designate. And the President may also require of such alien to enter into a bond to the United States, in such penal sum as he may direct, with one or more sufficient sureties to the satisfaction of the person authorized by the President to take the same, conditioned for the good behaviour of such alien during his residence in the United States, and not violating his licence, which licence the President may revoke whenever he shall think proper.

Sec. 2. And be it further enacted, That it shall be lawful for the President of the United States, whenever he may deem it necessary for the public safety, to order to be removed out of the territory thereof, any alien who may or shall be in prison in pursuance of this act; and to cause to be arrested and sent out of the United States such of those aliens as shall have been ordered to depart therefrom and shall not have obtained a licence as aforesaid, in all cases where in the opinion of the President the public safety requires a speedy removal. And if any alien so removed or sent out of the United States by the President shall voluntarily return thereto, unless by permission of the President of the United States, such alien on conviction thereof, shall be imprisoned so long as in the opinion of the President, the public safety may require.

Sec. 3. And be it further enacted, That every master or commander of any ship or vessel which shall come into any port of the United States after the first day of July next, shall immediately on his arrival make report in writing to the collector or other chief officer of the customs of such port, of all aliens, if any, on board his vessel, specifying their names, age, the place of nativity, the country from which they shall have come, the nation to which they belong and owe allegiance, their occupation and a description of their persons, as far as he shall be informed thereof, and on failure every such master and commander shall forfeit and pay three hundred dollars, for the payment whereof on default of such master or commander, such vessel shall also be holden; and may by such collector or other officer of the customs be detained. And it shall be the duty of such collector or other officer of the customs, forthwith to transmit to the office of the department of State true copies of all such returns.

Sec. 4. And be it further enacted, That the circuit and district courts of the United States, shall respectively have cognizance of all crimes and offences against this act. And all marshals and other officers of the United States are required to execute all precepts and orders of the President of the United States issued in pursuance or by virtue of this act.

Sec. 5. And be it further enacted, That it shall be lawful for any alien who may be ordered to be removed from the United States, by virtue of this act, to take with him such part of his goods, chattels, or other property, as he may find convenient; and all property left in the United States, by any alien, who may be removed, as aforesaid, shall be, and remain subject to his order and disposal, in the same manner, as if this act had not been passed.

Sec. 6. And be it further enacted, That this act shall continue and be in force for and during the term of two years from the passing thereof.

Jonathan Dayton, Speaker of the House of Representatives.

Th. Jefferson, Vice President of the United States and President of the Senate.

Approved June 25. 1798.
John Adams
President of the United States.

I certify that this act did originate in the Senate.

Attest,
Samuel A. Otis, Secretary

the post of minister of foreign affairs from the Directory, the five-man executive panel that governed France. Representatives of foreign governments who had business with the Directory approached Talleyrand first. The simplest, most efficient way to ensure that a representative's government enjoyed Talleyrand's good opinion, and that their business would be received favorably by the Directory, was to hand over a gift of cash. Talleyrand communicated the size of the sum he expected through one of his agents. Very quickly, this quid pro quo came to be understood and accepted among the diplomatic community in Paris, but no one had explained the custom to the emissaries from the United States.

Shortly after his inauguration in March 1797, in an effort to heal America's breach with France, President Adams selected three men to go to Paris. Elbridge Gerry of Massachusetts, fifty-three years old, had been one of the signers of the Declaration of Independence; Charles Pinckney of South Carolina, forty-four years old, was the U.S. minister who had been forced to leave France; and John Marshall of Virginia, forty-two years old, was a successful lawyer, a cousin of the pro-French Jefferson, and a future chief justice of the U.S. Supreme Court. Gerry, Pinckney, and Marshall's diplomatic experience was almost nonexistent, and they certainly had no experience dealing with a man as wily as Talleyrand.

Upon arriving in Paris, the Americans learned that before they could see Talleyrand they must first meet his agents—Jean Conrad Hottinguer, Pierre Bellamy, and Lucien Hauteval—three men who in the published reports of the American embassy's failed mission to Paris would be known, for discretion's sake, as X, Y, and Z. These three gentlemen informed the American delegation that their petition would be received favorably by the minister of foreign affairs if the United States government agreed to loan the government of France 32 million Dutch guilders (about $12 million) and present Talleyrand with a cash gift of 50,000 pounds sterling (about $250,000). Gerry, Pinckney, and Marshall were stunned by the casual manner in which Talleyrand's agents solicited these bribes, and they were incensed that their government should be expected to pay an exorbitant sum for the privilege of having France's minister of foreign affairs deign to confer with the official representatives of the president of the United States.

Hottinguer, Bellamy, and Hauteval were blasé about the bribe they demanded from the Americans. From their point of view, the United States was getting off easy. When the king of Portugal wanted to make peace with France, Talleyrand's price had been 8 million francs. Marshall and Pinckney were not impressed with the bargain, however, and they returned to the United States. Gerry stayed behind, hoping to win at least one or two concessions from the French and perhaps persuade Talleyrand to lower his price.

ILL-FAVORED FOREBODINGS
Talleyrand's demand for a bribe, coupled with the recent memory of the street battle in front of the president's house, convinced Adams and the Federalists that France was no longer a friend of the United States. By summer 1798, the Federalist-dominated Congress introduced a package of four new laws that would give the president and the federal government new powers to combat any threat to the nation. These four laws together are known as the Alien and Sedition Acts.

The first law Congress passed was the Naturalization Act. This law required immigrants to reside in the United States for fourteen years before applying for American citizenship. (The original waiting period had been five years.) The second law Congress passed was the Alien Act, by which Congress gave the president authority to deport any foreigner he believed was a danger to the peace and security of the United States. Under this law, the president was not obliged to give the suspect a hearing or even to state his reason for wanting the man or woman deported. The third law, the Alien Enemies Act, gave the president a new wartime power. He could label any citizen of a foreign power whose homeland was at war with the United States as an enemy alien. The fourth law, the Sedition Act, made it a crime to publish—or even to say out loud—anything "false, scandalous, or malicious" against the president of the

United States, Congress, or the U.S. government in general. Individuals found guilty of saying or publishing anything that held the government up to "contempt and disrepute" could be punished with two years in prison and a fine of $2,000 (about $34,000 in modern money).

The Alien and Sedition Acts were a flagrant violation of the First Amendment of the U.S. Constitution, but in fairness to President Adams, he did nothing to urge Congress to pass the legislation. By remaining silent on the subject, Adams gave the legislation his tacit approval, and when the legislation came to his desk, he signed it into law. Writing about the Alien and Sedition Acts years later, Adams said, "I knew there was need enough … and therefore I consented to them." Washington approved the passage of the Alien and Sedition Acts, too, and he deplored the protestations of the Jeffersonian Republicans who claimed that the new laws curtailed the liberties of the American people. Washington said that it was

in the nature of the Jeffersonian Republicans "to disturb the public mind with their unfounded and ill-favored forebodings." To Adams, Washington, and their fellow Federalists, the Alien and Sedition Acts were not an abridgment of rights, but a necessity for national self-preservation.

Of the four new laws, the Sedition Act got the most use. American newspapers in the late eighteenth century fed their readers a steady diet of vicious, scurrilous editorials and articles that attacked government officials. For example, Benjamin Franklin Bache, grandson of Benjamin Franklin and publisher of the Philadelphia newspaper, *Aurora*, had mocked Washington as the "Grand Lama," predicted that the first president would make "a bold push for the American throne," and at the end of Washington's administration asserted that the retiring president had been the cause of all of America's misfortunes.

Men like Washington, Hamilton, and Jefferson pretended they were not disturbed by such calumnies, but in truth the daily barrage of slurs, insults, and personal attacks stung. In September 1798, when Bache died in a yellow fever epidemic at age twenty-nine, Adams "eulogized" him, saying, "The yellow fever arrested him in his detestable career and sent him to his grandfather, from whom he inherited a dirty, envious, jealous, and revengeful spite against me."

THE MARTYR FROM VERMONT

In autumn 1798, Matthew Lyon, a congressman representing Vermont and a member of the Jeffersonian Republican party, returned home during a recess. Recently, Lyon had become a celebrity. In a quarrel with a Federalist congressman, Roger Griswold of Connecticut, Lyon had ended the argument by spitting in Griswold's eye. A few days later, Griswold retaliated by attacking Lyon on the floor of the House of Representatives, beating him savagely with his cane. It took several congressmen to pull the two men off each other.

In the days following the brawl, the Federalists in the House, especially those from New England, delivered one bombastic speech after another. Francis Dana of Massachusetts described Lyon as "a kennel of filth." Harrison Gray Otis, also of Massachusetts, asserted that Lyon had displayed conduct "which would not be suffered in a brothel or a den of robbers." The denunciations concluded with a bill, introduced by the Federalists, to expel Lyon from the House of Representatives. To the exasperation of the Federalists, it failed to gain the two-thirds vote required, and so "Spitting Lyon," as he was now called, kept his seat in Congress. Griswold and his fellow Federalists in Congress had failed to bring Lyon down, but Lyon had another enemy back home in Vermont.

Years earlier, in the Vermont state legislature, a Federalist named Nathaniel Chipman had mocked Lyon as "an ignorant Irish puppy." Lyon, true to form, lunged at Chipman, grabbed a fistful of his hair, and dragged him around the room. When Lyon moved on to Congress, Chipman remained in Vermont, becoming one of the most powerful Federalists in the state and developing a reputation as one of the most vindictive political power brokers in New England.

As Lyon rode across the border into Vermont, Chipman was waiting for him, armed with an indictment that charged Lyon with violating the Sedition Act. Specifically, Lyon had published a letter to the editor in the *Vermont Gazette* in which he attacked the administration of President Adams. Under Adams, Lyon wrote, "every consideration of the public welfare was swallowed up in a continual grasp for power, in an unbounded thirst for ridiculous pomp, foolish adulation, and selfish avarice." Because Lyon's letter met the Sedition Act's criteria by being "false, scandalous, or malicious," he was hauled off to trial in Rutland, Vermont, before a partisan Federalist judge. In his defense, Lyon argued that the Sedition Act was unconstitutional, which was an argument the court rejected. The jury found the congressman guilty, and the judge sentenced him to pay a $1,000 fine and serve four months in prison—but not the prison in Rutland. Instead, the judge sent Lyon to a filthy, dungeon-like prison in the town of Vergennes forty miles away.

The cell assigned to Lyon was a dank, fetid hole with an open privy in one corner. By the time Lyon was locked up, winter had come to Vermont, but his jailer refused to let him have a fire. Chipman, Griswold, and their Federalist friends may have been jubilant at Lyon's incarceration, but the Jeffersonian Republicans seized upon the wretched conditions of Lyon's imprisonment and in their newspapers cast him as a martyr suffering under the cruelty of the Sedition Act. The tactic of portraying Lyon as the victim of an unjust law worked. Although Lyon was serving a prison sentence at the time of the next congressional election, Vermont voters reelected him. Lyon, the brawler and jailbird, defeated the Federalists' candidate by more than 2,000 votes. As for his fine, Jeffersonian Republicans from Vermont and Virginia raised twice the amount needed. In February 1799, having served his four-month sentence, Lyon was a free man. He went straight back to Congress, where he took his accustomed seat on the House floor. A reporter for a Philadelphia newspaper who covered Lyon's return stated that the congressman looked "remarkably well for a gentleman just out of jail."

FRENCH AND IRISH INTRIGUERS While Lyon shivered in his frigid, stinking jail cell, gossips in Philadelphia were frightening each other with the rumor that France intended to take back the Louisiana Territory it had been forced to hand over to Spain in 1762. If a French army landed in New Orleans, what would stop them from invading American territory as well? In prose of the most vivid shade of purple, Federalist Congressman Fisher Ames of Massachusetts warned that the French army would visit "your houses and farms with fire, plunder and pillage! and your wives and sweethearts with ravishment and assassination, by horrid, outlandish sans-culotte Frenchmen!!" Any American man who failed to arm himself against the invaders risked being "torn limb from gut, and devoured alive by bloodthirsty cannibals."

Secretary of State Timothy Pickering claimed that the French consul in Philadelphia was scheming "to rally every sort of devil from the Mississippi to the Delaware" to overthrow the American government. Pickering urged Adams to invoke the Alien Act and arrest all French consuls in the United States. Adams refused. The consuls enjoyed diplomatic immunity, and he would not provoke an international incident and possibly a war with France by locking up its envoys.

Adams was ready, however, to use the Alien Act against another Frenchman, General Jean Baptiste Collot, whom the president described as a "pernicious and malicious intriguer." Collot had fought with Washington during the American Revolution. In 1793, he was governor of the French colony of Guadeloupe. When the British captured the island, as a courtesy they permitted Collot to seek sanctuary in the United States. During Collot's stay in America, he charted

portions of the Mississippi and Missouri rivers. It was widely (and wrongly) believed in Federalist circles that Collot was not an explorer but a schemer who planned to lead the frontiersmen west of the Appalachian Mountains in an insurrection against the United States and establish a French satellite nation. Another rumor held that Collot had said that if war broke out between America and France, he intended to be "one of the first to step forward and plunder the property of certain individuals." But when Adams authorized arresting Collot under the Alien Act, the general could not be found.

Collot had moved to Newark, New Jersey, where he was living under an assumed name. He gave himself away to Newark Federalists, however, when he took out a subscription to Bache's anti-Federalist, anti-Adams newspaper, *Aurora*. Happily for Collot, by the time he had blown his cover, France and the

United States were patching up their differences. Adams would not jeopardize the new détente by putting a French national on trial, so General Collot remained at large until, of his own free will, he booked passage on a ship and sailed home to France.

John Daly Burk was another likely target of the Alien Act. From his days as a student at Trinity College in Dublin, Burk would not curb his tongue. He had been expelled from Trinity for speaking against the doctrines of the established Church of Ireland and in favor of the French Revolution. In 1796, Burk emigrated to America, settling in Philadelphia, where he railed even against the country that had taken him in. One day, as Burk was in the midst of full-scale denunciation of the shortcomings of his new home, he exclaimed that he looked forward to the day when the French would invade the United States, because then "every scoundrel in favor of this government would be put to the guillotine." Burk's public outburst—when combined with the antigovernment articles he had published in a newspaper called the *Time Piece*—were enough to bring federal marshals to his door with an arrest warrant charging him with seditious libel.

Burk denied saying he wished every member of the Adams administration would be beheaded by the French, and he claimed he was the victim of a "contemptible informer." Nonetheless, the government was ready to proceed with his trial when one of Burk's friends, Aaron Burr, suggested to Adams and his cabinet that they could save themselves some trouble by simply deporting Burk to Ireland instead. The administration agreed, but Secretary of State Pickering mucked up the arrangement when he insisted that the U.S. government would not pay for Burk's passage. The point was still being disputed when Burk suddenly disappeared. He turned up years later in Virginia, where he was living under an assumed name and working as the principal of a school.

A NOTORIOUS LEGACY
The Alien and Sedition Acts had been born of the Federalists' fear that France would invade America or sponsor a revolution to overthrow the U.S. government, and their outrage over the scurrilous, antigovernment pieces that appeared daily in newspapers such as Bache's *Aurora*. Yet the Federalists were never aggressive in enforcing this legislation. No enemy aliens were deported, and barely twenty-five individuals were arrested on charge of seditions. Of these, only eleven were tried, and only ten were convicted. Furthermore, when the Alien Act expired in 1800 and the Sedition Act in 1801, Congress made no move to renew them. Jefferson began his presidency in 1801 by pardoning the ten men convicted under the Sedition Act.

Jefferson did not believe the federal government should be involved in cases of seditious libel, but he had no objection if the states wished to try such cases. In fact, Jefferson soon complained that newspaper editors had made him "a fair mark for every man's dirt" and that he now believed "a few prosecutions of the most prominent offenders would have a wholesome effect in restoring the integrity of the presses."

Adams and the Federalists had their reasons for passing the Alien and Sedition Acts. A bloody war with France appeared inevitable, the battle outside the president's house in Philadelphia confirmed their worst fears that agent provocateurs were at work in the United States, and every day Jeffersonian Republican newspaper editors savaged the federal government, undermining the respect and confidence the people ought to have in their elected officials. But the French invasion never came, and neither did a coup against the government.

The Alien and Sedition Acts discredited the Federalists, and the defeat of their incumbent candidate, Adams, in the presidential election of 1800 humiliated them. Hamilton might have been able, somehow, to reverse the Federalists' fortunes and lead them back into power, but he was killed in a duel with Burr in 1804. With the Federalists' political capital spent and their party leaders gone, they virtually disappeared from the American political scene. Tragically, the Alien and Sedition Acts became their legacy. They could have gone down in history as the party of the noble George Washington, but instead they became notorious for passing legislation that ran roughshod over the First Amendment. The Alien and Sedition Acts are remembered (fairly or not) as precursors to such violations of civil liberties as were seen in the Red Scare of 1919 to 1920 and the McCarthy era, among other periods.

CHAPTER 3

THE EMBARGO ACTS

THOMAS JEFFERSON

ON JUNE 22, 1807, THE AMERICAN FRIGATE USS *CHESAPEAKE* HAD JUST SAILED out of the harbor of Norfolk, Virginia, when the ship's captain, James Barron, thirty-eight years old, spotted a squadron of British ships anchored in Lynnhaven Roads. Suddenly one of the British ships, HMS *Leopard*, weighed anchor and pulled alongside the *Chesapeake*. Barron, who came from a seafaring Virginia family and who had already commanded the USS *United States*, was not intimidated by the *Leopard*, but he should have been. Barron had only taken command of the vessel the day before, his crew was inexperienced and poorly trained, his ship's deck was cluttered and untidy, and his powder was improperly stored in the ship's hold. Worse yet, the *Chesapeake* had only thirty-six cannons to the *Leopard's* fifty.

ALTHOUGH THE FRENCH NAVY HARRIED AMERICAN SHIPS ON THE HIGH SEAS ALMOST AS OFTEN AS THE BRITISH, THOMAS JEFFERSON CONTINUED TO REGARD FRANCE AS A FRIEND AND ALLY, AND GREAT BRITAIN AS A THREAT TO THE UNITED STATES.

For forty miles, the *Leopard* shadowed the *Chesapeake*, then it pulled ahead, blocking the path of the American vessel. When both ships had come to a halt, a small boat was lowered over the *Leopard's* side bearing a British lieutenant. Once aboard the *Chesapeake*, he informed Captain Barron that the Royal Navy suspected several deserters were serving aboard his ship, and he must submit to a search. Barron, indignant, refused to permit any such thing, and so the British lieutenant climbed back into his boat and had himself rowed to the *Leopard*.

A few minutes later, Barron and his officers saw the *Leopard's* gun ports fly open and the cannons run out. The panicky, ill-trained American crew was

entirely unprepared for an attack. For fifteen minutes, the *Leopard's* guns pounded the *Chesapeake*. Three American crewmen died in the barrage, and eighteen were wounded, including Captain Barron. Rather than see his ship reduced to splinters, Barron struck his colors and surrendered, at which time the same British lieutenant returned to the *Chesapeake* and dragged off four members of the crew he claimed were British subjects.

Barron patched up his wounded men and his damaged ship and limped back to Norfolk. When the citizens of the port town heard of the unprovoked attack on the frigate and the seizure of four crewmen, they called for a public meeting where they swore to assist no more British ships that entered American waters. They would not supply the British with pilots to help them navigate the Virginia coast, nor would they sell the British food and water. Before adjourning, the people of Norfolk established a fund to collect money for the widows and children of the sailors killed defending the *Chesapeake*. Five days after the attack, June 27, 1807, Robert MacDonald, one of the wounded crewmen, died. Four thousand ships' officers and sailors, members of local militia companies, and residents of Norfolk and the surrounding area formed an enormous procession to escort MacDonald's body to its grave.

It was common practice in wartime for British subjects to be impressed (forced) into service in His Majesty's Navy, but the "recruiters" did not stop there. James Madison, Thomas Jefferson's secretary of state (and successor as president), reported in 1806 that Britain had impressed 2,273 known American citizens into service in the Royal Navy. Britain claimed that it was only reclaiming its former subjects who, to avoid wartime service, had deserted the navy and joined the American merchant marine. Proof was difficult; American and British sailors looked the same and spoke the same language. But impressment was not the only source of conflict between the old country and the new.

A FOREIGN RELATIONS HEADACHE
From 1792 until 1815, France and Great Britain were in an almost continuous state of war. Initially the British— along with the Austrians, Prussians, Spanish, and other kingdoms—had gone to war to contain or push back the political instability the French Revolution had unleashed in Europe. A much greater threat emerged after Napoleon

ARMED WITH ONLY THIRTY-SIX CANNONS TO THE HMS *LEOPARD'S* FIFTY, AND MANNED BY A POORLY TRAINED CREW, THE USS *CHESAPEAKE* HAD NO CHANCE OF FIGHTING OFF THE BRITISH SHIP.

Bonaparte seized power in France in 1799. In the name of liberty, equality, and fraternity, Napoleon set out to "liberate" the nations of Europe from their kings and emperors. But Napoleon did not establish republics in the lands he conquered. Instead he consolidated them into a vast empire over which he reigned as emperor. (Napoleon crowned himself in a ceremony in Paris's cathedral of Notre Dame in 1804.) The one European power that held out against Napoleon was Great Britain, and as he tightened his grip on the Continent, the British lived in fear of a French invasion.

While France and Britain were locked in a life-or-death struggle that raged from the Nile to the Caribbean, the United States declared itself neutral and attempted to carry on normal trade relations with both countries. American commerce depended heavily on the exports U.S. ships carried to these markets. In 1803, such exports brought $32 million into the American economy; by 1807 that figured had jumped to $108 million. The French, of course, did not want any American goods going to Britain, and likewise the British did not want American goods reaching France. Both nations stopped American vessels on the high seas, seizing their cargo and sometimes expropriating the ships, too. Trying to persuade the British and the French to respect American neutrality and the right of American merchants to trade with both sides had preoccupied the two previous presidents. After Jefferson took office in March 1801, their foreign relations headache became his.

A critical event in the United States' tense relationships with England and France occurred at the Battle of Trafalgar, October 21, 1805, near Cape Trafalgar between Cádiz and the Strait of Gibraltar, in which Britain's Royal Navy under the command of Admiral Horatio Nelson crushed a French and Spanish fleet. The French and Spanish lost twenty-two of their twenty-seven ships, while the British lost none (although Lord Nelson was mortally wounded in the battle). The victory at Trafalgar gave Britain absolute supremacy in the Atlantic and the Mediterranean, which was a development that distressed President Jefferson. Ever since the people of Paris had stormed the Bastille prison on July 14, 1789, Jefferson had been outspoken in his support of the French Revolution.

Even after the revolution spiraled into the bloodshed and anarchy of the Reign of Terror, Jefferson still preferred the French republic, however chaotic, to Britain's entrenched system of monarchy and aristocracy. After the HMS *Leopard's* attack on the USS *Chesapeake*, Jefferson was ready to go to war to avenge the old injuries and injustices America suffered from the British and to prove to the world that his young nation was an up-and-coming power. In a letter to Philadelphia newspaper publisher William Duane, Jefferson wrote, "Now then is the time to settle the old and the new."

PRESIDENTIAL BRIEFING

(1743-1826)

• VICE PRESIDENT OF THE UNITED STATES UNDER JOHN ADAMS (1797-1801) AND THIRD PRESIDENT OF THE UNITED STATES (1801-9)

• BORN APRIL 13, 1743, IN ALBEMARLE COUNTY, VIRGINIA

• DIED JULY 4, 1826, AT MONTICELLO, VIRGINIA (THE SAME DAY JOHN ADAMS DIED)

• AUTHOR OF THE DECLARATION OF INDEPENDENCE (1776) AT CONTINENTAL CONGRESS

• IN INTERNATIONAL AFFAIRS, USED ECONOMIC POWER—SUCH AS THE WITHHOLDING OF TRADE—RATHER THAN MILITARY FORCE

• AUTHORIZED LOUISIANA PURCHASE (1803)

OUT OF HARM'S WAY

That summer of 1807, as President Jefferson weighed the option of going to war, there were about 2,500 American vessels at sea, manned by approximately 30,000 American sailors and carrying an estimated $100 million worth of goods as cargo. According to Jacob Crowninshield, a New England merchant and exporter, most of the American ships and the goods they carried were uninsured. Crowninshield gave as an example the ships and cargo that had sailed that year, 1807, from Salem, Massachusetts. Taken together, they were worth about $2.8 million, of which only $700,000 was covered by insurance. If the United States went to war, all of those vessels would become targets of the Royal Navy, many would be captured or destroyed, and the losses to American merchants and the shipping industry would be devastating.

Objections from Crowninshield and other advisers made Jefferson reconsider his war plans. He began to conceive of a guerrilla-style war in which all of America's ships would return home and be armed to raid British merchant vessels for a change. While new defenses were built along the U.S. coast, an American invasion force would march into British-held Canada. This strategy of harassment would, Jefferson believed, convince the British to respect the United States' neutrality, stop interfering with American merchant ships, and discontinue a practice Americans found especially galling: the seizure of American sailors on the pretext that they were British subjects. As with Jefferson's plans for all-out war with Britain, however, he never put these ideas into action, which was just as well because Congress was ambivalent about taking on the British, especially the seemingly invincible Royal Navy.

Jefferson did nothing until December 1807, when he received news from Britain and France that so disturbed him he felt certain the time had come at last to take action. London and Paris, already belligerents, suspected each other of benefiting unfairly from American trade and engaged in an escalating war of blockades that caught American commerce in the middle and threatened to strangle the U.S. economy, which depended heavily on exports. Britain closed all of Europe to American ships except those that had first passed through British customs. In addition, the British announced that they would be even more aggressive in pursuing their policy of "reclaiming" British subjects who had deserted to serve on foreign ships. Then Napoleon declared that any ships obeying the British orders would be "denationalized" and subject to seizure; France would attack and confiscate any U.S. ships carrying goods to or from the British Isles.

This double threat to American shipping shocked Jefferson. He described Europe as "a great madhouse [locked] in a paroxysm of insanity." The president had three options: The United States could submit to Britain and France's

NAPOLEON BONAPARTE CLAIMED HE WAS LIBERATING THE NATIONS OF EUROPE FROM THE EVILS OF MONARCHY. IN FACT, HE WAS CONSOLIDATING THEM INTO A VAST EMPIRE RULED BY HIM.

demands, it could go to war with one or both of them, or it could impose a total embargo of American trade. His chief priority was to keep the United States from becoming entangled in the Anglo-French war. Jefferson's friend and protégé James Madison argued that shutting down American overseas commerce would compel Britain and France to change their policies toward U.S. trading vessels. Madison's argument made sense to Jefferson, but he realized it would cause economic hardship. He described the embargo as "a temporary evil to save us from a greater." Although Jefferson was convinced that an embargo was America's best option, he did not act unilaterally. First, he discussed the matter with his cabinet. Then, with the cabinet's approval, Jefferson asked Congress to authorize an embargo, barring all American vessels from leaving American harbors to trade overseas. The Embargo Act was passed, almost without debate, on December 22, 1807. Jefferson imagined that by bottling up every American foreign-bound merchant vessel, he was "keeping our ships and seamen out of harm's way." But in pursuing that goal, Jefferson would seriously damage the American economy, striking everyone from farmers who could not sell their surplus cornmeal and flour overseas, to ship owners whose boats now sat idle at anchor, to dockworkers who had no cargo to load or unload, right on down to the bartenders at waterfront grog shops who lost their hard-drinking seafaring clientele. The embargo put 30,000 American sailors out of work.

In every major port city from Portsmouth, New Hampshire, to Savannah, Georgia, the story was the same: wharves piled high with bales of wool; barrels of potash, flour, and salted meat; hogsheads of rum; and crates full of other American-made merchandise—all ready for the markets of Europe, but no way to get them there. The bustling waterfronts became deserted. Coffeehouses, once packed with merchants and underwriters, went quiet. Meanwhile, in the fine mansions of Boston, New York, Philadelphia, and Baltimore, wealthy mercantile families saw their fortunes vanish almost overnight. Many people found such an economic burden intolerable, and so they broke the embargo.

"I WILL HAVE YOUR HEART'S BLOOD" It was noontime, August 1, 1808, as the crew of the *Black Snake*, a forty-foot sloop, eased their boat up to the shore of Vermont's Onion River and tied her to one of the trees that overhung the river. They were at Joy's Landing, about three miles north of Burlington. There, shielded from the hot August sun by the shade of the trees, Truman Mudgett, captain of the *Black Snake*, and his seven-man crew rested. The night before, they had made a successful run to Canada, delivering a boatload of potash to a buyer on the other side of the border. Potash was a useful ingredient in making lye soap and glass, and it was a good fertilizer. Now,

because of President Jefferson's embargo, the price of potash was rising. Before the embargo a 100-pound barrel of potash sold for about $8; before the embargo ended the price would skyrocket to $100 a barrel. Because the *Black Snake* could carry 100 barrels easily, this inflation in the price of potash was good news for Mudgett and his men.

Although smuggling was profitable, it was risky. So many residents of the northernmost regions of New York, Vermont, New Hampshire, and Maine had begun smuggling goods into Canada that Jefferson declared the whole region in a state of insurrection and ordered revenue men to patrol the rivers and lakes— especially Lake Champlain—and intercept the smugglers. To defend themselves against the government meddlers, Mudgett and his crew traveled well armed. Each man had a gun, and the boats were equipped with pikes to push away revenue cutters, three-foot-long clubs for hand-to-hand fighting, and a basket of rocks, each the size of a man's fist. In addition, the *Black Snake* carried a piece they called "the big gun," which was an eight-foot-long portable cannon that could fire fifteen musket balls at a time. Perhaps the crew's most valuable asset, however, was the backing of their neighbors, who would warn them whenever a revenue man was nearby. That is what happened early in the afternoon of August 1. As the smugglers sat in their boat cleaning their guns, a farmer approached with word that a revenue boat, the *Fly*, with a crew of fifteen under the command of Lieutenant Daniel Farrington, was looking for them.

"YOU DAMNED RED-COATED RASCAL!" SHOUTED CYRUS DEAN, ONE OF THE SMUGGLERS. "I WILL HAVE YOUR HEART'S BLOOD BEFORE YOU GO OUT OF THE RIVER."

Mudgett and his men climbed out of the *Black Snake* and concealed themselves in the high grass and among the trees on shore. From their hiding places, they saw the *Fly* approach, and they heard Farrington order his rowers to make for the *Black Snake*. As the revenue boat drew alongside the smuggler's sloop, Mudgett stepped out from behind a tree. "Don't lay hands on that boat," he cried. "I swear by God I will blow the first man's brains out who lays hands on her." In spite of the threat, Farrington climbed into the *Black Snake*, released the boat from her mooring, tied it to his own boat, and ordered his men to cast off. "You damned red-coated rascal!" shouted Cyrus Dean, one of the smugglers. "I will have your heart's blood before you go out of the river." As Farrington and his men rowed down the river, Mudgett and his men followed them, walking along the bank, shouting a steady stream of threats. They were all carrying their guns, and smuggler Samuel Mott had the big gun slung across his shoulders.

Still ignoring the smugglers, Farrington ordered his rowers to make for the opposite shore. As they pulled away, the smugglers began to fire. One of

Farrington's men, Ellis Drake, was struck by two musket balls in the head and tumbled dead into the river. Dean urged Mott to discharge his piece at the revenue men. Mott rested the cannon on a fence rail, took aim, and fired, killing two more of Farrington's men and wounding the lieutenant in the left arm, the right shoulder, and the forehead. Farrington staggered up the river bank, where he collapsed. His men, all unarmed, scattered for cover, while the smugglers made their escape across the river.

As news of the killings on the Onion River spread through the countryside, a local magistrate sent out officers to arrest Mudgett and his crew. Finding the smugglers to arrest them was relatively easy because they were well known in the region. But trying them was a different matter. Citizens of northern Vermont were so sympathetic to the smugglers that it was difficult to find an impartial jury. The jurors who were finally selected for the several trials (Dean, Mott, and Mudgett had asked to be tried separately) handed down inconsistent verdicts. Mudgett was released through a mistrial. Dean was sentenced to death and hung for inciting Mott to shoot the big gun. But Mott, who did the actual shooting that killed two men, was sentenced to a public flogging and ten years in prison.

The case did not end there, however. In October 1808, immediately after the trial of the *Black Snake* smugglers, Vermont voters went to the polls, where they showed their opposition to the embargo by ousting their Jeffersonian Republican governor and electing a Federalist.

ANTI-EMBARGO FERVOR

Before the embargo, Britain and France had been happy to do business with American merchants. Now, if they could not get flour, lumber, and other goods from the United States, they could find it elsewhere. For Napoleon, virtually all of Europe was his supermarket, and with the Royal Navy guarding the seas, English merchants could import goods from almost any corner of the world.

Jefferson imagined, however, that one place would be especially vulnerable to the American embargo—the British colonies in the West Indies. For decades the colonists in the Caribbean had relied upon regular American shipments of flour, salted meat, and other provisions that they could not produce in sufficient quantities for themselves. If the West Indies were suddenly cut off, they would appeal to Great Britain for help, and the best thing the crown could do, from Jefferson's perspective, was to promise to respect American neutrality. Once that promise had been made, American trade goods would flow again, and the people of the West Indies would not starve. In thinking through this scenario, however, Jefferson had failed to anticipate "leakages" by American smugglers.

In late December 1807, when word of the embargo reached the West Indies, the islanders panicked and began hoarding food supplies. The price of a barrel of flour, $8.25 before the embargo, soared to $40, with comparable inflation in the prices of cornmeal and salt. The panic did not last long, thanks to American smugglers, who, in January and February of 1808, slipped out of their harbors and made for the West Indies, with the holds of their ships crammed with food that they would sell at the new, sky-high prices.

A revenue collector in Philadelphia informed Albert Gallatin, secretary of the treasury, that from his port alone thousands of barrels of flour had headed to the Caribbean. Another revenue collector in Massachusetts complained that the bays and inlets of Cape Cod had become major launching points for ships smuggling goods to the British colonies. Because of these smugglers, the revenue collector said, the markets and storehouses of the British West Indies were "glutted with provisions" from New England. It is estimated that in New England alone, hundreds of ship owners were involved in smuggling.

To enforce the embargo, Jefferson ordered four American war ships, the *Hornet*, *Wasp*, *Argus*, and the unlucky *Chesapeake*, to patrol the sea lanes to the

West Indies. Rather than risk a confrontation with the U.S. Navy, the smugglers took their goods across the Atlantic to Europe instead. Meanwhile, as economic depression spread across the United States, angry public demonstrations erupted in the streets of the leading seaport towns, with crowds singing old Sons of Liberty songs from the 1770s. Anti-embargo fervor was so widespread that in Massachusetts, when forty people accused of violating the embargo were arraigned before a grand jury, the jurors refused to indict any of them.

By the time of the presidential election in November 1808, it was obvious to everyone—except the president himself—that Jefferson's embargo had become a national farce. On March 1, 1809, three days before Jefferson was scheduled to leave office, Congress repealed the Embargo Act. In an attempt to save face, the Jeffersonian Republicans—the majority party in Congress at the time—passed a Non-Intercourse Act that permitted American merchants to trade with anyone they liked, except the British and the French. But the Non-Intercourse Act proved to be no more effective than the discredited Embargo Act.

RUINED FORTUNES
Jefferson had convinced himself that the American public would endure any economic hardship imposed by the embargo out of a sense of patriotism. They might have, if Jefferson had gone to the people and explained his reasons for imposing the embargo. In what historian Merrill D. Peterson has described as "a critical failure of leadership," Jefferson never published an open letter or made a major address before Congress regarding his embargo policy. Consequently the farmers, manufacturers, ship owners, merchants, and sailors who suffered most from the embargo blamed Jefferson for all their troubles, and, the public looked upon the embargo as a high-handed intrusion of the federal government that was ruining their personal prosperity. From the public's point of view, Jefferson's revenue men were bullies, and the smugglers were heroes. Also, it did not escape the people's notice that the government's increasing penalties for violating the embargo and other attempts at enforcement were not exactly consistent with the president's political principles.

During the fifteen months the embargo was in effect, Britain and France did not experience enough economic hardship to make any of the concessions Jefferson expected the embargo would pry out of them. In the United States, however, the embargo strangled the economy. Treasury receipts dwindled, agricultural prices dropped—which was a consequence particularly harsh for the southern states—and many family fortunes and private businesses were ruined. For example, in Massachusetts by 1808 four-fifths of all merchants and others involved in import-export businesses were bankrupt or impoverished. In mid-1808 in Salem, a port that before the embargo had brought in 5 percent of the

annual revenue of the United States, a soup kitchen opened to feed the destitute; approximately 1,200 hungry men, women, and children came every day for the free meal. Little wonder that throughout New England, the region most involved in international commerce, there was open talk of seceding from the Union. The embargo also created a new class of criminals through its unintended encouragement of smuggling. The most damaging effect for Jefferson personally was that the embargo tarnished his reputation as the enemy of centralized government and the champion of the common people. As Jefferson prepared to leave the White House, the sixty-five-year-old president said, "Never did a prisoner, released from his chains, feel such relief as I shall on shaking off the shackles of power."

The Embargo Act had accomplished nothing, aside from plunging the United States into an economic depression. It certainly did not resolve America's quarrel with Britain over the impressment of sailors and the seizure of ships and cargo. And because Jefferson had not settled these issues, the United States moved a step closer to another war against the British.

CHAPTER 4

THE WAR OF 1812

JAMES MADISON

"SAVE THAT PICTURE!" THE FIRST LADY CRIED. "IF NOT POSSIBLE, DESTROY IT.
Under no circumstances allow it to fall into the hands of the British."

Dolley Madison's tone was peremptory, but there was no time to waste.
The British army had scattered a force of American militia and regular troops
at Bladenburg, just seven miles from Washington, D.C., and now they were on
their way to seize the undefended capital city of the United States. Most of the
city's inhabitants had fled, taking almost all the available wagons and carts with
them. There was no transport for the Madisons' personal possessions, let alone
the White House's valuable furniture. Even so, Dolley Madison wanted to save
the full-length Gilbert Stuart portrait of George Washington. Standing ninety-
five inches high and fifty-nine inches wide, the painting was enormous, and
some time earlier the White House staff had taken the precaution of screwing
the portrait directly to the wall. Now it would not come loose. In a last-ditch
effort to save the painting, Jean Sioussat, steward of the White House, climbed
a ladder, took out his penknife, and carefully cut the Washington portrait out
of its frame. With the painting saved, Dolley Madison grabbed one last
American relic—the Declaration of Independence—then hurried out to her
carriage and ordered her driver to head west toward Virginia, where she hoped
to find her husband. President James Madison had been with the American
troops that had tried, unsuccessfully, to keep the British out of Washington.

LIKE HIS MENTOR, THOMAS
JEFFERSON, PRESIDENT
JAMES MADISON NURSED
STRONG ANTI-BRITISH
SENTIMENTS. WHEN MADISON
RESOLVED TO GO TO WAR
AGAINST THE BRITISH,
JEFFERSON URGED HIM ON.

When the Americans scattered, the president escaped with them.

Dolley Madison made her escape late in the afternoon of August 24, 1814. In another hour or two, the British army entered Washington.

From a strategic or military perspective, Washington was of little consequence. In 1814, it was a village surrounded by marshes that bred clouds of mosquitoes. Augustus John Foster, Britain's minister to the United States immediately before war was declared, described the American capital as "an absolute sepulcher." Nonetheless, intent upon humiliating the Americans, the British commander-in-chief, Vice Admiral Sir Alexander Cochrane, marched his men into Washington with orders to destroy all government buildings.

According to the 1810 census, Washington had 8,208 inhabitants—5,904 whites, 867 free blacks, and 1,437 slaves. As word spread that the British were coming, almost the entire population abandoned the city. The British entered a virtual ghost town. When the British did encounter a Washingtonian, they behaved like gentlemen. There was no rape, murder, pillaging of private property, or burning of private homes. This came as a surprise, considering that one British commander, Admiral George Cockburn, had been so brutal in executing his scorched-earth policy in the Chesapeake Bay area that one well-to-do American had offered $1,000 for Cockburn's head, or $500 for either of his ears.

Cochrane's targets in Washington were the capitol and the executive mansion. By marching almost unopposed into town, Cochrane had humiliated President Madison in particular and the American people in general. By destroying the buildings that were the monuments of U.S. sovereignty, he would demonstrate just how foolhardy the upstart Americans had been to declare war against Great Britain.

At 9 P.M., a column of British troops climbed Capitol Hill and entered the chamber of the House of Representatives. They had expected something as austere as a New England meetinghouse, but architect Benjamin Latrobe had designed a building modeled on the splendor of ancient Rome, with a domed ceiling, fluted stone columns, and a magnificent sculpture of an American eagle with a twenty-one-foot wingspan over the speaker's chair. When the officers ordered their men to burn the place, some objected, insisting that a building so beautiful should be spared, but Cochrane was determined. The British soldiers piled the chairs, desks, and other furniture in the center of the House chamber, then set it alight. They repeated the process in the Senate and in the chamber of the Supreme Court, and they even burned the 3,000-volume collection of the Library of Congress. From Capitol Hill, the British made their way down the rutted, dusty track known as Pennsylvania Avenue to the president's house.

Inside, the officers and their arsonists found the table set for forty. Dolley Madison had expected a large party of guests for lunch that day, but she had been forced to flee Washington shortly after the servants had placed the meal on the table. It was all still there, and the wine, ale, and cider brought up from the cellar by Paul Jennings, one of the Madison family's personal slaves, still stood in their coolers. The meat and vegetables were safe from flies and mosquitoes under the silver domes that covered the dishes. Confronted with such a sumptuous meal, the British postponed burning the house, and they sat down to eat Madison's food and drink his wine. Once the meal was over, the officers sent four sailors upstairs with burning torches to set fire to the beds, hangings, and draperies. Downstairs, soldiers made a bonfire of Dolley Madison's gilded furniture. The British picked up a few souvenirs, but there was no looting in the executive mansion. Everything of value, as well as all of the Madisons' personal possessions, was burned.

ANOTHER WAR WITH THE BRITISH

Three issues had driven the U.S. Congress to declare war on Great Britain, and two of them had been simmering for years. The first was the repeated and intolerable impressment of American sailors. For more than a decade, the Royal Navy had stopped American ships on the high seas and seized members of the crew they insisted were deserters from the Royal Navy or at least British subjects. It is estimated that between 1803 and 1812—a time when Britain was at war with France—approximately 6,000 seamen were taken from American vessels and forced to serve on British warships. In response to formal objections from the United States government, the British agreed to release any wrongly impressed seamen once proof of citizenship had been established. Collecting such documents and submitting them to the proper authorities in England took months, and once the documents arrived in England, the review process dragged on for many months more.

Equally galling was the Royal Navy's interference in American trade. Although the United States had declared itself neutral in the war raging between Britain and France, the British seized cargos and sometimes U.S. merchant ships themselves if they were bound for a French port.

Then in 1810 a Shawnee chief named Tecumseh, along with his brother Tenskwatawa, who was better known as the Prophet, assembled a coalition of tribes to drive white settlers out of Illinois, Indiana, and Ohio. Many Americans were convinced that the British in Canada were behind this latest Indian war.

When Congress assembled in Washington, D.C., in November 1811, President Madison sent a message in which he reviewed all the outrages the United States had suffered from Great Britain, then concluded by urging Congress to put American citizens "into an armor and an attitude demanded by the crisis." In other words, President Madison

THE STAR-SPANGLED BANNER OF THE KEY POEM WAS MADE IN 1806 BY MARY PICKERSGILL OF BALTIMORE, AND ITS ORIGINAL SIZE—BEFORE RELIC-HUNTERS STARTED SNIPPING OFF PIECES—WAS 30 X 42 FEET.

was asking Congress for a declaration of war. For many years Madison had been a close observer of the ongoing troubles between Britain and the United States. During the administration of his friend, Thomas Jefferson, Madison had been an ardent proponent of an economic embargo, believing that sudden loss of American goods would force Britain to make concessions regarding impressments and impounding American ships and cargo. But the embargo had been a dismal failure: America suffered an economic depression, while the Royal Navy continued to harass American vessels. Now Madison's mind was made up. War was the only way to check British aggression and defend American interests.

The president's timing was ideal: Not only did his party, the Jeffersonian Republicans, dominate the House and the Senate, but among the newly elected congressmen were a band of hotheaded expansionists, mostly from western states, known as the "War Hawks," who threw their support behind Madison. Led by thirty-four-year-old Henry Clay of Kentucky and thirty-nine-year-old John C. Calhoun of South Carolina, the War Hawks were eager for another war with the British. Their idea was to conquer British Canada as a way to compel Great Britain to cease its interference with American trade and shipping.

Although only a freshman, Clay was elected speaker of the House, and under his leadership Congress enacted a series of measures to prepare for the coming conflict. They authorized the purchase of artillery, the construction of forts along the Atlantic coast, and the refitting of all U.S. vessels as warships. But Congress stopped short of declaring war. The United States still had envoys in Great Britain, led by William Pinkney of Maryland; perhaps Pinkney and his colleagues were having some success winning concessions from the British government. Congress decided to wait for the return of the USS *Hornet* from Great Britain.

The *Hornet* docked in New York City in May 1812 with Pinkney on board. The news he brought delighted the War Hawks. The British had made no

OVERLEAF: THE BRITISH BOMBARDMENT OF FORT MCHENRY IN BALTIMORE HARBOR INSPIRED FRANCIS SCOTT KEY TO WRITE "THE STAR-SPANGLED BANNER."

concessions whatsoever. Only days after the dispatches from the *Hornet* had been delivered into his hands, President Madison sent another message to Congress. One by one he listed all of Great Britain's offenses against the United States: The young nation's old antagonist had stifled American commerce, compelled American citizens to serve on British warships, and violated American waters. To this list Madison added the unproven charges that the British were inciting Chief Tecumseh and his allies against American settlers and that the British Crown was scheming to take over New England. Congressman Calhoun introduced a bill to declare war against Great Britain, and in just two days it passed the House by a vote of seventy-nine to forty-nine. The Senate followed suit, passing a declaration of war nineteen to thirteen.

Washington's leading newspaper, the *National Intelligencer*, exulted in the vote. The War Hawks' Congress was the equal of the "Immortal Congress" of 1776. "Under the auspices of the one this nation sprung into existence," the *Intelligencer*'s editor wrote, "under those of the other it will have been preserved from disgraceful recolonization."

GREEN OFFICERS AND RAW RECRUITS In spite of the bravado of

Madison, the War Hawks, and the newspaper editors, the United States was in no position to wage war against Great Britain. Its navy had only fourteen warships, and the army counted about 7,000 professionally trained troops. There were state and territorial militias, but the Federalist governors of New England refused to send their best fighting men against the British, and the military skills of the frontier militias had always been spotty.

Many of the military's senior officers owed their appointments to political patronage rather than as achievements won by victories on the battlefield. Even those who were veteran commanders from the American Revolution were now old men, who, as twenty-six-year-old artillery captain Winfield Scott described them, had "sunk into either sloth, ignorance, or habits of intemperate drinking." To attract recruits, Congress authorized sign-on bonuses that ultimately reached $124 in cash and 320 acres of land in the western territories. But nothing could be done about the inexperience of these green officers. Congressman Peter B. Porter of New York, a War Hawk and protégé of Clay, lamented that the latest crop of officers had come "fresh from lawyer shops and counting rooms." Even worse were the enlisted men—rough, raw, disorderly recruits who deserted on the slightest pretext, or none at all. Porter opposed going to war in the summer of 1812 because the nation was unprepared. American business interests, too, opposed going to war because of the disruption it would cause to trade and the economy. Desertion became so common during the first year of the war that President Madison promised a full pardon to any deserters who returned to duty.

COMMODORE OLIVER
HAZARD PERRY'S VICTORY
OVER A BRITISH FLEET IN
LAKE ERIE IN 1813 WAS ONE
OF THE FEW SIGNIFICANT
AMERICAN SUCCESSES
DURING THE WAR OF 1812.

In addition to lacking enough soldiers, Madison's government was also short on cash thanks to Jeffersonian Republican Congressmen who years earlier had repealed all internal taxes, including the much-hated whiskey tax. (See chapter 1, "George Washington: The Whiskey Rebellion.") When Jeffersonian Republican Congressmen suggested an increased tax on customs duties, Federalist Congressmen from the north, the primary market for imported goods, complained that their people were being unfairly burdened.

While Congress bickered over who should be taxed, Madison's Treasury secretary, Albert Gallatin, suggested that the federal government should borrow $16 million to pay for the war. Congress approved, authorizing the loan at 6 percent interest, but very few lenders stepped forward. Gallatin managed to raise about $8 million; another $7 million came from the Philadelphia firm of Parish and Girard, and John Jacob Astor, the richest man in America at the time, agreed to lend the government $2 million.

THE CANADIAN CAMPAIGNS

Once war had been declared, the Americans' first objective was Canada. As Clay explained later, "Canada was not the end, but the means—the object of the war being the redress of injuries, and Canada being the instrument by which that redress was to be obtained." Jefferson spoke for many Americans when he said that Canada was an easy target—"a matter of marching," as the former president put it, was all it would take to seize the country. After all, how could Canada, with only 500,000 people, stand against the 7.5 million who lived in the United States? Furthermore, the large French Catholic population that resented living under the rule of British Protestants was likely to join forces with the Americans. Once Canada was in American hands, the War Hawks argued, Britain would be willing to make concessions at last. The American plan was not to conquer Canada outright, but rather to occupy it and use it as a bargaining chip.

Secretary of War John Armstrong developed the strategy for the Canada campaign, and his primary goals were modest. U.S. forces would strike at Kingston and York (present-day Toronto), the two most important British naval bases in Canada, and at Fort George and Fort Erie, two strongholds that defended the Niagara River. Once the forts and naval bases were in American hands, they could be used to launch strikes against other British targets in Canada. Quebec and Montreal, however, were not on the hit list. Both cities were too well fortified, and no American commander was ready to risk an assault on them.

The secondary goal of this campaign was to control the Great Lakes. Because this part of U.S. territory was still virgin wilderness, the only way to transport men and goods was by water. Whoever controlled the lakes, controlled the U.S.-Canadian border.

The first American expedition into Canada attacked York. In April 1813, 1,700 American troops under the command of General Zebulon Pike (the explorer who in 1806 had climbed the Rocky Mountain peak in Colorado known ever since as Pike's Peak) stormed the town and captured it, but at a terrible cost. The British and Indian defenders of York lost 150 men, but the American death toll was 320. Most of the Americans were killed when the garrison's stores of gunpowder and ammunition exploded. General Pike, thirty-four years old, was among the dead. An eyewitness told how in the explosion "a large stone struck him in the forehead and stamped him for the grave." In retaliation for so many casualties, the Americans looted the town, then set fire to the government buildings. (The British would later cite this act of arson as their excuse for burning the United States Capitol and the White House.)

An American assault on Fort George and the neighboring town of Newark went well. Led by twenty-seven-year-old General Winfield Scott and twenty-eight-year-old Commodore Oliver Perry—fresh from his stunning naval victory over a British fleet on Lake Erie—American artillery pounded the fort into submission. The British commander, John Vincent, surrendered, then ordered British forces to evacuate three other forts along the Niagara frontier. It appeared that Jefferson's prediction of victory being as easy as marching was coming true.

The Americans failed to follow up on their victories and press their advantage, however. The British regrouped and, after defeating the Americans in two battles on the Canadian side of the border, crossed the Niagara River into New York State, where they committed terrible atrocities. They took Fort Niagara by surprise and bayoneted eighty American soldiers to death in their beds. At Lewiston, New York, the Indian allies of the British massacred the civilian inhabitants of the town, leaving their mutilated bodies scattered all across the countryside. Then the British moved on to Black Rock and Buffalo, which they burned to the ground.

In a bold move to regain the upper hand, the U.S. Department of War abandoned its misgivings about attacking the major Canadian cities and planned a campaign against Montreal under the leadership of Brigadier General Wade Hampton, a veteran of the American Revolution. Hampton had

4,500 men under his command, while Montreal was defended by 1,400 French Canadian militiamen. The campaign quickly fell apart. At the border, 1,000 American militia refused to cross into Canada. Nothing Hampton promised or threatened would persuade them to march into Canada, and so he left them behind. Once the remaining 3,500 Americans arrived at the outskirts of Montreal, they discovered massive defensive works that so intimidated the American forces that their first assault on the fortifications was feeble at best. The French Canadian defenders noticed, and raised a terrible commotion behind their breastworks, creating the impression that Montreal was defended by thousands of troops. That was all it took to scare the Americans off the field. Hampton gave up his campaign and retreated with his skittish army back across the border. After the debacle outside Montreal, the United States gave up all plans to occupy Canada.

THE BATTLE OF NEW ORLEANS
All night long on January 7, 1815, civilians of New Orleans had made their way slowly through a cold fog to the convent chapel of the Ursuline nuns to join the sisters in their dusk-to-dawn vigil of prayer to Our Lady of Prompt Succor, the city's patroness, for the success of the American army that defended the hundred-year-old city against the British. It was a very strange assortment of defenders: professional American troops, frontier militia, backwoods sharpshooters, free blacks of New Orleans, Choctaw Indians, plus a band of rough swamp pirates from Barataria Bay under the command of Jean Lafitte, the celebrated buccaneer and slave dealer.

Just as the Americans had hoped to use Canada as a bargaining chip with Great Britain, the British were attempting to occupy the Gulf Coast to use for the same purpose against the United States. The greatest prize along the coast was New Orleans, a wealthy city, its wharves and warehouses piled high with trade goods, and the gateway to North America via the Mississippi River. To take advantage of all the loot they expected to carry off after conquering the city, the British had brought cargo ships along with them.

Throughout December 1814, the British under General Edward Pakenham, an experienced military man and brother-in-law of the Duke of Wellington, Napoleon's conqueror at Waterloo, jockeyed for an advantageous position against General Andrew Jackson, the American commander. Jackson had first fought the British as a teenager during the American Revolution, and he had hated the redcoats ever since. When the boy was a prisoner of war, a British officer had slashed him across the face for refusing to shine the man's boots.

Almost the entire American force was dug in on the eastern bank of the Mississippi River behind earthworks that stretched from the river into a cypress swamp along the Rodriguez Canal at Chalmette, downriver from the city. The British had erected some defensive works, too, but it was plain that they intended to take the offensive in the battle, crush the ragtag Americans, and sweep into New Orleans. On the day of battle, January 8, 1815, General Pakenham had 5,300 trained regular troops, many of them veterans of the Napoleonic wars, to throw against General Jackson's 4,700 men, most of whom had no formal military training.

At dawn on January 8, a heavy fog drifting in from the river covered the plains of Chalmette. Delighted by this gift from nature, Pakenham ordered his 5,300 men forward. But suddenly the fog lifted, and the British were entirely exposed on the open field. Yet the Americans held their fire. At a steady pace the British marched forward. When they were 500 yards out from Jackson's earthworks, the American artillery opened fire. Grapeshot tore through the close-packed formations, but the British reformed their ranks and advanced. At the 300-yard mark, American riflemen opened fire. When the British were within 100 yards, American musket men sent a fresh hail of musket balls into the British ranks.

The relentless volleys of artillery and rifles from the American lines cut down the British by the score. Some turned and ran for their lives; others fell to the ground and played dead. As for General Pakenham, a round of grapeshot from an American cannon killed his horse and wounded him in the knee and arm. As one of his men helped him onto another horse, a second round of grapeshot struck the general and killed him. British General John Lambert assumed command, made a quick assessment of the situation, then ordered a retreat. When the shooting stopped, 2,000 British lay dead or wounded on the field. General Jackson had lost only eighty-three men.

The carnage outside New Orleans was the worst of the War of 1812, and, although Jackson and Pakenham could not have known it, the battle was entirely unnecessary. By a cruel irony, thirteen days earlier in the city of Ghent, in modern-day Belgium, on Christmas Eve, envoys from Great Britain and the United States had signed a peace treaty bringing the war to an end, though without settling any of the original disputes that had led to the war.

AT GREAT COST, BUT TO WHAT END? The War of 1812 lasted two years and eight months, yet in that brief time it cost the lives of about 20,000 American citizens. More than 17,000 lives were lost to disease in military camps, and an uncertain number of civilians were killed in war-related Indian raids such as the Lewiston massacre. Battlefield deaths ran to 2,260, and another 205 soldiers were executed for repeated acts of desertion. Approximately 4,400 American troops were wounded. In terms of financial

UNDER THE GUIDANCE
OF GENERAL ANDREW
JACKSON (IN FOREGROUND
ON HORSEBACK) 4,700
AMERICAN MEN—MOST OF
WHOM HAD NO FORMAL
MILITARY TRAINING—HELD
OFF 5,300 BRITISH TROOPS
IN A VERY BLOODY BATTLE
NEAR THE CITY
OF NEW ORLEANS.

costs, the war was almost ruinous. In 1812, the United States' national debt stood at $45 million, but by the end of 1815 it had skyrocketed to $127 million. Taxation to fund the war reached levels not seen again until the Civil War. Nonetheless, by 1814, the nation was on the edge of financial collapse, and by November of that year, the federal government was virtually bankrupt.

At the time the peace treaty was signed in 1814, neither the United States nor Great Britain had won a clear-cut military victory, yet the treaty was much more favorable to the British than to the Americans. The British did not promise to stop searching American ships, confiscating American goods, or impressing Americans sailors into service aboard British ships. The British did agree to vacate their forts in American territory and return any American territory its forces occupied, but those were the only concessions the American negotiators were able to win. The War of 1812 accomplished none of the goals President Madison had argued for so carefully when he called upon Congress to declare war against the British. American shipping was still vulnerable to the

Royal Navy on the high seas, and the most important government buildings in Washington, D.C., were burned-out shells. Only Jackson's stunning victory at New Orleans at the last minute took the sting out of the disaster.

President Madison's decision to go to war against Britain was a gross miscalculation. His belief that it would be simple to occupy and perhaps even annex Canada was flat-out wrong. He overlooked the size and strength of the Royal Navy that blockaded American ports and brought shipping along the Eastern seaboard to a virtual standstill. And like his predecessor in the White House, Jefferson, Madison had an exaggerated sense of how much trouble the United States could cause the British. Compared to the threat posed by Napoleon, the United States was insignificant. At the end of the war, the British gave up nothing, and all Madison had to show for his bravado was more economic hardship for his country, the shame of a burned capital, and the loss of 20,000 American lives.

CHAPTER 5

THE TRAIL OF TEARS

ANDREW JACKSON

ON ONE OF THE LAST DAYS OF MAY 1838, A CHEROKEE WIDOW NAMED OOLOOCHA was doing her housework while keeping an eye on her youngest children when she heard a commotion in the yard. On opening the door she saw a platoon of soldiers surrounding her house, their rifles pointing at her chest. One of the troopers had Ooloocha's mare, and several more soldiers were heading into the fields where members of her family were working. Then a handful of the armed men ran up the stairs of her house toward Ooloocha and the children. In a claim she filed four years later for the property she had lost in Georgia, she described what happened next. "They drove us out of doors and did not permit us to take anything with us," she testified, "not even a second change of clothes, only the clothes we had on, and they shut the doors after they turned us out. They would not permit any of us to enter the house to get [anything], but drove us off to a fort that was built at New Echota."

ANDREW JACKSON WAS AMBIVALENT ABOUT THE INDIANS. HIS ADOPTED SON WAS A CREEK, YET HE FELT THE U.S. GOVERNMENT WAS UNDER NO OBLIGATION TO RECOGNIZE THE TRIBES AS SOVEREIGN NATIONS.

The scene at the Cherokee widow's house was repeated throughout the Cherokee lands in Georgia—troops of soldiers descending on houses and fields, rounding up the inhabitants at gunpoint, and forcing them to travel on foot to one of the thirty-one forts the government had just built near major Cherokee towns. The Cherokee were forbidden to bring fresh clothes, and the soldiers would not even let them bring food, water, medicine, or blankets. They had to leave everything they owned behind—their crops, their livestock, and their personal possessions.

And in the chaos, terrible things occurred. One deaf Cherokee man who did not obey a soldier's command was shot dead. In one round-up, soldiers left a weak, sickly man about a hundred years old named Tik-i-kiski behind because he could not walk and they had no wagon to carry him. Several days later Tik-i-kiski, nearly dead of starvation, was found by some white children. The children's parents nursed the elder back to health, then brought him to the fort where his family was interned so he could make the journey west with them. On another occasion, when troopers approached a Cherokee house, two small children who were playing in the yard took fright and ran into the woods. The soldiers would not let their mother go search for them.

By the first week of June 1838, there were about 13,000 Cherokee scattered among the thirty-one stockades the state and federal governments had erected in the tribe's territory as military bases. Most of the stockades were in Georgia where the majority of the Cherokee lived, but there were stockades in Tennessee and one in North Carolina. There was not enough food, and there was not enough space inside the forts' buildings to house all the detainees. In some places, the soldiers pitched tents for the Cherokee, but in others the Indians slept on the bare ground, with no blankets to warm them, and nothing to shield them from the rain. Meanwhile unscrupulous white men and women were looting the Cherokee's houses, farms, and shops, and even violating Cherokee graves to steal silver jewelry from the bodies of the dead.

A SIMPLE, CLEAN SOLUTION

The years after the War of 1812 were a boom time in the United States, especially for farmers in the western territories. State governments had invested in canals and highways, and steamboats—the latest mode of transportation—began plying the Ohio, the Mississippi, and other rivers of the West. For the first time, settlers in the far-flung regions of the country had a cheap, reliable way to get their goods to the markets of the East. As farming and raising livestock became more and more profitable, more and more settlers poured into the western lands. In 1810, Indiana and Illinois had a combined population of 37,000; by 1830 their numbers had leapt to nearly half a million. Mississippi and Alabama enjoyed a similar population explosion—from about 40,000 in 1810 to about 445,000 in 1830.

An obstacle to these pioneers was various Indian nations who had long inhabited millions of acres of land in all of these states. As corn farmers in the North and cotton planters in the South looked to expand their holdings, the pressure on the Indians to sell became intense. And when some tribes, such as the Cherokee, refused to sell, the settlers appealed to the federal government to clear off the Indians.

Andrew Jackson first became involved in Indian removal after he had led U.S. troops—and their Cherokee allies—to victory over the Red Stick Creeks in the Creek War in 1813 and 1814. As part of the treaty between the Creeks and the United States, the Indians ceded twenty-three million acres of their homeland in Georgia and Alabama. Impressed by Jackson's achievement, the government sent him to negotiate four more treaties with four different Indian tribes. Jackson, a dutiful man, did as he was asked, but he felt it an enormous waste of time. When the first settlers had come to America in the 1600s, the Indians had the upper hand in terms of military strength, but that was no longer the case. As the U.S. army had proven time and again, it could crush any Indian uprising east of the Mississippi. In a letter to President James Monroe in 1817, Jackson advanced the argument that since the circumstances of the Americans and the Indians had changed entirely, it was time for the federal government to abandon the pretense that the Indians were sovereign nations; the Indians were subjects of the United States. The way Jackson saw it, the simplest, cleanest solution would be for Congress to pass legislation authorizing the confiscation of Indian land.

President Monroe was not comfortable with the idea of an all-out land-grab. Instead, he attempted two policies that were poles apart. First Monroe sent delegates to various Indian tribes to try to persuade them to give up their lands east of the Mississippi for new lands west of the river. About 3,000 Indians accepted the government's offer, but the majority of the tribes rejected it. The second approach was an attempt to diminish the tensions between whites and Indians by encouraging the tribes to assimilate into American society: to live in houses, farm, adopt American-style clothing and names, and establish schools, newspapers, and a government modeled on the American system.

The Cherokee, Creek, Choctaw, Chickasaw, and Seminoles—known as the "Five Civilized Tribes"—made a good-faith attempt to assimilate into American society while retaining certain aspects of their traditional culture. In spite of the huge track of real estate the Creeks turned over to the Americans, the five tribes still inhabited a considerable portion of northern Georgia, as well as land in Tennessee and North Carolina. Here they attempted to straddle two worlds. Most became fluent in English; many could read and write in English and in their own language after Cherokee scholar Sequoyah invented an Indian alphabet; a sizable number converted to Christianity; and wealthy landowning Cherokee imitated their white neighbors by buying and selling African slaves. Yet in spite of the five tribes' attempts to enter mainstream American society, the pressure on them to sell their land to whites was constant. The Cherokee,

PRESIDENTIAL BRIEFING
(1767-1845)
• GENERAL AND SEVENTH PRESIDENT OF THE UNITED STATES (1829-37)
• BORN MARCH 15, 1767, WAXHAW SETTLEMENT, SOUTH CAROLINA
• DIED JUNE 8, 1845, NEAR NASHVILLE, TENNESSEE
• IN THE WAR OF 1812, JACKSON BECAME A NATIONAL HERO THROUGH A DEVASTATING DEFEAT OF THE BRITISH AT THE BATTLE OF NEW ORLEANS, 1815
• ELECTED PRESIDENT IN 1828. ALLOWED THE TAKING OF INDIAN LANDS IN GEORGIA, FLORIDA, AND ALABAMA; ENCOURAGED WESTWARD EXPANSION AND RECOGNIZED THE INDEPENDENCE OF TEXAS FROM MEXICO

LEGISLATORS SUCH AS DANIEL WEBSTER, HENRY CLAY, DAVY CROCKETT, AND MASSACHUSETTS CONGRESSMAN EDWARD EVERETT (SHOWN HERE), OPPOSED THE INDIAN REMOVAL ACT—CALLING IT A MERCENARY ATTEMPT TO STEAL LAND AND A SHAMELESS INSTANCE OF BAD FAITH ON THE PART OF THE FEDERAL GOVERNMENT. NONETHELESS, CONGRESS PASSED THE ACT ON MAY 28, 1830, AND PRESIDENT JACKSON SIGNED IT INTO LAW.

for example, passed legislation that made it a crime for any Cherokee to sell his land to an American. In 1821, the penalty was a $150 fine; by 1829, the Cherokee had elevated the penalty to the death sentence.

"THEY MUST YIELD"
The election of Jackson to the presidency in 1828 encouraged the Georgia legislature to take action against the Cherokee nation. The state annexed all Cherokee land in Georgia and nullified all acts of the Cherokee legislature. Alabama and Tennessee soon followed Georgia's lead.

Now that he was president, Jackson had to put into action the policy he had advocated as early as 1817. In an address to Congress in 1829, Jackson made appeals to both law and the sympathies of his audience. The tribal governments were in violation of the Constitution, he said, and quoted the text, "No new State shall be formed or erected within the jurisdiction of any other State." As for the Indians themselves, their condition was pitiable. "They have been made to retire from river to river and from mountain to mountain," Jackson said, "until some of the tribes have become extinct and others have left but remnants to preserve for awhile their once terrible names." The president continued, "I suggest for your consideration the propriety of setting apart an ample district west of the Mississippi, and without the limits of any State or Territory now formed, to be guaranteed to the Indian tribes as long as they shall occupy it, each tribe having a distinct control over the portion designated for its use." Jackson urged Congress to enact this policy of relocating the Indians because "humanity and national honor demand [it]."

Inspired by the Georgia law and with the full approval of President Jackson, the U.S. Congress passed a bill that stripped all Indians east of the Mississippi of all their land; as compensation, the tribes would receive land across the Mississippi River in territory outside any of the states.

AS TERRIBLE AS THESE REMOVALS WERE, JACKSON DID NOT INTEND TO INFLICT A "FINAL SOLUTION" ON THE INDIANS, NOR IS THERE EVIDENCE THAT HE WANTED TO EXTERMINATE THEM.

Daniel Webster, Henry Clay, and Davy Crockett were among the members of Congress who opposed the Indian Removal Act, denouncing it as a mercenary attempt to steal land, not to mention a shameless instance of bad faith on the part of the federal government, which had treaty obligations with the tribes. Congressman Edward Everett of Massachusetts reminded Congress that the people they were about to drive from their homes were "the old and the young, wives and children, the feeble, the sick [who were to be] dragged hundreds of miles, over mountains, rivers, and deserts, where there are no roads, no bridges, no habitations." At such a thought, Everett said, "the imagination sickens." In spite of these protests, Congress passed the Indian Removal Act on May 28, 1830, and Jackson signed it into law. By the time Jackson left office in 1837, approximately 46,000 Indians had been forced westward to the Indian Territory (present-day Oklahoma), and thousands more were scheduled for removal.

As terrible as these removals were, Jackson did not intend to inflict a "Final Solution" on the Indians, nor is there evidence that he wanted to exterminate them. In some respects, Jackson was more open-minded than many of his contemporaries. For example, he did not object to marriages between whites and Indians. His adopted son, Lincoyer, was a Creek orphan. But as a man with a deep attachment to states' rights (rights that have not been expressly given to the federal government by the U.S. Constitution or forbidden to the states), Jackson rejected absolutely the notion that an independent Indian nation could exist within the borders of a sovereign state such as Georgia or Alabama. That is why he held out an alternative to the Indians: If they swore allegiance to the United States and the state in which resided, they could stay and keep their land. If they insisted on setting their tribal law above the law of the states, then they would have to go.

While President Jackson was willing to accept the Indians' allegiance, he did not in any way regard them as equals. In Jackson's annual message to Congress that he delivered on December 3, 1833, he presented his reasons for advocating a policy of removing the Cherokee from their homeland to territory west of the Mississippi:

> My original convictions upon this subject have been confirmed by the course of events for several years, and experience is every day adding to their strength. That those tribes can not exist surrounded by our settlements and in continual contact with our citizens is certain. They have neither the intelligence, the industry, the moral habits, nor the desire of improvement which are essential to any favorable change in their condition. Established in the midst of another and a superior race, and without appreciating the causes of their inferiority or seeking to control them, they must necessarily yield to the force of circumstances and ere long disappear.

CHEROKEE CHIEF JOHN ROSS FOUGHT ALONGSIDE THEN GENERAL ANDREW JACKSON DURING THE CREEK WAR TWENTY YEARS EARLIER, BUT WHEN HE VISITED THE WHITE HOUSE IN 1834 TO ASK THE PRESIDENT FOR $20 MILLION COMPENSATION FOR THE EIGHT MILLION ACRES OF LAND THE CHEREOKEE WERE BEING FORCED TO ABANDON, HE WAS VILIFIED BY JACKSON AND HIS REQUEST WAS DISMISSED AS "PREPOSTEROUS."

The Cherokee responded to the Georgia and congressional legislation by going to court. One of the provisions of the Georgia law required that all white adults who wished to live in Indian territory apply to the state for a license. It was an odd requirement, but the Georgia legislators knew that white Protestant pastors of Indian congregations were helping the Cherokee resist the government's attempts to confiscate their land. Samuel A. Worcester, a seventh-generation clergyman from Vermont, was one of seven ministers who refused to apply for such a license. They were arrested, tried, and sentenced to four years of hard labor. The convicted ministers appealed their case to the U.S. Supreme Court. On March 3, 1832, the court led by Chief Justice John Marshall ruled in *Worcester v. Georgia* that the state of Georgia had no authority to seize Indian land or abrogate Indian legislation or place an obstacle in the way of American citizens who wished to pass in and out of Indian territory because such actions were delegated exclusively to the Congress of the United States.

The Court's decision liberated the ministers from prison, but that did not help the Cherokee. Georgia may have had no right to take the Indians' land, but Congress did, and the Supreme Court did not overturn or declare unconstitutional the Indian Removal Act passed by Congress and signed by the president. The Cherokee were running out of options.

THE CHIEF AND THE PRESIDENT John Ross's blue eyes and brown hair came from his Scots ancestors, but he was one-eighth Cherokee. He had grown up in Cherokee territory and learned to straddle both worlds. In his twenties, Ross began to identify himself with the tribe, immersing himself in the politics of the Cherokee nation. In 1827, the tribe elected him principal chief.

Ross was the model of Monroe's assimilation program. He was a wealthy man who lived like other wealthy southern planters—in a comfortable home with twenty slaves working in his fields and tending his house. In addition to farming, Ross had a trading company, and between these two sources of income he became one of the wealthiest men in the Cherokee nation.

As the state and federal governments pressed the Cherokees to give up their lands, Ross offered his people reassurance. "Friends," he said, "I have great hopes in your firmness and that you will hold fast to the place where you were raised. Friends, if you all unite together and be of one mind, there is no danger."

But in fact there was a very real danger that the Cherokee would be forced out of their homes, whether or not they all stood together, and so Ross went see President Jackson. Ross was optimistic because he had fought with Jackson years earlier at the Battle of Horseshoe Bend—the decisive battle of the Creek War in which 3,000 U.S. troops, led by Jackson and assisted by Cherokee warriors under Chief Junaluska, overpowered 1,000 Creek, slaughtering 800. Ross imagined he would be welcomed as a brother-in-arms. But in fact, Jackson despised Ross as "a great villain" and regarded him as the head of a mixed-race elite in which true Cherokee blood had been diluted. In spite of Jackson's dislike, however, he agreed to meet Ross.

Promptly at noon on February 5, 1834, Ross arrived at the White House and was shown in to the president's office. Ross began with an earnest appeal: "Your Cherokee children are in deep distress ... because they are left at the mercy of the white robber and assassin." He drew the president's attention to a lottery operated by the state of Georgia in which Cherokee land was the prize. Then, inexplicably, Ross shifted from appealing to the president's sense of fair play and began to make demands. Ross wanted the U.S. government to expel white settlers from old Cherokee lands near the border area of Georgia, Alabama, Tennessee, and North Carolina, and he wanted the U.S. army posted in the area to protect the tribe from white squatters.

Jackson was furious, but he suppressed his rage. In a calm voice he stated candidly that as expressed in the Indian Removal Act of 1830 it was the policy of his administration that the entire Cherokee nation must relinquish their lands and move to new territory that the government would assign them west of the Mississippi River. Ross replied that if they must go, then he wanted a cash payment of $20 million from the U.S. government. It was a staggering sum, equal to the national debt, but Ross insisted that it was a fair price given that the Cherokee were being forced to abandon eight million acres of land, including land on which gold had recently been discovered.

Now the president made no effort to conceal his anger. He dismissed Ross's demand for $20 million in compensation as "preposterous." If the principal chief could not talk sensibly, Jackson believed there was no point in continuing their discussion. Realizing that he had antagonized the president, Ross backtracked, saying he had confidence that Congress would make a fair offer, and he would accept it on behalf of his people. Jackson promised that he would support any cash award approved by the Senate's Committee on Indian Affairs. A few days later, while Ross was still in Washington, Senator John P. King of Georgia, chairman of the Committee on Indian Affairs, informed Ross that the government was prepared to offer the Cherokee nation $5 million.

Ross's visit to Washington was an unmitigated disaster. He had in essence agreed to the removal of his people from their land, and he had promised to accept whatever cash settlement the U.S. government decided to award the Cherokee nation. In an effort to save face, Ross rejected the Senate's offer of $5 million, saying that when he had agreed to accept a cash award from the government, he had not imagined the Senate would insult the Cherokee by offering such a paltry sum.

Another year passed. The Cherokee showed no sign of leaving their homeland, and the federal government was not yet ready to use force to drive them out. A large delegation of Cherokee chiefs traveled to Washington to ask for their own meeting with Jackson. Addressing his guests as "brothers," Jackson launched into a lengthy speech intended to persuade the Cherokee to see the wisdom of relocation. "Most of your people are uneducated," he said, "and are liable to be brought into collision at all times with your white neighbors. Your young men are acquiring habits of intoxication. With strong passions … they are frequently driven to excesses which must eventually terminate in their ruin. The game has disappeared among you, and you must depend upon agriculture and the mechanic arts for support. And yet, a large portion of your people have acquired little or no property in the soil itself. How, under these circumstances, can you live in the country you now occupy? Your condition must become worse and worse, and you will ultimately disappear, as so many tribes have done before you." Their only option, Jackson concluded, was to go west.

The Cherokee chiefs left the White House as dispirited as Ross had been a year earlier. Jackson was determined to have their land, and he had the power to take it.

THE TREATY OF NEW ECHOTA
To combat the influence of Protestant pastors such as Samuel Worcester who were urging the Cherokee not to abandon their homeland, President Jackson brought in a minister who would represent the government's point of view, the Reverend John Schermerhorn, a Dutch Reformed minister from New York and a trusted friend of the president's. (Schermerhorn had been a guest at the Hermitage, Jackson's plantation outside Nashville, Tennessee, on more than one occasion.) Beginning in 1832, Schermerhorn advised the Cherokee to accept the inevitable, make the best deal they could with the government, and move peacefully to the Indian Territory. Schermerhorn found support among three prominent Cherokee: Major Ridge, a wealthy planter; John Ridge, Major Ridge's son; and Elias Boudinot, the founder and editor of the tribe's newspaper, the *Cherokee Phoenix*. These men comprised the "treaty faction," Cherokee who believed they were powerless to resist the federal government.

Before Christmas 1835, Reverend Schermerhorn traveled to New Echota, Georgia, the capital of the Cherokee nation. There he issued a dramatic call for "a council of all the people" to discuss the newest treaty offered by the U.S. government. Among other terms, the government agreed to subsidize the removal of the Cherokee to the Indian Territory, to support them for their first two years in residence there, and to pay $4.5 million in compensation to the tribe (an adjustment of the $5 million offered previously). The overwhelming majority of Cherokee signified their contempt for the treaty by refusing to attend Schermerhorn's meeting: Of the 13,000 Cherokee, only 300 to 400 men, women, and children came. Schermerhorn delayed the meeting for several days, hoping more people would come, but they never did. With no other recourse open to him, Schermerhorn declared the council in session and after what he considered a suitable period of discussion, called for a vote. The men who were present voted, seventy-nine to seven, to accept the treaty and move to the west. Schermerhorn forwarded the results to Washington.

The absent Cherokee sent their own message to Jackson and the Senate— a resolution, signed by 12,000 Cherokee, denouncing the Treaty of New Echota. Jackson ignored the appeal, although some of the most prominent men in the Senate did pay attention to it. Senators Webster and Clay denounced the Treaty of Echota as blatantly unjust. Standing on the floor of the Senate,

Webster rebuked his Democratic colleagues for having "no concern for Indian rights, so far as I can perceive." In spite of such protests, the Treaty of New Echota passed by a single vote, and five days later Jackson signed it into law. The Cherokee were informed that they had two years to pack up and travel to the Indian Territory.

In a speech to his supporters Principal Chief Ross said, "We will not recognize the forgery palmed off upon the world as a treaty by a knot of unauthorized individuals, nor stir one step with reference to that false paper."

THE START OF THE TRAIL
Members of the tribe who sided with the Ridges and Boudinot, who accepted the Treaty of New Echota, became known as the "treaty Cherokees." The federal government permitted them to organize their own removal and dispensed the necessary funds. Under these almost privileged conditions, about 2,400 Cherokee headed west to the Indian Territory, though they were plagued by hardship and tragedy. One group of 900 Cherokee lost eighty-one of their members, fifty of them to cholera. Another group of 365 treaty Cherokee suffered from heavy rain and snowstorms. Fifteen members of this party died along the way, eleven of them children younger than eight years old. Meanwhile in Washington, preparations were under way to force the remaining 10,600 Cherokee off their lands.

To its credit, Congress tried to ameliorate the removal. It authorized $65,880 per 1,000 Cherokee to supply food, clothing, and other provisions for the journey, as well as one wagon and five horses for every twenty Cherokee. The congressional committee that supervised the removal named Lewis Ross, Principal Chief John Ross's brother and a well-respected merchant in his own right, as its agent for the removal. In other words, Congress would pay Lewis Ross for supplying the wagons, horses, food, and other necessities for the journey.

General Winfield Scott was outraged by the congressional committee's arrangements for the removal, which he characterized as "extravagant." He argued that providing a wagon and five horses for every twenty Cherokee was wasteful because, on average, among 1,000 Cherokee there were to be found "at least 500 strong men, women, girls, and boys not only capable of marching twelve or fifteen miles a day, but to whom the exercise would be beneficial." As for naming Lewis Ross the government's agent for the removal, Scott complained that Congress had given Ross a monopoly while barring "highly respectable [white] citizens" from bidding for the contract. In spite of General Scott's objections, the congressmen authorized the funds for the removal and kept Lewis Ross on as their agent.

The government overlooked one crucial facet of the removal. Congress and the military knew that the removal of the tribe would begin in late May, yet

OVERLEAF: THIS PORTRAYAL OF THE TRAIL OF TEARS IS INCORRECT. FEW OF THE INDIANS WENT ON HORSEBACK OR IN COVERED WAGONS—MOST WALKED THE ENTIRE DISTANCE FROM GEORGIA TO OKLAHOMA.

most of the forts were ill prepared for a sudden influx of thousands of Indians. They were short on everything from axes to tents to blankets to cooking pots. Such shortfalls would not have mattered, of course, if the Cherokee had been permitted to bring these useful items from their own homes.

As it happened, Jackson was no longer in the White House when the removal began. It was his handpicked successor, Martin Van Buren, who put into operation a policy Jackson had initiated at the beginning of his first term. From retirement at his plantation, Jackson wrote to Van Buren urging him to get on with the removal of the Cherokee. Van Buren replied that Jackson had nothing to fear, that the removal would proceed, and that he would not grant any extensions. The way the new president saw it, the Cherokee had already two years to pack and move.

"READY TO DROP INTO THE GRAVE" The flatboat moored at Ross's Landing (present-day Chattanooga) on the Tennessee River was already full, but the nervous soldiers drove more and more Cherokee men, women, and children up the gangplank. Suddenly everyone heard a loud, long cracking sound as the massive timbers of the flatboat began to break. Pandemonium erupted on the boat, and the horrible sound of the timbers breaking up was drowned out by shrieks, wails, and angry cries as the terrified immigrants all surged toward the gangplank, desperate to return to shore. Incredibly, no one was hurt or killed, and all the Cherokee made it safely off the crippled flatboat.

To accommodate the 800 Cherokee, the soldiers roped six flatboats to a steamship that carried the Indians safely down the Tennessee River to the next stop on the sad journey, Decatur, Alabama. Meanwhile the army herded the next detachment, 875 Cherokee, to the riverbank. No boats waited for them, but rather than take them back to the fort, the soldiers insisted the Cherokee spend the night where they were, exposed to the dank night air and plagued by swarms of mosquitoes. The next day, six more flatboats and a steamboat arrived to carry them away.

They brought with them dysentery, measles, whooping cough, and other contagious diseases that had begun in the wretched, overcrowded conditions of the forts. Malnutrition, physical exhaustion, and exposure to the elements made even healthy adults susceptible. A man from Maine who encountered one detachment of Cherokee on what has become known as the Trail of Tears recorded, "A great many go on horseback and multitudes on foot—even aged females, apparently nearly ready to drop into the grave."

Sadly, the government's originally generous provision for the removal of the Cherokee did not play out as planned. Often, expected deliveries of food and other supplies were stolen by middlemen who sold the goods for profit.

The number of wagons, which General Scott had thought unnecessary, now proved to be insufficient to carry the sick and the weak as well as the fodder needed for the horses. Adding to the Indians' troubles, all along the route they were routinely overcharged by settlers who managed toll bridges or operated ferries. Not all whites were pitiless, however. Some religious congregations opened their churches and schoolhouses to shelter Indians for the night. In some towns, doctors did what they could for the sick and the dying, and farmers and other landowners gave the Cherokee permission to forage for firewood and hunt game on their property.

SAD LEGACY

How many died? The number is uncertain. Dr. Elizur Butler, a Protestant minister who accompanied the Cherokee, estimated that 4,000 perished along the trail, and this figure is the one cited most often in history and reference books. Chief Ross believed 424 died, while a government official in the Indian Territory (Oklahoma) set the death toll at 1,645. Because many deaths in the forts as well as the deaths of newborns and infants less than six months old may have gone unrecorded, it is impossible to give an accurate number.

It is an indelible stain on the reputation of Jackson that he would compel more than 13,000 men, women, and children—from newborns to dying old men and women of a tribe that had been an ally of the United States against the Creek War only a generation before—to leave their homes and all their personal belongings and walk (in most cases) nearly 1,000 miles to begin new lives in a strange and comparatively desolate country. Jackson's action cost the lives of hundreds, possibly thousands, and caused unimaginable pain and hardship to every Cherokee forced to make the journey. In one respect Jackson was correct. In Oklahoma, the Cherokee did survive as a nation. But given how smoothly the Cherokee had earlier adopted mainstream American culture, it is likely that they could have survived quite well if they had been left alone to live in their ancestral homelands.

CHAPTER 6

REPEAL OF THE MISSOURI COMPROMISE

FRANKLIN PIERCE

A WARM, HUMID WIND WAS BLOWING AS JOHN BROWN, A WIRY, STEEL-EYED abolitionist from upstate New York, led seven men through the dark to the cabin of James P. Doyle, a proslavery man from Tennessee. It was about eleven o'clock on the night of May 24, 1856, when they reached the house near the Pottawatomie Creek in Franklin County, Kansas. As the eight armed men headed toward the door, two savage bulldogs charged out of the darkness. James Townsley and Frederick Brown—one of John Brown's sons—unsheathed their cutlasses and stabbed one dog to death while the other scampered away into the brush.

John Brown stepped up onto the porch and knocked on the cabin door. From inside, Doyle called out, "Yes? What is it?" Brown called back, "Can you tell me the way to the Wilkinson place?"

As Doyle opened the door, Brown and his men burst into the cabin. Huddled together stood Mahala Doyle, her young daughter, and her three sons: twenty-two-year-old William, twenty-year-old Drury, and fourteen-year-old John. As Brown's men grabbed Doyle and his three sons, dragging them out of the door, Mahala Doyle pleaded for the life of at least her youngest boy. Brown relented and returned the teenager to his mother.

The three Doyle men were forced down the road, about 100 yards from the cabin; there two more of Brown's sons, Owen and Salmon Brown, drew their

HISTORIANS STILL DEBATE WHETHER JOHN BROWN WAS AN ABOLITIONIST MARTYR, OR A TERRORIST, BUT THEY AGREE THAT HE WAS A CATALYST OF THE CIVIL WAR.

80

A FORCE OF 800 PROSLAVERY
MEN BURNED AND LOOTED
THE TOWN OF LAWRENCE,
KANSAS, LEAVING IN RUINS
THE TOWN'S TWO NEWSPAPER
OFFICES, THE HOME OF
THE GOVERNOR, AND
THE LANDMARK FREE
STATE HOTEL.

cutlasses and attacked their defenseless prisoners. Doyle and his eldest son, William, died relatively quickly in the road, but Drury tried to escape. He died horribly, with his head slashed open and his arms hacked off.

Leaving the bodies where they lay, the killers walked a half mile to the Wilkinson cabin. At the door, Brown tried the same ruse again, this time asking for directions to Dutch Henry's Tavern. Wilkinson, more wary than James Doyle had been, shouted the directions through the door, but Brown insisted he step outside and show him the way. At first Wilkinson hesitated, but when Brown threatened to break down the door, he unbolted and let the strangers in. Mrs. Wilkinson, who was sick with measles, recalled later, "The old man [John Brown], who seemed to be in command, looked at me, and then around at the children." Mrs. Wilkinson remembered him as "a tall, narrow-faced, elderly man" in travel-stained clothes, wearing a black cravat and a straw hat.

Mrs. Wilkinson begged Brown to spare her husband's life. He ignored the sick woman. Wilkinson begged Brown to let him fetch a neighbor to tend his wife. Brown refused. Impatient to get on with their bloody work, Brown and his men hustled Wilkinson outside in his stocking feet, not even waiting for him to put on his boots. About 150 yards from the cabin, Thomas Weiner and Henry Thompson, one of Brown's sons-in-law, inflicted deep gashes in Wilkinson's head and side before slitting his throat to finish him off.

Their final stop along Pottawatomie Creek was the cabin of James Harris. It was after midnight, and Brown gave up his pretense of being a lost traveler; instead, he broke down the door. Harris was in bed with his wife and child. Staying with them were three men: Jerome Glanville, a stranger who had been given hospitality for the night, and two acquaintances, William Sherman and John S. Wrightman, who had bought a cow in the neighborhood. Glanville, Wrightman, and Harris were spared after they swore that they were not proslavery, but Sherman—who refused to make such a vow—was dragged off into the dark. Weiner and Thompson killed him, then tossed his body into the creek. Harris found it floating there the next morning, with the skull cut open and the left hand nearly hacked off, just attached to the wrist by a bit of skin.

"KILL EVERY GOD-DAMNED ABOLITIONIST"
John Brown regarded his attack on the proslavery settlers along Pottawatomie Creek—a night of terror that became known as the Pottawatomie Massacre—as a righteous act of vengeance. About a month earlier, in April 1856, 800 proslavery men had attacked the antislavery town of Lawrence, Kansas, destroying the town's two newspaper offices, burning the home of the governor and the landmark Free State Hotel, and carrying off about $150,000 worth of valuables and merchandise looted from the town's homes and businesses. About the same time, news arrived from Washington, D.C., that Senator Charles Sumner of Massachusetts, one of the most outspoken champions of the abolitionist cause, had been attacked and almost beaten to death on the floor of the Senate by Congressman Preston Brooks of South Carolina. In John Brown's mind, these two incidents justified his raid on the proslavery settlement along Pottawatomie Creek.

For two years, the Kansas Territory had been in a state of violent upheaval. The day President Franklin Pierce signed into law the Kansas-Nebraska Act of 1854, sponsored by Senator Stephen A. Douglas, which granted to the citizens of the territory the right to decide whether their state would be slave or free, he set off a stampede of proslavery and antislavery (or "free soil") settlers from as far away as New England, each side vying to fill the state with its own supporters. The proslavery voters got there first, with hundreds of them pouring over the border from Missouri, establishing property claims so they could vote in the first territorial election. By a margin of 5,516 to 791, they elected a proslavery delegate to Congress, then elected a territorial legislature that made it a crime in Kansas to so much as speak against slavery. As the

PRESIDENTIAL BRIEFING

(1804–1869)

• FOURTEENTH PRESIDENT OF THE UNITED STATES (1853–57)

• BORN NOVEMBER 23, 1804, IN HILLSBORO, NEW HAMPSHIRE

• DIED OCTOBER 8, 1869, IN CONCORD, NEW HAMPSHIRE

• NICKNAMED "HANDSOME FRANK" AND KNOWN AS THE "HERO OF MANY A WELL-FOUGHT BOTTLE"

• REOPENED THE VOLATILE ISSUE OF SLAVERY EXPANSION AND QUICKENED THE COMING OF THE CIVIL WAR BY SIGNING THE KANSAS-NEBRASKA ACT (1854), REPEALING THE MISSOURI COMPROMISE

• APPEASED SOUTHERNERS BY APPOINTING AS WAR SECRETARY JEFFERSON DAVIS, FUTURE PRESIDENT OF THE CONFEDERATE STATES OF AMERICA

• REVILED BY HIS OWN (DEMOCRAT) PARTY, THE ONLY ELECTED PRESIDENT TO BE DENIED RENOMINATION BY HIS PARTY

antislavery settlers arrived, the situation in Kansas became bloody, with frequent ambushes and murders that took at least fifty-five lives and perhaps as many as 200. David Atchison, a fire-breathing senator from Missouri, urged the proslavery men of Kansas "to kill every God-damned abolitionist in the district," while the Reverend Henry Ward Beecher of New York shipped 1,500 rifles to antislavery settlers in Kansas so they could defend themselves.

The trouble began when President Pierce gave his approval to a move in Congress to repeal the Missouri Compromise, or rather the Missouri

Compromises, because there were two of them, one ratified in 1820 and another in 1850. The first, hammered out in Congress in 1820, settled the question of where slavery could expand in the Louisiana Territory. Everything above the latitude of 36° 30´ would be free territory, but slavery would be permitted south of that line. The one exception, or compromise, was Missouri, which was above the cutoff line but was admitted to the Union in 1821 as a slave state.

By 1846, northerners were becoming anxious about the South's rapidly increasing power in Congress and in the Electoral College. Since 1821, four states (Missouri, Arkansas, Florida, and Texas) had been admitted as slave states, while only two new free states (Michigan and Iowa) had joined the Union. The northerners' anxiety rose higher after the U.S. victory in the Mexican-American War of 1846 to 1848, when Mexico ceded vast new territories to the United States, most of which lay below the 36° 30´ dividing line. Representative David Wilmot of Pennsylvania wanted to tack on an amendment to a House appropriations bill that would ban the expansion of slavery into any territory once held by Mexico. Predictably, the amendment, known as the Wilmot Proviso, stirred up intense opposition from the South, led by John C.

CALHOUN ISSUED A WARNING TO HIS NORTHERN COLLEAGUES: IF THEY PASSED THE WILMOT PROVISO, THEY WOULD UNLEASH UPON THE LAND "POLITICAL REVOLUTION, ANARCHY, CIVIL WAR."

Calhoun, the senior senator from South Carolina. In February 1847, Calhoun, sixty-five years old and dying of tuberculosis, rose to speak against the Wilmot Proviso. Age and poor health had stripped him of the handsome looks he had enjoyed as a young man. Senator Henry Clay of Kentucky described Calhoun that day as appearing "careworn, with fevered brow, haggard cheek and eye."

Calhoun based his argument on the notion of private property: Just as Congress could not enact a law barring a man from taking his household goods, his horses, or his other property into a new territory, neither could Congress bar a man from taking with him his human property—in other words, his slaves. Then Calhoun issued a warning to his northern colleagues: If they passed the Wilmot Proviso, they would unleash upon the land "political revolution, anarchy, civil war."

The debate dragged on for another three years, but ultimately Congress dropped the Wilmot Proviso and enacted a new Missouri Compromise, the Compromise of 1850. Senator Clay, the author of this compromise, was himself a slave owner, but he tried to find a middle ground to satisfy both the proslavery and the free soil factions in Congress. Clay's compromise, steered through Congress by senators Stephen Douglas and Daniel Webster, consisted of five

PROSLAVERY MEN FROM MISSOURI KNOWN AS "BORDER RUFFIANS" SURGED INTO KANSAS WHERE THEY REGISTERED TO VOTE IN THE TERRITORY'S FIRST ELECTION. BY A MARGIN OF 5,516 TO 791, THEY ELECTED A PROSLAVERY DELEGATE TO CONGRESS.

parts. First, California would enter the Union as a free state. Second, Texas would relinquish the lands west of the Rio Grande, which would become the New Mexico Territory. Third, under the principle of popular sovereignty, the inhabitants of the New Mexico Territory would decide for themselves whether to admit slavery into their territory. Fourth, slavery would continue to be legal in Washington, D.C., but the buying and selling of slaves would be abolished. And, fifth, under the new Fugitive Slave Act (1850), all citizens of the United States, whether in the North or the South, would be required by law to help capture and return runaway slaves to their masters.

THE RIGHTS OF SLAVE OWNERS Within four years, Clay's compromise lay in ruins. The Fugitive Slave Act galvanized abolitionists, while the doctrine of popular sovereignty gave the proslavery advocates a new legislative weapon for extending slavery into new territory. Since the nineteenth century, there has been a general impression that the Fugitive Slave Act drove people in the North to a state of near insurrection, with angry mobs descending on slave catchers and liberating fugitive slaves—and indeed there were such cases. For example, in fall 1851 a mob stormed the police station in Syracuse, New York, where a slave named Jerry was being held. The mob freed Jerry and helped him escape to Canada. About the same time, in Christiana, Pennsylvania, a large crowd of free blacks and whites confronted Edward Gorsuch, a Maryland slave owner who had come north to reclaim two runaways. As part of the crowd rescued Gorsuch's slaves, someone opened fire, killing Gorsuch and badly wounding his son. Local authorities arrested forty-five white men, but all were acquitted.

Historian Stanley W. Campbell, author of *The Slave Catchers: Enforcement of the Fugitive Slave Law, 1850–1860*, conducted a study of the enforcement of the Fugitive Slave Act. He found that 90 percent of all captured runaways—about 300 slaves—were sent back to the South. Yet it was the dramatic confrontations between slave catchers and irate crowds that made newspaper headlines, not the routine return of runaways back to the South. Although instances of public resistance to the Fugitive Slave Act were rare, they received the most attention and convinced Southerners that Northerners would never respect their rights.

Respect for the rights of slave owners was a pillar of President Pierce's administration. He was a New Hampshire man, but unlike many of his fellow New Englanders, he was no abolitionist. (If he had been, he couldn't have been elected.) In Pierce's inaugural address delivered on March 4, 1853, he did his utmost to reassure the South. "I believe that involuntary servitude as it exists in the different states of this Confederacy [the United States, not the Confederate States of America], is recognized by the Constitution. I believe that it stands

IN HIS INAUGURAL ADDRESS PRESIDENT FRANKLIN PIERCE DECLARED THAT SLAVERY "STANDS LIKE ANY OTHER ADMITTED RIGHT, AND THAT THE STATES WHERE IT EXISTS ARE ENTITLED TO EFFICIENT REMEDIES TO ENFORCE THE CONSTITUTIONAL PROVISIONS."

like any other admitted right, and that the states where it exists are entitled to efficient remedies to enforce the Constitutional provisions. ... I fervently hope that the question [of slavery] is at rest, and that no sectional or ambitious or fanatical excitement may again threaten the durability of our institutions or obscure the light of our prosperity."

One of the chief goals of Pierce's foreign policy was certain to delight the South. He wanted to buy Cuba from Spain. Previous presidents had tried to acquire the island too, but they had all been turned down. For example, James K. Polk had offered the Spanish Crown $100 million for Cuba. Proslavery advocates in the South had talked about introducing slavery into the lands conquered from Mexico, but slavery and a plantation system already existed in Cuba. It is estimated that there were about 400,000 black slaves in Cuba in 1853. If Cuba were annexed, with an eye toward eventually admitting it as a state, it would give the South even more political muscle. In the end, Pierce had no more luck persuading Spain to sell Cuba than Polk had had. It must have been a disappointment to southern politicians, but Pierce's approval of a new piece of domestic legislation would console them.

APPEASING THE F STREET MESS By 1854, Senators Clay, Webster, and

Calhoun—once a great triumvirate who dominated the Senate in the 1830s and '40s—were all dead. Among the rising stars in national politics was the forty-one-year-old senator from Illinois, Stephen A. Douglas. Friends called him the "little giant," a tribute to his physique (although only 5 feet 4 inches tall, Douglas had a bull chest and broad shoulders) as well as his skills as a leader of the Democratic Party. In 1850, Douglas had worked with Clay and Webster to get the revised Missouri Compromise through Congress, but now he worked to have that compromise repealed. Although Douglas was a native of Vermont and a senator from Illinois—both free states—he owned property in Mississippi that was worked by about 140 slaves, a fact he preferred to keep quiet. Douglas had also bought real estate in Chicago, an up-and-coming Midwest city, but one that would never see a real economic boom until it became a railway hub connecting the cities of the East with the settlements of the West.

In the 1850s, everyone was talking about a transcontinental railroad. If it were to be built, the federal government would have to open up the Kansas-Nebraska Territory for settlement by winning land concessions from the Indian tribes and sending in surveyors to establish proper boundaries. Farmers, land speculators, and investors in railroads were all in favor of such a measure, but congressmen from the southern states were cool to the idea. The entire Kansas-Nebraska Territory lay above the 36° 30′ line, so slavery would not be permitted there. Douglas was chairman of the Senate's committee on the territories, and his

IN THE MISSOURI COMPROMISE OF 1850, HENRY CLAY, WHO WAS HIMSELF A SLAVEOWNER, TRIED TO FIND A MIDDLE WAY THAT WOULD SATISFY BOTH THE PROSLAVERY AND ANTISLAVERY FACTIONS IN CONGRESS. HE IS SEEN HERE PRESENTING HIS COMPROMISE TO THE U.S. SENATE.

fellow Illinois Democrat, William A. Richardson, was chairman of the House of Representatives' committee on the territories. Together Douglas and Richardson wrote two bills, which were substantially identical, to open the Kansas-Nebraska Territory for settlement. Richardson's bill sailed through the House, but Douglas's bill was stymied by southern senators. Leading the opposition were four Southerners—James M. Mason and Robert M. T. Hunter of Virginia, Andrew P. Butler of South Carolina, and David R. Atchison of Missouri. They were, respectively, chairmen of the foreign relations, finance, and judiciary committees, while Atchison was president pro tem of the Senate. Collectively they were known as the "F Street Mess," because all four gentlemen boarded in the same house on F Street. (One of the meanings of "mess" is a group of people who eat together, or the place where they eat, as in a mess hall.)

Atchison expressed the feelings of his fellow mess-mates and of the South when he told Douglas that he would see Nebraska "sink in hell" before he voted for the territory to be carved into free states. The Southerners' price for passage of the Kansas-Nebraska Act was the repeal of the Missouri Compromise—both the 1820 and the 1850 versions. The 36° 30′ line of demarcation must be abolished, and the settlers, under the doctrine of popular sovereignty, must be permitted to vote on whether their territory would be slave or free.

THE SUNDAY AFTERNOON CALLERS

To repeal both compromises, Douglas and his allies in Congress needed the support of the president. On a Sunday morning in January 1854, members of Douglas's and Richardson's committees called on Jefferson Davis, the secretary of war (and the future president of the Confederate States of America), and begged him to persuade Pierce to see them that day. (On religious principle, Pierce disliked conducting any business on the Sabbath.) Davis, who understood the significance of the legislation, agreed to make a personal appeal to the president. With the congressmen in tow, Davis went to the White House, where he called on Pierce in the rooms reserved for the First Family. For Davis's sake, the president set aside his usual rule and went down to meet with his visitors.

NEWS THAT THE PRESIDENT HAD THROWN HIS SUPPORT BEHIND REPEAL STUNNED THE NORTH AND THE ANTISLAVERY PEOPLE. SAM HOUSTON, A LEADER OF TEXAS'S WAR AGAINST MEXICO IN THE 1830S AND NOW U.S. SENATOR, RECOGNIZED THAT REPEAL WOULD "CONVULSE THE COUNTRY FROM MAINE TO THE RIO GRANDE.

Pierce had said in his inaugural address in 1853 that the Compromise of 1850 had settled the question sufficiently for him to govern the country in peace. But now here were some of the most influential men in Congress paying a personal visit to ask him to endorse a repeal of the compromise. Ultimately, two things prompted Pierce to support the repeal: his own faith in popular sovereignty and his desire to win the Senate's support for his plan to annex Cuba. If repeal of the 1850 Compromise was the price for a little political horse trading, then Pierce would pay it. While the congressmen watched, Pierce wrote out the articles calling for repeal at his own hand.

News that the president had thrown his support behind repeal stunned the North and the antislavery people. Sam Houston, a leader of Texas's war against Mexico in the 1830s and now U.S. senator, recognized that repeal would "convulse the country from Maine to the Rio Grande ... I, as a southern man, repudiate it." But on this point Houston stood virtually alone. As the future vice president of the Confederacy, Alexander H. Stephens, said later, "Never was an act of Congress so generally and so unanimously hailed with delight at the South."

In the North, news of the proposal to repeal the Compromise of 1850 met with cries of outrage. Six northern congressmen—including Charles Sumner, Salmon P. Chase, and Joshua Giddings—teamed up to write a denunciation of the plan. Repeal would be a "gross violation of a sacred pledge," they said. It would take the unsullied territory of Kansas and Nebraska and transform it into a "a dreary region of despotism, inhabited by masters and slaves." But Senator

ALTHOUGH A NATIVE OF
VERMONT AND A SENATOR
FROM ILLINOIS, STEPHEN
DOUGLAS OWNED PROPERTY
IN MISSISSIPPI THAT WAS
WORKED BY ABOUT 140
SLAVES, A FACT WHICH HE
LABORED TO KEEP QUIET.

George Badger of North Carolina argued in favor of the repeal from a distinctly personal point of view. "If some Southern gentleman," he said, "wishes to take the old woman who nursed him in childhood and whom he called 'Mammy' into one of these new territories for the betterment of the fortunes of his whole family—why, in the name of God, should anybody prevent it?" On May 30, 1854, the Kansas-Nebraska Act passed both houses of Congress: in the Senate by a vote of 37 to 14, and in the House by a vote of 113 to 100. Within days Pierce signed it into law.

By throwing his support behind the Kansas-Nebraska Act, Pierce handed the proslavery faction a victory and enraged abolitionists. In Framingham, Massachusetts, the abolitionist firebrand William Lloyd Garrison delivered a scathing speech against the U.S. Constitution's guarantees regarding slavery. Holding up a copy before his large audience, Garrison denounced the Constitution as "a covenant with death, and an agreement with hell." Then he set fire to the document, crying, "So perish all compromises with tyranny!" as the crowd erupted with thunderous applause.

The effect of the Kansas-Nebraska Act went well beyond flamboyant gestures. As seen in the Pottawatomie Massacre and the Sack of Lawrence, the repeal of the compromises unleashed a near civil war in the Kansas territory, a shocking warm-up to an even more horrifying conflict to come. From a political point of view, Pierce did serious damage to his own Democratic Party, as it lost almost all of its influence in the North. The Whig Party, which had opposed the act, died out almost overnight in the South, and dwindled away in the North, as its members eventually joined the new Republican Party. But the most significant, most enduring effect of Pierce's endorsement of the Kansas-Nebraska Act was to reawaken the old hatreds between North and South, the proslavery and antislavery factions, and to push the nation one giant step closer to civil war, a four-year fratricidal holocaust that would take about 620,000 lives and leave half a million wounded.

CHAPTER 7

THE ATTEMPT TO ANNEX SANTO DOMINGO

ULYSSES S. GRANT

ULYSSES S. GRANT SAW SANTO DOMINGO AS MUCH MORE THAN A REFUGE FOR FREEDMEN: IT WAS IDEALLY SITUATED FOR A NAVAL BASE, AND IT WOULD BE A GOOD COALING STATION FOR SHIPS TRAVELING BACK AND FORTH BETWEEN THE U.S. AND THE PORTS OF CENTRAL AND SOUTH AMERICA.

LATE ON THE NIGHT OF OCTOBER 29, 1869, MEN WEARING WHITE ROBES AND white hoods broke down the door of the Colby house, then dragged Abram Colby, a former slave who had just been elected to the Georgia legislature, out of bed. As Colby's wife, mother, and young daughter watched, the intruders wrestled him out of the door. The child ran up, pleading for her father's life. In reply, one of the hooded strangers drew a pistol, waved it in front of the little girl's face, and threatened to shoot her dead.

Out in the woods, the men stripped Colby naked and whipped him with sticks and leather belts. As they beat him, they damned him for voting for Ulysses S. Grant and turning the black people of the state against white Southerners. Three years later, in testimony before a joint House and Senate committee on incidents of violence in the old Confederacy, a congressman asked Colby if he could identify any of his assailants. He said he could. "Some are first-class men in our town," Colby recalled. "One is a lawyer, one a doctor, and some are farmers."

After beating Colby for three hours, the Klansmen left him to die in the woods. Colby survived the attack, but the injuries he suffered that night crippled him. "They broke something inside me," Colby told the congressional committee. "I cannot do any work now."

The beating of Colby is just one instance of a wave of violence that raged across the South during the years 1865 through 1877, the period known as

Reconstruction. For those dozen years following the end of the Civil War, the federal government attempted to ease the transition of African Americans from slavery to life as free citizens, while at the same time trying to bring white Southerners who had rebelled against the Union back into the mainstream of American political life.

Shortly after assuming the office of president following the assassination of Abraham Lincoln in April 1865, Andrew Johnson, himself a Southerner, declared, "White men alone must manage the South." That policy was undermined in April 1866 when both houses of Congress passed the Civil Rights Act, which guaranteed that all adult male citizens of the United States would enjoy the same rights "without distinction of race or color, or previous condition of slavery or involuntary servitude." Johnson vetoed the bill, but Congress overrode his veto. Within days, white mobs throughout the South attacked blacks as well as white Republicans. Three days of anti-black rioting in Memphis, Tennessee, left forty-eight people dead and hundreds of black homes, churches, and schools ransacked or destroyed. In New Orleans, a white mob attacked a meeting of black citizens and white Republicans, killing forty. Out in the countryside, the Ku Klux Klan targeted white teachers who had opened schools for black children and adults, and black churches where pastors taught their newly emancipated congregations how to assert their newly recognized civil rights.

"Impudent negroes," as the Klan called them, who acted as if they were the equal of their white neighbors, or who had achieved a modest degree of success, were particular targets of the Klan. Klansmen in Mississippi beat a former slave who had taken to court a white man who owed him money and would not pay the debt. In Florida, Klansmen whipped an entire family of black farmers—including the children—for daring to farm their own land rather than work as sharecroppers for a white landowner. In the Piedmont district of North Carolina, one judge tallied up the outrages committed against black people in his jurisdiction: twelve murders, nine rapes, fourteen cases of arson, and more than 700 beatings. Among those beaten was a 103-year-old woman.

"LET US HAVE PEACE"
Late in 1865, after a brief inspection tour of the conquered South, General Ulysses S. Grant urged President Johnson to adopt a lenient policy with the former Confederates. Grant was more pragmatic than progressive, and many of his recommendations made sense. He understood that the sight of black troops in Union uniforms would enrage most Southerners, so he recommended that Washington send only white soldiers to the South. "White troops generally excite no opposition," he wrote to Johnson, "and therefore a small number of them can maintain order in a given district." Grant urged the president to avoid any policy that would be perceived by the white

PRESIDENTIAL BRIEFING

(1822-1885)

• UNION GENERAL AND EIGHTEENTH PRESIDENT OF THE UNITED STATES (1869-77)

• BORN HIRAM ULYSSES GRANT ON APRIL 22, 1822, IN POINT PLEASANT, OHIO

• DIED JULY 23, 1885, AT MOUNT MCGREGOR, NEW YORK

• IN THE CIVIL WAR, BROKE CONFEDERATE CONTROL OF THE MISSISSIPPI RIVER BY CAPTURING VICKSBURG (1863)

• ELECTED PRESIDENT ON THE REPUBLICAN TICKET (1868) AND PRESSED FOR RADICAL RECONSTRUCTION IN THE SOUTH

• REELECTED (1872), SECOND TERM PLAGUED BY THE PANIC OF 1873, AS FIRST TERM WAS BY SCANDALS

AFRICAN AMERICANS WHO WERE PROSPEROUS, WHO ASSERTED THEIR RIGHTS, OR WHO OTHERWISE OFFENDED SOUTHERN SENSIBILITIES BECAME TARGETS OF THE KU KLUX KLAN AND OTHER WHITE VIGILANTE GROUPS.

Southerners as "humiliating to them as citizens." On the other hand, Grant felt that a resentful, rebellious spirit was so pervasive among Southerners that they could not yet be "intrusted [sic] with the law-making power." At the same time that Congress was debating whether to grant full voting rights to former slaves, Grant was recommending that white Southerners be disenfranchised. It may have been a sensible recommendation at the time, but it virtually guaranteed that Republicans would take over the state governments, confirming in the minds of Southerners that they were under occupation, stoking their resentment, and fueling their hatred of the freedmen.

Almost every day, Republican governors in the South heard fresh accounts of acts of violence and terror committed by white Southerners against former slaves. In 1868, W. A. Patterson, a freedman, wrote to Governor William W. Holden of North Carolina, "The ku kluks klan [sic] is shooting our familys [sic] and beating them notoriously. We do not know what to do." Governors like Holden did not know what to do either. Under normal circumstances, they would have called out the state militia to find and arrest the outlaws, but no white man of the South would serve in such a militia. Black men would enlist, but most governors had no confidence that new recruits could stand up against the battle-hardened Confederate veterans who comprised the Klan. Even more terrible was the thought of igniting a race war in the South.

When the Republicans nominated Grant as their candidate for president in 1868, the Klan launched an intimidation campaign to keep black voters from the polls. An Arkansas congressman, three members of the South Carolina legislature, and several delegates to state constitutional conventions were assassinated. In Camilla, Georgia, an all-black "Vote for Grant" election parade was attacked by 400 armed white men under the command of the county sheriff. They opened fire on the parade, killing and wounding more than twenty. In St. Landry Parish, Louisiana, a huge white mob rampaged through the countryside, murdering approximately 200 black farmers and sharecroppers. The Republican Party leadership in Georgia and Louisiana did not know what to do, and neither did their candidate, General Grant, other than to take as his campaign slogan the plea, "Let us have peace."

A REFUGE FOR BLACK AMERICANS Grant won the election, but the peace he longed for did not come. Southern blacks were still under attack from the Klan and white mobs. In 1869, President Grant proposed a solution—the annexation of Santo Domingo in the Caribbean, the present-day Dominican Republic, as a refuge and colony for former slaves. At the time, Santo Domingo had a population of approximately 200,000, a very large percentage of which was of African descent. Grant felt certain that Santo Domingo, a country that

covered 18,816 square miles, could support "the entire colored population of the United States, should it choose to emigrate." That would have meant the relocation of about six million black Americans, but Grant believed that among others of their race in Santo Domingo the American freedmen could prosper, safe from the attacks of bitter white Southerners. "The prejudice [of color] is senseless to me," Grant said, "but it does exist." Because it was obvious to the president that whites and blacks could not live in peace, the prudent solution appeared to be the relocation of black Americans out of the United States.

Grant was not the first U.S. president to propose or endorse the idea of colonizing free blacks outside of the United States. In a meeting with black leaders at the White House on August 14, 1862, Abraham Lincoln had spoken candidly about the unlikelihood that most white Americans would be willing to live peacefully and on terms of equality with black Americans. "Your race suffer very greatly, many of them, by living among us," Lincoln told the delegation. "There is an unwillingness on the part of our people, harsh as it may be, for you free people of color to remain among us." Lincoln suggested that his guests return to their communities and urge free black men and women to emigrate to colonies the United States hoped to establish in Honduras or Nicaragua. Once these first settlers were established in Central America, Lincoln believed, many thousands, even millions, more would follow after the Confederacy was defeated and the slaves were free. One of the delegates told Lincoln, "This is our country as much as yours, and we will not leave it." When Frederick Douglass, the foremost spokesman of black Americans, heard of Lincoln's plan, he charged the president with "contempt for Negroes."

In spite of the opposition from blacks, the federal government went forward with the idea of starting a colony for freedmen, although it would have to be in Haiti because the governments of Honduras and Nicaragua refused to accept the emigrants. Congress appropriated $600,000 for the colony, and government agents recruited 453 black men, women, and children, to lay the foundation of the first settlement. That was in 1863. In less than a year, eighty-five members of the colony had died of smallpox or starvation, and the government was obliged to send a ship of the U.S. Navy to rescue the malnourished survivors.

There is a common misconception that President James Monroe (1817–1825) sponsored an effort to colonize free American blacks in Africa. It is not true. The colonization movement was begun in 1816 by Paul Cuffee, a prosperous Quaker merchant of mixed African and Native American ancestry, who transported thirty-eight free blacks aboard one of his own ships to Freetown in Sierra Leone. Cuffee died the next year, but his project was adopted by the American Colonization Society (ACS), a Protestant philanthropic organization that had the support of Bushrod Washington (nephew of

George Washington), Henry Clay, Daniel Webster, Andrew Jackson, and Richard Bland Lee and Edmund Lee (uncles of Robert E. Lee), among other distinguished politicians. The ACS believed that colonizing American blacks in Africa would give them a home where they could prosper, free from the prejudices of white Americans, while at the same time bringing Christianity and Western civilization to the tribes of Africa. Clay, who chaired the first meeting of the ACS, put the following question to the distinguished attendees: "Can there be a nobler cause than that which, while it proposes to rid our own country of a useless and pernicious, if not a dangerous, portion, of its population, contemplates the spreading of the arts of civilized life, and the redemption from ignorance and barbarism of a benighted portion of the globe?"

In 1822, the first colony of American blacks settled on the western coast of Africa in what is now Liberia. The settlers named their capital Monrovia, in honor of James Monroe, who was president of the United States at the time of their emigration. This has led to the misapprehension that the Monroe administration was behind the colonization plan. In fact, naming the capital Monrovia was the settlers' tribute to their former home. The same motivation would cause them to adopt a flag modeled on the American flag.

A VISIT FROM THE PRESIDENT
The evening after New Year's Day, 1870, President Ulysses S. Grant wrapped himself in his winter cloak, strode out of the White House, and walked across Lafayette Square, alone, to call on Senator Charles Sumner of Massachusetts. Sumner had first come to Congress in 1851. Nineteen years later, he was one of the most influential men in the Senate, and he was revered among abolitionists and freedmen as a living martyr. In 1856, during the Senate debate on the proposed Kansas-Nebraska Act, Sumner had delivered a blistering speech in which he took aim at one of the bill's outspoken defenders, Senator Andrew Butler of South Carolina. Butler, Sumner informed his fellow senators, had "a mistress who, though ugly to others, is always lovely to him; though polluted in the sight of the world, is chaste in his sight—I mean, the harlot, Slavery." Two days later, as Sumner sat at his desk working his way through a pile of correspondence, Preston Brooks, a congressman from South Carolina and Butler's nephew, marched into the Senate chamber. He beat Sumner with his cane over the head until he fell bleeding and unconscious to the floor. Sumner's injuries were so severe it took him three years to recover.

Grant and Sumner were not close friends; their personalities were too much at odds. Sumner had a flair for melodrama; his speeches tended to be bombastic. Grant was reserved, and he spoke plainly. Both were accomplished men, and they were proud of their achievements, but in Sumner's case this natural pride expressed itself as vaunting egotism. A visitor once confided to

SENATOR CHARLES SUMNER OF MASSACHUSETTS LED THE OPPOSITION IN THE SENATE TO THE ANNEXATION OF SANTO DOMINGO, ARGUING THAT PRESIDENT GRANT HAD BULLIED AN IMPOVERISHED, MILITARILY WEAK NATION INTO HANDING OVER ITS INDEPENDENCE TO THE UNITED STATES.

Grant that Senator Sumner had no faith in the Bible. The president replied, "That's because he didn't write it."

On the evening of January 2, President Grant was willing to put aside differences and do what no American president had ever done—to go in person, unannounced and unescorted, to make a personal appeal to a senator for his support. Sumner was at home, dining with two newspapermen. The sudden, unexpected arrival of the president surprised the senator and his guests, but Sumner recovered his poise, asked Grant to join them at the table, and offered him a glass of sherry. Grant took the seat, but declined the wine. Then he explained the purpose for his call. He wanted the treaty for the annexation of Santo Domingo to pass; as chairman of the Senate's Foreign Relations Committee, Sumner's support for the treaty would be invaluable. Sumner replied, "I expect Mr. President to support the measures of your administration."

Grant was content. He wished the gentlemen a good evening and walked back across Lafayette Square, believing that he had received Sumner's assurance that he would back the Santo Domingo treaty.

A SCHEME THWARTED

To Grant's mind, Santo Domingo had much more to recommend it than merely as a refuge for abused freedmen. The country's main harbor, Samana Bay, was large, deep, and ideally situated for a naval base that could protect U.S. interests in the Caribbean and Central America. It would make a good coaling station, too, for merchant ships traveling back and forth between the United States and the ports of Central and South America. And the United States would not have to conquer the country. Santo Domingo's president, Buenaventura Baez, told Grant's envoys that he was ready to turn over his nation to the United States. The deal was straight forward, even a bargain. The United States would pay $1.5 million—the amount of Santo Domingo's outstanding debts—as well as send President Baez the sum of $100,000 and a small arsenal of weapons. Baez was even willing to hold a public referendum on the question of annexation so that no one could accuse Grant of imperialism.

Grant had yet another motive for offering African Americans a safe haven in Santo Domingo: If the freedmen left en masse, the South would be deprived of its primary workforce. Once the black man was gone, Grant said, "his worth here would soon be discovered, and he would soon receive such recognition as to induce him to stay." In other words, once white Southerners realized they needed black labor, they would stop terrorizing them.

Meanwhile, President Baez prepared for the nationwide referendum on the annexation question. On February 19, 1870, approximately 16,000 voters went to the polls, and about 90 percent of them voted in favor of annexation. For

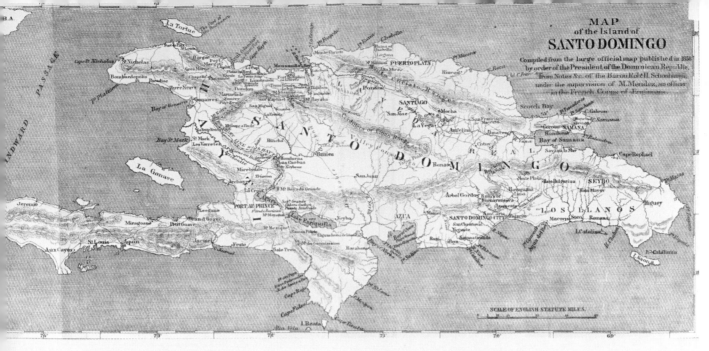

MAP
of the Island of
SANTO DOMINGO

Compiled from the large official map published in 1858
by order of the President of the Dominican Republic,
From Notes &c. of the Baron Robt H. Schomburgk,
under the supervision of M. Mendez, an officer
in the French Corps of Engineers.

SCALE OF ENGLISH STATUTE MILES.

Grant and Baez, it was a very satisfying result, although Baez had taken an added precaution to ensure that the vote was favorable. As Baez admitted to Major Raymond Perry, an American agent in Santo Domingo, he had put out the word that any man who voted against annexation would be banished or shot.

When the Santo Domingo treaty was presented to the Senate Foreign Relations Committee, Chairman Sumner did not obstruct it but let it come before the full Senate for debate. And there he buried it. Grant felt betrayed, but Sumner always claimed that his reply the night the president called upon him had been noncommittal. It could be read that way, but what later turned out to be Sumner's vehement determination to kill the Santo Domingo annexation plan stunned and angered Grant.

During the debate, Sumner claimed that by acquiring Santo Domingo the United States would saddle itself with a nation where political upheavals were almost a daily occurrence. Sumner believed Santo Domingo's debt was greater than $1.5 million (although he had no proof), and he characterized Baez as a "political jackal." As for President Grant, Sumner damned him for bullying an impoverished, militarily weak nation into handing over its independence to the United States. Sumner warned that Grant wanted to graft an "imperial system" onto the American form of government. And then, working himself into one of those oratorically florid moments for which he was famous, Sumner charged that if America annexed Santo Domingo, it would be the first step in "a dance of blood."

In June 1870, the Senate voted on the Santo Domingo treaty. Deadlocked at 28 to 28, the treaty failed to win the two-thirds required for approval. Senator Sumner had won.

IN 1869, THE CARIBBEAN ISLAND OF SANTO DOMINGO HAD A POPULATION OF APPROXIMATELY 200,000, A VERY HIGH PERCENTAGE OF WHICH WAS OF AFRICAN DESCENT.

Writing later about his annexation policy in his memoirs, Grant said, "What I desired above all was to secure a retreat for that portion of the laboring classes of our former [slave] States, who might find themselves under unbelievable pressure ... And I believed that the mere knowledge of that fact on the part not only of the freedmen but of their former masters, would serve to prevent anything like widespread injustice."

THE DEBATE OVER THE ANNEXATION OF SANTO DOMINGO BROUGHT OUT A RASH OF NASTY, HATEFUL, ELITIST RHETORIC, EVEN FROM REFORMERS IN THE NORTH WHO HAD ONCE SYMPATHIZED WITH THE PLIGHT OF THE SLAVES. IT MARKED THE BEGINNING OF THE END OF THE EGALITARIAN IDEAL OF RECONSTRUCTION.

It must have been disheartening for the freedmen that President's Grant solution to the killings and other outrages they suffered at the hands of the Klan was not an all-out effort to enforce the law, but rather a scheme to encourage the victims to leave the country—as though the upheaval in the former Confederacy was all their fault, or nothing could be done about it. But there was another, entirely unexpected result of Grant's plan to annex Santo Domingo. Confronted with the prospect of eventually admitting to the Union a territory compromised almost entirely of black citizens, the treaty's opponents in Congress and elsewhere drew upon the familiar racist arguments that Southern Democrats, slave owners, and Klansmen had been using for years. Republican Senator Carl Schurz of Missouri, a Union veteran who had fought at Chancellorsville and Gettysburg, asserted that due to the tropical climate, the inhabitants of Santo Domingo naturally descended into "shiftlessness." Edwin L. Godkin, editor of the *Nation* magazine, scoffed at the notion that "ignorant Catholic Spanish negroes" could ever become sober, productive American citizens. Charles Francis Adams Jr., grandson of John Quincy Adams and great-grandson of John Adams, not only denied that the people of Santo Domingo would be an asset to the United States, but he also rejected the entire idea of granting voting rights to all adult male citizens. "Universal suffrage," Adams argued, "can only mean in plain English the government of ignorance and vice. It means a European, especially Celtic, proletariat on the Atlantic coast, an African proletariat on the shores of the Gulf and a Chinese proletariat on the Pacific." The debate over the annexation of Santo Domingo brought out a rash of nasty, hateful, elitist rhetoric, even from reformers in the North who had once sympathized with the plight of the slaves. It marked the beginning of the end of the egalitarian ideal of Reconstruction.

Grant's Santo Domingo annexation plan was a full retreat, first from the Republican Party's belief that the emancipated black population of the

BUENAVENTURA BAEZ, PRESIDENT OF SANTO DOMINGO, WAS PREPARED TO TURN OVER HIS NATION TO THE U.S. IN RETURN FOR $1.6 MILLION AND A SMALL ARSENAL OF WEAPONS.

1865

former Confederacy could enter the mainstream of American life, and second from the federal government's policy that white Southerners must respect the civil rights of African Americans because they were now full citizens of the United States. The scheme to ship the former slaves to Santo Domingo was in essence a public statement by the president of the United States that blacks and whites could not live peaceably in the same communities, that the acts of violence committed by the Klan and other vigilante groups like them were regrettable but were to a degree understandable, and that he, Ulysses S. Grant, would not defend the rights of black Americans nor ensure that they enjoyed the full protection of the law. Legislatures throughout the former Confederacy took the president's hint, as it were, and a year later, after federal troops were withdrawn and Reconstruction came to an end, enacted a new body of state laws and local ordinances to enforce segregation of the races and restrict the civil rights and civil liberties of African Americans.

GRANT'S SCHEME TO SHIP FORMER SLAVES TO SANTO DOMINGO WAS A PUBLIC STATEMENT BY THE PRESIDENT THAT BLACKS AND WHITES IN THE UNITED STATES COULD NOT LIVE PEACEFULLY IN THE SAME COMMUNITIES. IT WOULD BE A PRECURSOR TO A NEW BODY OF LEGISLATION, AT THE STATE AND LOCAL LEVELS, THAT WOULD ENFORCE SEGREGATION AND RESTRICT THE CIVIL RIGHTS OF AFRICAN AMERICANS FOR YEARS TO COME.

CHAPTER 8
THE PULLMAN STRIKE
GROVER CLEVELAND

THE TELEGRAM ARRIVED ON JULY 2, 1894. UPON RECEIPT, THERE WAS NO QUESTION what U.S. Major General J.M. Schofield wanted from General Nelson Miles, who was in command of the forces stationed in and around Chicago. "You will please make all necessary arrangements confidentially," Schofield wrote, "for the transportation of the entire garrison at Fort Sheridan—infantry, cavalry, and artillery—to the lake front in the city of Chicago."

SOME BELIEVE THAT PRESIDENT GROVER CLEVELAND ACTED TOO SLUGGISHLY IN HIS RESPONSE TO THE PULLMAN STRIKE; WHILE OTHERS SAY CLEVELAND SHOULD HAVE KEPT HIS NOSE OUT OF THE PRIVATE LABOR DISPUTE. EITHER WAY, CLEVELAND CAME OUT OF THE STRIKE AND SUBSEQUENT RIOTS WITH AMERICAN BLOOD ON THE LEGACY OF HIS PRESIDENCY.

Since workers at the Pullman Palace Car Company, a railcar manufacturing plant in Pullman, Illinois, twelve miles from Chicago, had gone on strike in late June, the situation had turned riotous and deadly. Schofield wanted troops ready to march at President Grover Cleveland's command.

General Miles was headquartered in Chicago when he received the telegram and was ordered back to Washington immediately. As Miles made his way east later that day, the general received several additional telegrams along the way, each describing what had taken place in Pullman since he had left. Now Miles was being ordered to report directly to Secretary of War Daniel Lamont for a meeting with Lamont, President Cleveland, and other members of the president's cabinet.

Miles was one of the nation's top military commanders, known as the "Winner of Bloodless Victories" for his record of low troop casualties during battle. Born in 1839, Miles had been a volunteer in the Union Army in the Civil

War and had been wounded four times. He had a thick, salt-and-pepper mustache, a stocky build, and a reputation as a vain show-off. Years later, Theodore Roosevelt would nickname Miles "The Brave Peacock."

Lamont was the well-educated son of a wealthy New York farmer, but he walked away from Union College to enter journalism. His life in politics began when New York Democratic Party leader Samuel Tilden recruited Lamont as a clerk for the state party office. After that, Lamont worked his way up to military secretary of New York, appointed by then-governor Grover Cleveland. In 1884 when Cleveland was elected president, Lamont followed him to Washington.

When Miles arrived at Lamont's office, the secretary explained that the situation in Pullman had gotten worse.

The Pullman Palace Car Company was the largest and most prosperous industry in the country specializing in

ENTREPRENEUR GEORGE PULLMAN BUILT A CITY IN RESPONSE TO THE GROWING NEED FOR LABORERS TO WORK AT HIS RAILCAR MANUFACTURING PLANT. AT ITS PEAK, PULLMAN RAILCAR MANUFACTURING EMPLOYED SOME 4,000 WORKERS, MANY OF WHOM BELIEVED PULLMAN WAS NOTHING MORE THAN A MISER AND SWEATSHOP OWNER WHO WAS GETTING FILTHY RICH OFF OF HIS UNORGANIZED WORKFORCE.

luxurious sleeping cars designed for the savvy and discriminating, wealthy traveler. To step into a Pullman car was to enjoy the comforts of home. The company employed thousands of mechanics, engineers, and laborers, many of whom lived minutes from the plant in Pullman, a city George Pullman saw as a model town, one he hoped would be replicated throughout America. The Pullman company, Miles said, "had accumulated great wealth and national prominence."

The way most people saw it, working for Pullman and living in his city didn't sound half bad. But most had based their opinions on the propaganda Pullman had been putting forth. This was one of the reasons why the strike had taken place to begin with. Pullman workers had been treated with indignity and deprived of fair wages, and a majority had walked out on a man they believed ran his city and business like a dictator. Pullman would give an employee a house to live in, then attach his or her wages for the mortgage or rent. He went so far as to charge fees for using the town library. Ministers were expected to pay to rent the town church.

During 1893, the country suffered a major economic depression, the Panic of 1893, which threw four million people out of work. (The Panic of 1893 had been set off when foreign investors and U.S. businessmen liquidated their paper assets and demanded gold.)

That decline in commerce took a grave toll on George Pullman's business. By the end of the year, he laid off nearly 66 percent of his workforce. For those remaining, life at Pullman became unbearable. Without warning, Pullman reduced their pay. A ten-hour payday in 1893 had been, on average, $2.63 for mechanics and $1.66 for all other Pullman employees. A year later, mechanics were making $2.03, with the remaining pulling in, again, on average, approximately $1.47.

President Cleveland did little to step in and manage the depression, noting that it was a common occurrence inside the ebb and flow of an economy and would work itself out in due time. Cleveland blamed the depression on the Sherman Silver Purchase Act and the McKinley Tariff of 1890, and he openly repeated his stance that the federal government had no business getting involved with private industry.

WILDCAT WALKOUT
The Pullman Palace Car Company officially went on the books in 1867. By 1893, Pullman had a workforce of 4,000 employees and a town named after him that he had built from the ground up. Around town, Pullman wasn't liked all that much. "My father worked for the Pullman company for thirteen years," said Jennie Curtis, a Pullman employee. "I paid his rent to the Pullman company up to the time he died. I was boarding at the time of my father's death. He being laid off and sick for three months, he owed the Pullman company $60 at the time of his death for back rent. The company made me, out of my small earnings, pay that rent due to my father."

Pullman was using the country's economic instability to justify an enormous pay cut. Workers could certainly understand a reduction due to the depression, but cutting wages by one-third was heartless, especially when the rents Pullman was collecting stayed the same. In some cases, the employees' bills even increased.

On May 11, 1894, a wildcat strike, or unauthorized work stoppage, broke out in Pullman. Eugene V. Debs, founder and president of the American Railroad Union (ARU), didn't necessarily want a strike; instead he wanted the ARU to speak with Pullman on behalf of his employees. Debs insisted that he and the American Railroad Union be allowed to negotiate with Pullman management before a full-scale walkout. A strike, he explained to the irate workers, had to be voted on and sanctioned by the ARU.

PRESIDENTIAL BRIEFING

(1837–1908)

• TWENTY-SECOND AND TWENTY-FOURTH PRESIDENT OF THE UNITED STATES (1885–89 AND 1893–97)

• BORN STEPHEN GROVER CLEVELAND ON MARCH 18, 1837, IN CALDWELL, NEW JERSEY

• DIED JUNE 24, 1908, IN PRINCETON, NEW JERSEY

• GOVERNOR OF NEW YORK (1883–85)

• SUPPORTED LOWER TARIFFS AND CIVIL SERVICE REFORM, REDUCED CIVIL WAR PENSIONS, AND SIGNED THE INTERSTATE COMMERCE ACT (1887)

• THE ONLY U.S. PRESIDENT TO SERVE TWO NONCONSECUTIVE TERMS

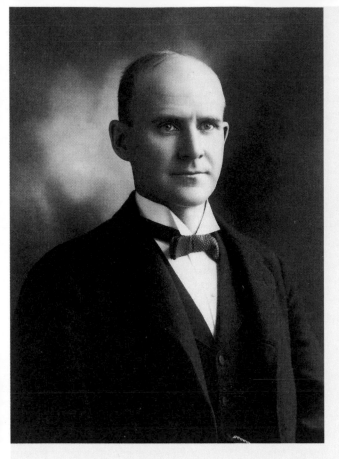

Pullman workers didn't care. That night, they sat up in front of the plant and refused to go back to work without a wage increase and changes in Pullman city. As Debs walked the picket line and talked to striking Pullman employees, he was astounded by the stories he heard of men losing their lives to faulty equipment and the hundreds of injuries sustained by employees who were forced to work under dangerous conditions. Nonetheless, Debs promised strikers that he would do whatever he could to make things better, but they must agree to go back to work.

But it was far too late for that. Pullman employees felt they had been mistreated and underpaid long enough. Their faith in the company was broken and beyond a quick fix. They were tired of being Pullman slaves. So by the end of the month, Debs convinced the ARU to vote and support the Pullman workers and put an end to their attempts to arbitrate between the two sides.

As the strike went into June, Pullman union members prohibited any train tugging a Pullman car to travel into or out of Pullman or Chicago. The only exception, Debs pointed out, was government trains carrying mail. The union founder certainly didn't want the military to get involved, and he knew that if the mail wasn't allowed to pass through town, President Cleveland would be forced to step in.

By June 29, however, what had been a local strike had turned into a national movement across the upper Midwest and Southwest, and it was growing bigger every day. Railcar engineers and workers walked off the job in support of Pullman workers. It was said that some 50,000 railway workers went on strike during that same week in late June. On top of that, locals who supported the rail strike were now stopping railcars in many major cities, effectively shutting down the entire railway system. The delivery of mail nationwide was soon grounded. In his Libertarian analysis of the Pullman strike, noted scholar and author Dr. Chris Sciabarra reported that there was $2.5 billion worth of transportation property available around the country—all of which had now been rendered idle. President Cleveland was being pressured to take control, but he refused to get involved, citing his determination to stay out of private labor disputes.

President Cleveland had his own agenda. At the time, he was in the process of trying to reduce the tariff and keep various other campaign promises he had made. He couldn't get his hands dirty with a labor dispute. Not now. He had a relationship with big business to protect. No matter which side he took, the outcome would influence his future. There was also the problem of going over the heads of town officials and the governor of Illinois, who Cleveland knew to be on the side of the strikers. So in light of keeping his standing clean, Cleveland handed the strike over to his attorney general, Richard Olney, who had always been a good friend to the railroads. (As a Boston attorney representing railroad interests, Olney wrote in a letter to railroad magnates in 1887, "The [Interstate Commerce] Commission ... is or can be made, of great use to the railroads. It satisfies the popular clamor for a government supervision of railroads, at the same time that that supervision is almost entirely nominal.")

CHECK THE THREATENED REVOLUTION Secretary of War Lamont and

General Miles hastily made their way across Lafayette Park onto the grounds of the White House on the afternoon of July 3, not long after Miles returned from Chicago. Besides President Cleveland, also attending the meeting would be General Schofield, Attorney General Olney, and Secretary of State Walter Quintin Gresham. Earlier, dispatches had been received, Miles reported, "from prominent men in the East, urging some measure be taken to check the threatened revolution in Chicago." Cleveland was getting backed into a corner by the wealthy anti-labor elite who had helped elect him.

Reports indicated that innocent bystanders and Pullman strikers were being murdered and maimed by malicious crowds fired up by the pure energy created inside the swell of the strike. One man was pulled from his engineer's seat and stoned to death by hundreds of rioters, while terrified passengers, noses pressed against the glass, looked on from inside the railcar. Apparently the mob was angry because the engineer had not shown solidarity with the union by refusing to drive his train. With clashes of violence breaking out wherever trains and mobs crossed paths, not to mention thousands of impatient, angry Pullman strikers chanting and tossing stones, it was clear that President Cleveland would need to do something. But the president was adamant. He would not send in troops unless Illinois governor John Altgeld requested military assistance.

Altgeld, in turn, would soon make it clear: Stay out of our business. Writing to the president in a telegram some weeks later Altgeld said, "Surely the facts have not been correctly presented to you in this case ... Waiving all questions of courtesy, I'll say that the state of Illinois is not only able to take care of itself, but it stands ready to furnish the federal government any assistance it may need elsewhere."

During the closed-door meeting at the White House, General Miles sat and listened as the talk centered on sending in 200 soldiers. The idea was to have the men march down Chicago's Michigan Avenue in a show of force. Miles later said that the president and the attorney general believed that with the troops, "the disturbance would be over and the trouble ended." It is presumed that Olney and the others discussed having federal judges issue injunctions against strike activity, in combination with sending in the troops. But there is no record of any of the president's advisors telling him during this particular meeting that sending in troops would likely escalate the violence. However, one has to assume that competent, intelligent men running the country would have known as much.

The strikers were poor, out-of-work laborers, and they were seething mad—men and women whose livelihoods had been sucked from them by a man they viewed as a miser. Most had nothing to lose. Miles knew better than to assume that a show of force by 200 soldiers would end the strike. A veteran of the Civil War, he had seen good men in desperate situations resort to savagery. If the president was serious about resolving the dispute, it was going to take a *lot* more than a couple hundred soldiers.

Attorney General Olney, who as a lawyer in Boston had represented large railroad companies, had a vested interest in the outcome of the strike. He held rail stock and had friends running some of the country's most profitable railroads. The General Managers Association (GMA), an organization of twenty-four railroads that had terminals in Chicago, now represented the Pullman company, and it wanted to end the strike quickly. As June turned to July and the strikers' numbers grew, the GMA set some rather unfair ground rules in place, sending out warnings of the immediate termination of workers who refused to drive railcars. The group also reached out to Attorney General Olney, who made it clear that strikers could quit their jobs if they disagreed with the treatment. No one was forcing anyone to work.

With that sort of rhetoric, Olney and Cleveland were merely playing politics, acting as if the strike was going to resolve itself with only a small military investment on their part. Americans were not ignorant. Most knew when the government was superficially conciliating a situation. Moreover, Cleveland had maintained support for the railroads throughout his term. He wasn't about to disappoint them now. In addition, Olney knew how to get into the middle of a problem and get it resolved without a public relations disaster. He initiated an injunction from the federal court, granted on July 2, which declared the strike unlawful. In a sense, Olney and Cleveland made it a federal crime to walk a picket line. On the morning of July 3, the White House was informed that Pullman laborers, as expected, had failed to return to work. Thus, according to the law, striking workers who refused to return to work were committing a crime. Olney then announced that Eugene Debs would be arrested on conspiracy charges and contempt of court for ignoring injunctions against strike activity. Debs was sentenced to six months in the Woodstock, Illinois, jail.

In theory, it all sounded perfect. The union might back down once it realized Debs was in jail, and, it was hoped, the mobs would disperse and the country's railways would be back in business. Cleveland could pat Olney on the back in front of reporters and take credit for a job well done, with no political cost to his reputation.

Near the end of the meeting, however, Miles pointed out that the Sub-Treasury, which housed more than $20 million in government funds, was at risk of being overtaken by rioters near Pullman. Before the meeting adjourned, Cleveland changed his mind, telling Miles, "Return immediately to Chicago and take such measures as would ensure the maintenance of law and order—and especially the authority of the United States." Thus, the president had gone from at first not wanting to get involved in the Pullman mess at all, to sending in 200 soldiers, to finally allowing Miles to use his own discretion in keeping the peace.

DARK NIGHTS

From Buffalo to Kansas, Nebraska to Texas, as if preparing for war, troops were assembled and informed that a state of martial law had been declared, though without an official proclamation. The president had made a decision to use massive military force.

Arriving in town on July 4, General Miles saw a once thriving Chicago of law-abiding citizens now occupied by some 3,000 infantry and cavalry, all at attention, awaiting orders to move on nearby Pullman. After Miles greeted his men, he mobilized the troops, as he later wrote, "in the most strategic positions."

Acting on behalf of President Cleveland, General Schofield issued a dispatch from Washington alerting commanders outside Chicago to the facts that had been agreed upon the previous day:

> It having become impracticable, in the judgment of the President, to enforce by ordinary course of judicial proceedings, the laws of the United States, you will direct ... [an] entire command at once to the city of Chicago ... there to execute the orders and processes of the United States court, to prevent the obstruction of the United States mails and generally to enforce the faithful execution of the laws of the United States.

It was 10:15 A.M. when troops arrived at Forty-Seventh Street and Stock Yards, directly on the outskirts of Pullman city limits. Initially, the arrival of the military was met with a quiet sense of defeat. An ominous feeling of displeasure was in the air, alongside an eerie calmness, but surprisingly, troops had no trouble maintaining peace and order.

The following morning, however, the mood changed. As the sun rose, a mob of thousands appeared over the horizon. When the armed troops stood their ground, the mob proceeded to overturn railcars, burn station houses, and continue on a rampage that extended for at least three miles along the coastline of Lake Michigan, "destroying property indiscriminately," one general's report said. Soon, the strikers began torching buildings and railcars full of merchandise.

As the morning progressed, the crowd swelled to 10,000, outnumbering troops three to one, yet now they had amassed into a line two miles long and a half mile wide—a human fence ready to do battle.

The president, supervising the situation from Washington, ordered the Illinois National Guard and additional troops from bordering states to converge

on Pullman and Chicago. Throughout the evening, the fires grew, and the crowds became more disorderly and irritated. The local police reported that at least twenty men were killed as fires raged and buildings crumbled.

In his book *Striking for Life: Labor's Side of the Labor Question*, John Swinton, a progressive reformist for the labor movement who spent nearly forty years as a journalist, blamed the violence on President Cleveland's decision to send in troops. "It was a dark night for freedom," Swinton wrote, "for labor, and for the Republic when a Democratic President took sides with the enemy."

According to Swinton, political leaders in Illinois were quite "offended by the President's action, as they had again and again given assurance of their ability to maintain order under all circumstances." Before President Cleveland's troops were sent in, there were intermittent episodes of violence, but nothing too orchestrated.

AS SOON AS THE PRESIDENT'S MILITARY FORCES ARRIVED, STRIKING WORKERS AND UNRULY, RIOTOUS MOBS BEGAN TORCHING RAILCARS AND BURNING BUILDINGS AND TOSSING STONES AT ANYONE WHO SEEMED TO BE ON THE SIDE OF GEORGE PULLMAN. NONETHELESS, SUPPORT FOR PULLMAN WORKERS INCREASED ACROSS THE NATION.

Swinton said that Cleveland's choice to send in troops was "uncalled for" and an "unjustifiable intermeddling … which [would] soon be settled in favor of the Unionists, through the rare genius, pacific policy and masterly strategy of their leader, Eugene Debs." Swinton called the Pullman strike a conflict between the "capitalist rings" (the railroads), the "blockhead [George] Pullman," and the "corrupt bosses of both political parties," against the working-class men and women that made America what it was. There was no room in a labor dispute for the president of the United States and the military.

ACROSS THE COUNTRY, MOBS AND STRIKING RAILCAR WORKERS SUPPORTING THEIR BRETHREN IN PULLMAN CITY BEGAN SABOTAGING RAILCARS BY DISMANTLING RAILCAR SWITCHES, FORCING COLLISIONS AND DEATHS NATIONWIDE.

DEATH, WORK, AND TAXES
The Pullman debacle was the first national strike in American history. In President Cleveland's defense, there was no precedent of this magnitude on which to base a response. Some people later claimed that Cleveland should have acted sooner, before the strike got out of hand, or perhaps sent in an envoy to act as a mediator between Pullman and the strikers.

But he of course did neither.

In any event, by day's end on July 6, 1894, American forces would make history by firing on and killing American citizens. As it happened, U.S. marshals and American military forces moved in and tried to take back the town of Pullman. In doing so, soldiers killed six to eight men, according to an official report of the incident. Many more deaths were later attributed to the strike, though it was impossible to point a finger at which law enforcement group—if any—was responsible.

On July 8, President Cleveland issued a proclamation in haste, making it clear that he was cautioning "all good citizens ... against aiding, countenancing, encouraging, or taking any part in such unlawful obstructions, combinations, and assemblages." Anyone refusing to abide by the order would be subject to arrest. The troops in Pullman and Chicago, in addition to those across the country, were given full authority, the president wrote, to "act with all the moderation and forbearance consistent with the accomplishment of the desired end."

The violence came to a slow end in Pullman and Chicago, but it escalated in other parts of the nation. In the days following the president's proclamation, the White House received dispatches from North Dakota, Montana, Idaho, Oregon, Washington State, Wyoming, Colorado, Utah, Nevada, California, and New Mexico. Most echoed what Idaho governor W.J. McConnell wrote:

> Domestic violence in the form of an unlawful conspiracy to destroy life and property exists in Shoshone County, Idaho. Armed men in such force that I am powerless to aid the civil authority in restoring order. Citizens residing in the county are deprived of the equal protection of the laws guaranteed by the Constitution. The legislature of the state cannot be convened at this time. The presence of regular troops is absolutely necessary. I therefore call upon you to direct that at least two companies of regulars be stationed in said county until order is restored and the laws recognized.

By the end of July, trains were running again, commerce was literally back on track, and the U.S mail was being delivered. President Cleveland assigned a commission to investigate and assess the outcome and the reasons why the strike turned into a pitched battle that temporarily crippled the country's transportation system. Known as the President's Strike Commission, Commissioner of Labor Carroll D. Wright, John D. Keenon of New York, and Nicholas E. Worthington of Illinois could never pinpoint a direct cause of the destruction or identify one specific group responsible for the damages. What it did

conclude, however, was how much the strike cost America, as well as the railroads, estimating that Pullman employees lost somewhere around $350,000 in wages. In addition, railroad workers in and around Chicago who participated in the strike lost about $1.4 million more. But more than any of that, the commission concluded, "On the plea of upholding the law and protecting life and property, the General Managers' Association … asked for and obtained the judicial and military arms of the federal government to crush the strike." Moreover, the commission further stated that "the facts obtained by the investigating commission appointed by Mr. Cleveland showed that there was very little disorder at Chicago [and Pullman] up to July 3, when the federal troops appeared on the scene." On top of that, according to the Chicago fire department's official report, "the total damage up to July 6 had been less than $6,000."

The commission reported twelve as its official number of people "shot and fatally wounded," a number few agreed with, considering that hundreds had died from being caught in burning buildings, hit by falling debris, or crushed by the crowds, while others were beaten to death and stoned, with perhaps thousands more dying under residual circumstances throughout the country. The commission recommended that Congress pass a federal law prohibiting employers from firing striking workers or "blackballing" labor union supporters. Born strictly out of the Pullman strike, the Erdman Act, passed in 1898, provided "voluntary mediation of railroad labor disputes and recourse to a board of arbitration." Congress passed the law specifically in response to "growing public opposition to the use of federal troops to put down strikes."

Writing about the strike in 1921, historian David Saville Muzzey called it the "most serious industrial struggle in the history of our country." Surely, beyond changing the way labor disputes were later settled, the Erdman Act was likely a direct result of the Pullman strike. American labor and industry, in addition, changed drastically as big business became wealthier, and union membership grew—enormously—from 447,000 to 2.1 million members between 1897 and 1904.

The precedent set in Pullman certainly made government less likely to get involved in labor disputes and encouraged businesses to hire special management teams to deal with unions and labor spats. The rise of the union, in general, helped increase blue collar wages and broaden public support for the American workforce, as support for the capitalists who hired them waned. Yet it would take years for corporate America to accept these changes. Suffice it to say that socialism was on the rise as the twentieth century dawned. In fact, Eugene V. Debs, who had played such a pivotal role in Pullman, emerged from his six-month prison term a radical socialist, running for president five times on a ticket that included his new title as the principal talking head for the Socialist Party of America.

CHAPTER 9

"A SPLENDID LITTLE WAR" WITH SPAIN

WILLIAM McKINLEY

TO A TWENTY-THREE-YEAR-OLD FROM RURAL NEBRASKA, IT SEEMED LIKE A marvelous adventure. President William McKinley had decided to launch what his secretary of state was to call "a splendid little war" against the crumbling Spanish empire in the Caribbean and the Pacific. McKinley had sounded a call for 125,000 volunteers to help carry out this patriotic mission. William Walter Grayson, eager to leave the small town of Beatrice and its surrounding wheat-fields behind him, was among the first to sign up. Thus, on the hot, sticky night of February 4, 1899, with less than six months' sporadic training and carrying an old Springfield rifle with which he was barely familiar, Private Grayson found himself nervously patrolling a lonely, dusty stretch of road on the island of Luzon in the Philippines.

Grayson and his equally green Nebraska buddy, Private Orville Miller, were part of an eight-man detail guarding an ill-defined perimeter separating American forces from an irregular contingent of Filipino insurgents. Americans and Filipinos had stood together in the opening days of "McKinley's War." But now Filipinos asserting their independence and an American occupation army were staking rival claims to territory around Santa Mesa, a Manila suburb at the confluence of the Pasig and San Juan rivers north of Manila. They had taken up opposing positions and confronted each other warily and even hostilely, shouting epithets and insults across the lines. The

dividing line was a waterpipe bringing water to the city, and a rickety bridge crossing the pipe. Under no circumstances, the young sentries were told, were intruders to be permitted to cross the pipeline and that artificial boundary.

Trudging along the road, swatting voracious mosquitoes and griping about the stifling humidity, Grayson and Miller suddenly perked up their ears. They heard, or thought they heard, rustling sounds in the vicinity of the bridge. They peered into the darkness; they seemed to see ill-formed figures resembling a man moving in the shadows. Grayson raised his rifle. "I had been trained in 'Corporal of the Guard,'" he said later. "I called out, 'Who goes there?'"

"Alto!" came back a thickened, mocking voice. Grayson cocked his rifle. "Halt!" he called out again. "Alto!" the voice mimicked. Now he was sure he could see a man's figure some fifteen feet away, coming toward him. Menacingly, he thought. "Well, I thought, the best thing I could do was to shoot him," he recalled afterward. Thus Private Grayson fired the opening shot of what was to become America's bloodiest, costliest, and most savagely fought conflict between the Civil War and World War II.

"REMEMBER THE MAINE!"
"Why is the president's mind like his bed?" went a satiric joke in turn-of-the-century Washington. "Because someone has to make it up for him before he can use it." On February 15, 1898, the American battle cruiser USS *Maine* blew up in the Havana harbor in the Spanish colony of Cuba, taking the lives of 264 American sailors. A great howl went up in the U.S. press and on Capitol Hill for revenge against Spain. That nation was already on

THE USS *MAINE* SAT ON THE BOTTOM OF HAVANA HARBOR IN 1898 AFTER A MASSIVE EXPLOSION THAT KILLED 264 AMERICAN SAILORS.

bad terms with the United States because of its brutal colonial policy in Cuba, only ninety miles from the U.S. mainland, so it was immediately suspected of committing the dastardly deed (which was later found to have been caused by a defective boiler). "War!" exhorted the sensationalist Hearst and Pulitzer newspapers, demanding a retaliatory strike against the "cowardly" Spanish.

As "Remember the Maine!" echoed across the country, Congress pressed the president for a declaration of war. McKinley dithered and fudged, asked advice, consulted, and sidestepped the issue without really deciding. Finally, more than two months after the sinking, an impatient Congress approved a declaration virtually on its own and forced the president's hand. Seventeen thousand American troops landed in Cuba in June with little opposition. Within six weeks, with Theodore Roosevelt legendarily waving his cowboy hat and leading his volunteer Rough Riders up San Juan Hill, the Spanish surrendered. The United States suffered fewer than 250 casualties, well over half of them from heat prostration or mosquito-borne diseases. America occupied the island, but under a stern Congressional mandate that Cuba must become independent and only temporarily a U.S. protectorate. America also occupied the nearby Caribbean island of Puerto Rico.

One other plum remained on the Spanish imperial tree. Covetous American eyes focused on the Philippines in the far Pacific. The 7,000-plus islands of the archipelago ("half of them underwater at high tide," goes the Philippine joke) had been colonized by Spain after Ferdinand Magellan's circumnavigation of the globe in 1521 and converted to Christianity by Spanish friars. The capital and largest city, Manila, had for several centuries been headquarters for a flourishing galleon trade that brought choice silks and jewels of the Orient to America and Europe.

The islands were thought to be rich in undeveloped resources, cheap fodder for America's thirsty and booming factories. Located off the South China coast, they would be a stepping-stone to new international markets for American commerce. Besides, with Spain defeated, the islands and their supposed riches might be gobbled up by the acquisitive British, French, or Germans, or the increasingly expansionist Japanese, to the detriment of American interests. Indeed, Germany had sent five warships to scout Manila harbor, allegedly planning to establish an imperialist monarchy with a German prince at its head. Emphatically planting the Stars and Stripes in Asia would notify the older nations of Europe that the upstart United States was now a global power to be reckoned with.

The United States had already posted an Asiatic fleet under Commodore George Dewey in Hong Kong to protect American Pacific shipping. Even before the declaration of war, Navy Secretary John D. Long, goaded by his rambunctious young aide, Roosevelt, had sent Dewey a peremptory cable:

PRESIDENTIAL BRIEFING
(1843–1901)

• TWENTY-FIFTH PRESIDENT OF THE UNITED STATES (1897–1901)

• BORN JANUARY 29, 1843, IN NILES, OHIO

• DIED (ASSASSINATED) SEPTEMBER 14, 1901, IN BUFFALO, NEW YORK

• UNION ARMY VETERAN OF BATTLE OF ANTIETAM (SHARPSBURG), 1862

• ELECTED IN 1896: STRONGLY PRO-BUSINESS, RAISED TARIFFS, PURSUED OPEN DOOR WITH CHINA, AND CLEARED WAY FOR BUILDING OF THE PANAMA CANAL

• RELUCTANT TO ENTER THE SPANISH-AMERICAN WAR (1898); THE UNITED STATES, VICTORIOUS, ACQUIRED THE PHILIPPINES, PUERTO RICO, AND GUAM; UNDER MCKINLEY THE UNITED STATES BECAME A WORLD POWER

• ASSASSINATED BY AN ANARCHIST IN 1901

COLONEL THEODORE
ROOSEVELT (FRONT ROW
CENTER) AND HIS VOLUNTEER
"ROUGH RIDERS" ROUTED
THE SPANISH COLONIAL
ARMY IN A FURIOUS CHARGE
UP SAN JUAN HILL.

In the event of declaration of war with Spain, your duty will be to see that the Spanish squadron does leave the Asiatic coast, and then offensive operations in the Philippine islands.

After war was declared, Long and Roosevelt cabled Dewey again, this time with McKinley's knowledge:

Proceed at once to Philippines. Commence operations against Spanish squadron. You must capture or destroy.

"YOU MAY FIRE WHEN READY, GRIDLEY"
On April 28, Dewey's fleet sailed for the Philippines. The result was one of the shortest and most one-

sided battles in naval history. The antiquated Spanish fleet consisted of only nine vessels. Most were armed with antique cannons, crewed with half-trained personnel, and top-heavy with aging officers who had never fought a sea battle, all compounded by egregious errors by the Madrid high command. Instead of remaining near their Cavite base, protected by its shore batteries, they were ordered into Manila Bay to shield the capital. Dewey caught them there at dawn on May 1 and drew up in a line of battle. "You may fire when ready, Gridley," he famously ordered the captain of his flagship, USS *Olympia*. The U.S. warships opened fire with their longer-range cannons, paused for a leisurely breakfast, then resumed shelling the hapless and hopelessly outgunned Spanish until noon. All but one of the Spanish warships went to the bottom of Manila Bay, and the last was so heavily damaged it had to be scuttled.

DEWEY BROUGHT WITH HIM A SLIM, SLIGHT FILIPINO WITH A CHARISMATIC LEADERSHIP TOUCH, EMILIO AGUINALDO.

Meanwhile, Dewey put ashore a landing party of sailors and Marines to secure the city. They were greeted enthusiastically by Filipinos who had been fighting the Spanish since 1896. Dewey brought with him a slim, slight Filipino with a charismatic leadership touch, Emilio Aguinaldo. Aguinaldo's followers quickly took over much of Manila and fanned out into the country-side. On June 12, 1898, a date still celebrated as Philippine Independence Day, Aguinaldo proclaimed the Philippine Republic, which was the move that was to bring Grayson from the American Great Plains to the Philippine boon-docks.

Grayson's teachers back in Nebraska had never mentioned the Philippines. He was not alone in his ignorance. "I could not have located those darned islands within two thousand miles," President McKinley said, and he sent an aide out for an atlas. Then he issued his call for volunteers to serve two years "unless the war should end sooner." While the nation scrambled for arms and equipment for the new recruits, first falling back on leftovers from the Civil War and frontier fighting, Grayson was sworn into the 54th Nebraska Volunteer Infantry. By late summer, fingering his newly issued rifle, Grayson boarded a troopship for the month-long voyage across the Pacific.

"ALTO!" FOLLOWED BY THE CLICK OF A RIFLE BOLT After Private

Grayson fired that steamy night, he heard a thump like a body falling. Private Miller raised his rifle and cocked it, too. Grayson heard a sound like the click of a rifle bolt. "Then two Filipinos sprang out of a doorway not more than twenty feet from us," Grayson later described. "I called 'Halt!' Miller fired and dropped one. I saw another

EMILIO AGUINALDO, A
SMALL-TOWN BUSINESSMAN
AND MAYOR, HAD BEEN
FIGHTING THE SPANISH
COLONIAL REGIME SINCE
1896 AND ROSE THROUGH
THE RANKS TO LEAD
THE INSURGENCY.

one was left, so I fired. Well, I think I got my second Filipino that time."

Grayson and Miller dashed back to the other members of their detail. "Line up, fellows!" Grayson shouted. "The natives are in here all through these yards!" Grabbing their rifles, the others rushed forward, firing indiscriminately at noises and shadows that might be a large Filipino attacking force. Grayson ran back to the main American encampment and spread the alarm. "Wake up, Colonel!" one officer shouted to a sleeping Colonel Frederick Funston. "The ball has begun!" Other soldiers began firing, with very little return fire, until the shooting died away about 2 A.M. and they were told to stop wasting ammunition. The Americans took their first casualties. Two South Dakota volunteers were killed, possibly from friendly fire.

The following morning, Aguinaldo sent emissaries to negotiate for peace. The American commander, General Elwell S. Otis, would have none of it. "Fighting having begun, it must go on to the bitter end," he said grimly. Grayson soon got his first taste of combat. The Nebraskans, behind a heavy artillery barrage from a Utah artillery unit, cleared Aguinaldo's "Army of Liberation" defenses along the San Juan River. Joined by regiments from Colorado and Tennessee, they swept up San Juan del Norte hill and by day's end controlled a ridgeline overlooking Manila. The opening battle of what was to become a lengthy war was far from over. It went on for four days, involving regular army and volunteer units and was one of the bloodiest in the entire war. Americans, including the Nebraskans, suffered 238 casualties, forty-four of whom were killed or died of wounds. The Army "estimated" 4,000 Filipino casualties. The Army of Liberation was completely driven out of Manila. Aguinaldo withdrew and regrouped his forces around his headquarters in Malalos, to the north.

AND NOW WHAT? Military success had already compelled McKinley to confront what he found most difficult about being president: He had to make a decision. Now that the Philippines had seemingly dropped into America's lap, what was to be done with them? Should the United States, itself the product of anticolonial revolution, renounce its traditions and annex the Philippines as its

first overseas colony? The Philippines, after all, were nearly 8,000 miles from the American homeland. Its people were very different in culture, religion, development—and complexion—from most Americans. Or should America guarantee Philippine national independence, as Aguinaldo insisted Dewey had promised in bringing him back from Hong Kong to lead the insurgency? And what of those greedy Germans and British, with their warships lurking around, waiting to pounce? They posed a real threat to American Pacific interests. Shouldn't the nation stand up to them?

Loud voices pulled McKinley in all directions. An Anti-Imperialist League—led by the industrialist Andrew Carnegie, former president Grover Cleveland, and celebrity author Mark Twain—held rallies, demonstrations, and torchlight processions protesting possible annexation. "I should hate to see the eagle place his talons on any other land," Twain wrote. Even Senator Mark Hanna, the industrialist who had guided the docile McKinley to the presidency, expressed misgivings. But in the Senate, the eloquent Albert Beveridge rallied the pro-annexation faction with a ringing oration about America's destiny, and that ultimate voice of imperialism had weighed in with an inflammatory speech urging America to "take up the white man's burden" and bright light, democracy and Christianity, to the supposedly benighted and darker-skinned Filipinos. Moral arguments were advanced as well. The United States had indeed encouraged the aspirations of the Philippine insurgency; less than granting them independence would be going back on America's word. The American Protestant missionary spirit spoke up, too. It proclaimed that it was America's "religious duty" to take over the islands and civilize and Christianize a backward, heathen people—ignoring the fact that most Filipinos were already Christian, albeit Roman Catholic.

Alternate solutions were urged on McKinley. Perhaps the United States could just settle for possession of Manila itself. The city would function under the U.S. flag as a seaport, coaling station, and trade outpost, perhaps with a small naval base at Subic Bay. That would follow the model of several European imperial nations, such as Britain, with its long-term lease at Hong Kong. A limited solution might quiet the anti-imperialist protests; it would seem more like a business arrangement.

Or America could annex only Luzon, and not the other 7,000 islands. That might also dampen opposition and simplify questions of U.S. jurisdiction. All these suggestions had drawbacks, however. Taking only Luzon would amputate the nation and leave it easy prey for the other imperialists to pick off the islands, one by one. And taking only Luzon would hardly satisfy those land-grabbers hell-bent on building an American empire.

APPEALING TO THE ALMIGHTY McKinley specialized in soaring patriotic speeches, filled with flag-waving and references to divine providence. In his youth, McKinley had aspired to be a Methodist minister. In his present dilemma, there seemed only one thing to do. McKinley had to ask for divine help. And so— as he was to relate over and over later—he retired to his White House bedroom, knelt at the foot of the bed, and "asked Almighty God for light and guidance."

McKinley ruminated that it would be cowardly and dishonorable to restore the islands to Spanish rule and bad business and discreditable to relinquish them to commercial rivals such as Germany or France. "There was nothing left for us but to take them all, and to educate the Filipinos, and uplift them and civilize them, and by God's grace do the very best we could by them, as our fellow-men for whom Christ also died."

The president had dispatched five commissioners to Paris to work out a treaty with Spain under international auspices. Now he instructed the commissioners to stand fast on the issue of annexation; there was to be no compromise or partial takeover. The Philippines must be ceded to the United States lock, stock, and barrel—all 7,000 of them. "The cession must be of the whole archipelago, or none," McKinley cabled the commissioners. "The latter is inadmissible, and the former must therefore be required." When the Spanish negotiators balked, McKinley authorized the commissioners to suggest a $20 million buyout. The near-bankrupt Spanish government capitulated. The president ordered that official maps be redrawn to mark the Philippines as U.S. territory. Then he set out to bombastically sell the country on the new imperialist policy. The November elections brought gains for the president's Republican Party, seeming to confirm the country's support.

On December 10, 1898, after what one senator described as "the closest, hardest political battle I have ever known," the Senate approved annexation, and the treaty, by the margin of a single vote. Ratification came only after some severe arm-twisting and fulsome promises of future support by the White House. Predictably, there was a great uproar. Annexation was said to totally violate the nation's founding principles. Twain roared angrily that the U.S. flag should be redesigned. Paint the stripes black and replace the field of stars with a skull and crossbones, he raged. William Jennings Bryan, McKinley's opponent in 1896 and again in 1900, declared, "We said we are going to bring prosperity and democracy to the Filipinos. But we had better not educate them, because they might learn to read the Declaration of Independence."

McKinley insisted colonialism was not his policy at all. Instead, in a Christmas proclamation, he declared that it would be a case of "benevolent assimilation." In what became known as the "benevolent assimilation procla-

mation," McKinley pulled out his most glittering and reassuring oratorical flourishes: "Our earnest and paramount aim is to win the confidence, respect, and affection of the Philippine people by proving to them that the mission of the United States is one of benevolent assimilation."

Aguinaldo was outraged. Inspired by the anti-imperialist rhetoric and his study of American democracy, he had firmly believed that the Senate would reject the treaty. Now he felt betrayed. Aguinaldo declared a new Republic of the Philippines, with its capital at Malalos, and he had himself inaugurated as the newly independent nation's first president. He decreed a new form of warfare, giving up on set-piece battles of the type triggered by Grayson's initial gunshots. Instead the Army of Liberation would rely on guerrilla tactics, "flying columns"

DUG IN AND LAYING DOWN A FIELD OF FIRE (ABOVE), AMERICAN INFANTRY MORE OFTEN CONFRONTED GUERRILLA TACTICS AND HIT-AND-RUN RAIDS.

(independent military units assigned to a particular mission, which may be a cavalry or sometimes field artillery in addition to infantry), and hit-and-run raids. The new government officially declared war on the United States. Although the United States named it the "Philippine Insurrection," implying a revolt against legitimate authority, to Filipinos the fighting was (and still is) labeled the "Philippine-American War," a conflict between two sovereign nations.

In 1899, American generals were experienced in wide-open Plains warfare against mounted Indian tribes. Operations where the enemy was concealed in thick jungle or lying low in rice paddies were simply unknown. Cavalry and artillery were of little use when there were few roads and few fixed enemy positions. Nor was the army prepared for a war in which a foremost enemy was debilitating and mysterious tropical disease. At any given moment, half of a unit's men might be suffering from malaria, parasitical disorders, dysentery, typhoid, or even cholera, not to mention venereal disease.

The Army of Liberation retreated northward, ambushing Americans in the mountain passes as they followed. American troops fanned out onto the other major islands, meeting savage resistance from additional insurgent groups. With few uniforms and somewhat undisciplined organization, Americans complained that they could not distinguish friend from foe; often men toiling in the fields turned out to be armed warriors who suddenly produced weapons, attacked unsuspecting Americans, and then returned to work. When villages were suspected of hiding guerrillas, Americans simply burned the villages and turned their guns on the inhabitants.

"WE SAID WE ARE GOING TO BRING PROSPERITY AND DEMOCRACY TO THE FILIPINOS. BUT WE HAD BETTER NOT EDUCATE THEM, BECAUSE THEY MIGHT LEARN TO READ THE DECLARATION OF INDEPENDENCE."

Troops on both sides were accused of—and investigations substantiated—horrifying atrocities and torture. Wounded soldiers were savagely beaten and often shot. Children were killed where a village supported the insurgency. One instance, still angrily remembered a century later, was General Jacob "Howlin' Wilderness" Smith's campaign on the island of Samar. Smith received his nickname because he told troops to turn the island into a "howlin' wilderness." "I want no prisoners," he shouted. "I want you to kill and burn! Kill and burn! Kill all persons capable of bearing arms against the United States." Asked at what age a person would be considered "capable," he replied, "over the age of ten."

Filipinos admitted to hideous atrocities of their own, including a massacre of American troops in which insurgents disguised as women mourners at a funeral suddenly produced machetes and hacked American soldiers to death, then mutilated the bodies and sprinkled them with sugar to attract ants and animals.

America continued to pour money and human lives into the cauldron. Eventually more than 270,000 men saw action. McKinley was reelected in 1900 with "Rough Rider" Roosevelt as his running mate, but America was growing war weary. What was a peace treaty, after all, if men were still fighting and dying in a far-off land? Cries to bring the boys home resounded in Congress and in the newspapers. The volunteers, it was said, had done their duty and should be released. The harvest was coming; their families needed them on the farms.

Yet the war seemed stalemated. Then in a spectacular feat of derring-do, Colonel Funston and a small handful of hand-picked Filipinos and Americans crept into Aguinaldo's mountain hideout, kidnapped the insurgent leader, and whisked him back to Manila in a gunboat hidden off shore. Two weeks later, at the occupiers' headquarters in Malacanang Palace, Aguinaldo swore an oath of allegiance to the United States, renounced the revolution, and called on followers to lay down their arms. "Let the stream of blood cease to flow; let there be an end to tears and desolation," he said.

For all intents and purposes, the war ended there, although organized resistance didn't stop until 1904 and there were still pockets of fighting on the Muslim island of Mindanao as late as 1913. Grayson was long since back in Nebraska. The 54th Volunteers had been devastated in the early fighting and by disease, and the unit was down to less than half strength when they were pulled out and shipped home. Grayson was working in a Beatrice inn and fulminating about General Otis's "bullheadedness" in rebuffing Aguinaldo's peace gestures after the "pipeline incident."

MOURNING COMRADES WHO HAD BEEN TORTURED AND KILLED BY INSURGENTS, U.S. INFANTRYMEN VOWED REVENGE—AND OFTEN TOOK IT.

YOUNG MAN WITH A WEAPON
On September 1, 1901, the president of the United States traveled to Buffalo to officially open the Pan-American Exposition. He delivered a trademark McKinley bombastic speech, then began to clasp hands with a line of well-wishers. One clean-shaven, neat-appearing young man confronted him with a handkerchief wrapped around the proferred hand. Leon Czolgosz, a lone-wolf anarchist, fired two shots from a concealed pistol, and McKinley slumped to the ground. He was taken to the fair's emergency hospital, where an operation was performed to close his abdominal wound, but the bullet could not be retrieved. At first the president rallied and

Judge

ENTERED AT THE POST-OFFICE AT NEW YORK AS SECOND-CLASS MATTER. COPYRIGHT 1899 BY ARKELL PUBLISHING COMPANY. TITLE REGISTERED AS A TRADE MARK.

GRANT HAMILTON—

seemed on the way to recovery. But infection set in. Three weeks after the shooting, McKinley died, and Roosevelt became president. The following July 4, the new president declared the war officially over.

The consequences of McKinley's fateful and poorly thought-out decision were immense. Apart from the $7 billion expense (in modern money), the war had cost more than 7,000 casualties, who were killed in action, wounded, or struck down by disease, plus uncounted others requiring lifetime care.

Astonishingly, the conflict forged a lasting bond between the two nations. The United States made good eventually on its promise of national independence. An American-style government was established in 1916, and the Philippines became a self-governing commonwealth in 1935. Filipinos fought valiantly side by side with American troops in World War II, succumbed by the thousands in the infamous Bata'an Death March, and endured four years of brutal Japanese occupation that left the proud city of Manila in ruins. The nation became fully independent in 1945. The last American military bases on Philipiline soil were returned in 1999, a hundred years after McKinley's pledge of "benevolent assimilation."

CHAPTER 10

THE PUNITIVE EXPEDITION INTO MEXICO

WOODROW WILSON

DEMOCRAT WOODROW WILSON HAD ALWAYS PUBLICLY PLEDGED A "WATCHFUL WAITING" POLICY, STAYING OUT OF MEXICO'S POLITICAL AFFAIRS; BUT BEHIND THE SCENES, WILSON WAS MAKING PROMISES TO MEXICO'S GOVERNMENT—AND WHEN MEXICAN BANDIT PANCHO VILLA ATTACKED AN AMERICA TOWN, WILSON WAS FORCED TO TAKE MILITARY ACTION.

MAUD WRIGHT WAS WASHING DISHES IN THE KITCHEN OF HER HUMBLE RANCH house in Hernandez, Mexico, when she heard a commotion outside. It sounded like horses galloping up the pathway. Men were yelling and talking over one another.

Maud dried her hands on her apron, picked up her baby, and then went to the door to see what was going on. It was March 1, 1916, near dusk. Colonel Nicholas Servantes and a band of twelve men had ridden into Hernandez in search of supplies. Servantes was one of revolutionary leader Pancho Villa's most obedient commanders. Villa and his revolutionary army rode north, heading toward the U.S. border, and were prepared to invade Columbus, New Mexico. Servantes and his group had strayed from the trail and would catch up with Villa later that night.

"Do you have any food to sell?" one of the men asked Maud, whose husband, Edward, was in the nearby town of Pearson purchasing supplies. It wasn't uncommon for men to drive up the trail and be in want of meat, flour, or clean water, but Maud could see that these men were nothing more than poker-playing, cigar-chomping, whiskey-drinking bandits.

One of the men stepped forward. He said they were Mexican President Venustiano Carranza's soldiers, but Maud didn't believe it. Carranza had been a Mexican governor who was installed as president after several battles for power in Mexico City. Carranza's reign had somewhat stabilized what had been

a government in absolute disarray. Many were behind Carranza, including U.S. President Woodrow Wilson. Nevertheless, Maud was certain the men at her door were not affiliated with Carranza.

"I have only a little bit of flour and meal," she said.

Servantes dismounted and walked toward the doorway. The others followed. Servantes asked, "I might buy some food for my men?"

As Maud contemplated how to deal with Servantes, her husband, Edward, showed up with two pack mules and a young Mexican farmhand. Edward and Maud had moved to Hernandez in pursuit of work, had a child, and were quite content with their modest ranch.

For years, the Mexican government had been in a state of disorder. Revolutions had risen out of Mexico City and spread all across the country. Although the hostilities Mexico faced were not new—the country had been in varying states of instability since attaining independence from Spain in 1821— President Wilson's Republican adversaries, who were more inclined toward an isolationist, noninterventionist foreign policy, were irate with him for not keeping his nose out of Mexican politics. Just eight days after Wilson was

FAMED OUTLAW *BANDITO* PANCHO VILLA (SECOND FROM RIGHT IN THE FRONT ROW) BECAME ONE OF WOODROW WILSON'S BIGGEST PROBLEMS AS WILSON BEGAN TO QUESTION HIS DECISION TO HELP MEXICO.

inaugurated in 1913, he had pledged a new outlook for the country and America's relationship with Carranza, noting, "One of the chief objects of my administration will be to cultivate the friendship ... of our sister republics of Central and South America ..." He also once remarked, "I am going to teach the South American Republics to elect good men!" Yet, as much as Wilson claimed to understand the scope of Mexico's problems, he said publicly that he had no tolerance for revolutionaries. "We can have no sympathy with those who seek to seize the power of government to advance their own personal interests and ambition." He was speaking of Pancho Villa. The president's critics, however, suspected he might get America involved where it didn't belong.

Maud was taken prisoner, and her child was given to the farmhand's wife. (Maud would be reunited with her child after Villa let her go a week later.) Maud's husband, Edward, and the farmhand were executed by Villa's men. Maud Wright's kidnapping was the beginning of what would soon turn into a problem for President Wilson with Mexico that would have worldwide repercussions.

POWER HUNGRY

The problems that President Wilson inherited in Mexico started before he took office in 1912. The revolution led by Francisco Madero was already gathering momentum and spreading throughout Mexico. Francisco Madero ran against Porfirio Díaz in Mexico's 1910 presidential election. Realizing he was going to lose, Díaz had Madero jailed to keep him from running. Díaz won the election, but many Mexicans understood he had stolen it. Meanwhile, Madero issued a call to arms, urging Mexicans to rally against Díaz. This was the beginning of the Madero revolution.

Pancho Villa was born Doroteo Arango, in Durango, Mexico, in 1887. He supported Madero, but soon broke from the group and went off on his own, with hundreds of followers who believed that Villa could offer them something better than Madero or Díaz. Some said Arango had changed his name to Villa after murdering a man (who had reportedly raped his sister) and fleeing into the mountains to avoid arrest. According to the *American National Biography*, however, young Arango took the name of Francisco Villa, a sierra bandit with whom he rode, after the elder Villa was killed in a shootout, in order to establish his leadership over the remnants of the gang—thus becoming Francisco "Pancho" Villa. Since that time, Villa had been known as a *bandito*. Still, Villa had a strong sense of loyalty; he would never fight against his old friend, Madero, for example. Instead, Villa joined Victoriano Huerta, one of Madero's former field commanders, who had instigated a takeover of Mexico City. In turn, Madero ordered Villa to be jailed for insubordination. Villa spent a year behind bars before escaping to the United States. As Villa monitored the situa-

PRESIDENTIAL BRIEFING
(1856–1924)

• TWENTY-EIGHTH PRESIDENT OF THE UNITED STATES (1913–21), GOVERNOR OF NEW JERSEY, AND PRESIDENT OF PRINCETON UNIVERSITY (1890–1902)

• BORN THOMAS WOODROW WILSON ON DECEMBER 28, 1856, IN STAUNTON, VIRGINIA

• DIED FEBRUARY 3, 1924, IN WASHINGTON, D.C.

• ELECTED 1912, FIRST SOUTHERN PRESIDENT SINCE ANDREW JACKSON AND THE ONLY DEMOCRAT BETWEEN 1896 AND 1932

• SIGNED CLAYTON ANTITRUST ACT (1914) AND ESTABLISHED FEDERAL RESERVE (1914) AND FEDERAL TRADE COMMISSION (1914)

• AT PARIS PEACE CONFERENCE (1919) AFTER WORLD WAR I, PUSHED FOR "PEACE WITHOUT VENGEANCE" IN THE VERSAILLES TREATY

• DRAFTED A COVENANT FOR A LEAGUE OF NATIONS, WHICH WAS REJECTED BY THE U.S. SENATE

• AWARDED THE NOBEL PRIZE FOR PEACE IN 1919

-WELL NAMED-

W.A.Rogers

AFTER PRESIDENT WILSON ACKNOWLEDGED VENUSTIANO CARRANZA'S TAKEOVER OF MEXICO CITY IN 1914, PANCHO VILLA FLED INTO THE NORTH COUNTRY TO BEGIN PLANNING HIS REVENGE. SOON AFTER, UNDER THE ORDERS OF WILSON, U.S. GENERAL JOHN PERSHING STAGED A MASSIVE SEARCH FOR VILLA AND HIS BAND OF OUTLAWS.

tion from across the border, he learned that Huerta had engineered a coup and ultimately deposed Madero, which opened up an opportunity for Villa to return and perhaps have a position of power himself.

President Wilson had tried to stay out of the mess that had become Mexico's government, telling Americans that it wasn't the United States' business to get involved. However, behind the backs of his political adversaries in Washington and the American people, Wilson closely monitored Mexico's affairs. U.S. ambassador to Mexico, Henry Lane Wilson, known as an "aggressive advocate of dollar diplomacy," fell in with Huerta and his ruthless administration. Ambassador Wilson disliked Madero and became embroiled in Huerta's plan to overthrow him, which involved President Wilson.

What caused President Wilson the most anguish as he tried to manage the situation was that Germany and England made it known that they supported Huerta. It seemed the world was screaming for the United States to intervene, but as far as the rest of the world knew, Wilson maintained neutrality. Incidentally, there had not been a free election in Mexico for years. There was an arms embargo in place, which prevented Huerta from building an army of any strength. By 1914, Ambassador Wilson, who was in disagreement with the president on most policies dealing with Mexico, resigned, and John Lind took his place. Lind and President Wilson met frequently. After each meeting, the president generally gave a statement as to what had transpired. The situation in Mexico was tense. Americans were eager to know what was going on, but the president was silent about the change of ambassadors. Wilson told the *New York Times* on January 4, 1914, "The Huerta government is slowly being crushed, not only by the Constitutionalist forces, but by its own isolation, and that inevitably it must fall."

Once again, the president's public policy was "let them handle their own problems," while talking about the need for an immediate election in Mexico—one in which Wilson asserted Huerta could *not* take part or the United States would intervene militarily.

Huerta laughed at the president's proclamation, and he held an election in October, which he made sure he won.

President Wilson had spoken out on this contentious issue eight days after his inauguration, telling Congress on March 12, 1913, "Huerta, the bitter, implacable foe of everything progressive and humane in Mexico... openly defied the authority of the United States ... and laughed to scorn the high idealism which lay behind it." Wilson knew Huerta had seized the government. Now, as Germany made it known it was befriending Huerta's regime, Wilson was under pressure to step in and fix things.

Many criticized Wilson's persistent, "watchful waiting" policy, a phrase he coined and frequently used to describe his restraint from using force in Mexico despite the turmoil. Many of the president's critics in Congress were now prepared to combat his policies, which had done little to free the repressed people of Mexico. As much as Wilson said he wanted to keep America out of Mexico, he was determined to stay involved in shaping Mexico's future.

WITH PRESIDENT WILSON ACKNOWLEDGING CARRANZA'S TAKEOVER, VILLA PLEDGED TO DO TO AMERICA WHAT IT HAD DONE TO HIM AND HIS PEOPLE. SO HE FLED INTO THE NORTH COUNTRY AND BEGAN BUILDING AN ARMY.

On August 20, 1914, Carranza and his army took control of Mexico City. A year later, Wilson made the declaration that America would recognize Carranza's regime as a suitable governing body. Wilson's approval of Carranza's government infuriated Villa, who had hoped that Carranza would include him in the new government. Additionally, Villa had a friend in Washington, Consul George Carrothers, who had been telling him that it was possible the Wilson administration would recognize Villa's efforts if his revolution took over Mexico City. But now Carranza, a leader Villa despised, was in power. With President Wilson acknowledging Carranza's takeover, Villa pledged to do to America what it had done to him and his people. So he fled into the north country and began building an army.

BATTLE CRY According to one witness, on the night of March 8, 1916, a week after Colonel Servantes and his men had ridden into Hernandez to steal supplies and kidnap Maud Wright, Villa had one intention in mind: To kill everybody in the United States.

Up until this point, Villa had roamed throughout the countryside in civilian clothes so as not to draw attention to himself. It had been nearly two years since Carranza had established his presidency. Still furious about this, Villa had been building and training his army, staging small incursions and causing great havoc in northern Mexico—all with the thought he would one day strike in America to get back at Carranza and Wilson.

Villa was said to have worn a "queer little round straw hat" on most days leading up to his invasion of New Mexico. He was also seen routinely riding a small mule, blending amiably into the northern populace. But on March 8, Villa emerged from his tent quite a different man. Instead of appearing like a peasant, he showed himself a majestic and gallant military leader, clad in a flashy new military uniform and sitting high atop his brilliant sorrel charger as he addressed his army. There were 1,500 men standing behind him—some claimed double that number—as he led a charge toward the American border.

As Villa and his men rode from Torreon toward the United States near Columbus, New Mexico, they'd stop and camp for no more than three-hour intervals. Most of the men were exhausted. Many hadn't slept more than an hour at a time, generally in the saddle or with their heads against tree stumps. Several of Villa's men confided secretly that they were thinking of abandoning the revolution, saying they were tired and had been at it for far too many years.

As they closed in on Columbus, Villa's commanders ordered soldiers to kill any American they ran up against—except women and children.

By 4:00 P.M. on March 8, Villa and his men were inside the American border. As they crossed into Columbus, Villa shouted, "Make torches of every man, woman, and child to be found," apparently overturning his earlier order to spare the lives of women and children.

The fighting in Columbus started soon after, as Villa's army rushed American cavalry troops stationed nearby. A reconnaissance group had gone in the previous night and scouted the area, making note that Villa's initial attack would not meet much resistance (which proved to be true). But as American troops from the north got word and rushed south, the fighting became intense. "Villa sent his troops across the tracks," Maud explained, "… soon I saw buildings on fire. Then the American troops apparently got into action, and in a little while, the Mexicans came back."

"Viva Villa!" became a common battle cry Villa's men shouted as they charged. Scores of Villa's revolutionaries abandoned the cause, however, as Villa rode among them, cursing and threatening to shoot any man who ran away.

DEAD OR ALIVE Accounts varied, but Villa reportedly killed between seventeen and twenty American soldiers, and wounded nearly seventy-five. Columbus, New Mexico, was partly burned to the ground. Members of Congress had warned the president something like this would happen sooner or later if he did not stop meddling in Mexico's affairs.

As plans were made to send in a group of American regulars to track, capture, or kill Villa, Congress had some rather harsh words for the president. Wyoming Republican Frank Mondell, after being asked by Illinois Democratic

Adolph Sabath what he would do about Mexico, said, "I would first put in a Republican Administration that would not meddle with the domestic affairs of that country!" The president, Mondell continued, brought these new troubles upon the American people himself "by seeking to dictate in Mexican affairs."

Democrat Martin Foster tried backing up the president, but he couldn't stray from the facts: "I do not believe it is the duty of our government to send our boys into Mexico and plunge this country into war."

Indeed, it was too late. The president had wasted time by placating the Mexican government, then turning around and telling the American people he was staying out of its affairs. Republicans believed his Mexican policies had made America weak. In addition, the new concern was that if troops were sent in on what Wilson was calling a "punitive expedition" for Villa, who would protect them? If America didn't wage war with Mexico, how could Wilson expect soldiers to find and execute Villa? The Mexican people would not tolerate Americans rummaging through their villages.

Meanwhile, Carranza issued a statement. In part, he said, "My government sincerely regrets this affair and asks the American people to be patient."

Republicans saw an opportunity to prove how Wilson's failures had put America in a position of being forced into war with Mexico—thus igniting tensions with Germany, Japan, and England, adding fuel to an already volatile world situation.

Wilson's secretary of war, Lindley Garrison, had resigned on February 10, saying, "It is evident that we hopelessly disagree upon what I conceive to be fundamental principles." Wilson waited three weeks before choosing the former mayor of Cleveland, Newton Baker, an admitted pacifist, to fill Garrison's role. Theodore Roosevelt supporter George Perkins was incensed and wrote into the *New York Times*, commenting, "Wilson has told us to believe he was hunting for the most competent man ... at last he appoints an ardent pacifist, a man who promptly states that he knows nothing whatever about the duties he is to perform." Summing up what most Americans felt, Perkins ended the editorial by saying, "Mr. Wilson adds a fresh page to the

FRANCISCO PANCHO VILLA SAID HE WANTED TO "KILL EVERYBODY IN THE UNITED STATES" THAT HE CAME IN CONTACT WITH AFTER AMERICAN PRESIDENT WOODROW WILSON SANCTIONED CARRANZA'S TAKEOVER. HE BECAME ONE OF THE MOST WANTED MEN IN ALL THE WORLD.

chapter of shame and humiliation, which he is writing into the history of the United States."

Under pressure, on March 15, a week after the attack on Columbus, Wilson sent Commander John J. Pershing into Chihuahua, Mexico, with 11,000 men, artillery units, newfangled field radio transmitters, machine guns, and the 1st Aero Squadron. Wilson released a statement saying that Carranza had "invited" the Americans into Mexico. As it turned out, Pershing's troops ventured some 300 miles into Mexican territory, and they were opposed wherever they went. At one point, a clash broke out with Carranza's men in which nine American soldiers were killed. Moreover, a majority of the Mexican people were uninterested in helping Americans.

Pershing, a Missouri native who had fought in the Philippines against Emilio Aguinaldo's staunchly disciplined insurgents, was the best choice Wilson could have made.

A spurious report that Villa had been killed surfaced on April 16. Yet, fewer than four weeks later, Villa and his bandits emerged and initiated a second raid on American soil in Boquillas and Glenn Springs, Texas. In the aftermath of Villa's raids, President Wilson ordered Texas, New Mexico, and Arizona militia units, along with regular U.S. troops, to secure the border and protect American interests at any cost. Still deep inside Mexican territory, General Pershing and his men were told by Carranza's Mexican government to retreat north, or face certain attack from all sides.

Between June and July scores of African-American cavalry troops were taken prisoner and killed in various parts of Northern Mexico by Carranza's military forces. On July 21, Pershing sent a message to President Wilson, noting how chaotic and uncertain the situation had become. Field intelligence had told Pershing that Villa had regrouped and now had more than 18,000 men behind him. They were at that moment heading south, toward Pershing, prepared to go up against the entire American force. This, on top of Carranza's troops beginning to squeeze him on both sides, did not put Pershing in such a stable position to defend American interests or find and execute Villa. In addition, the armed intervention by Pershing had aroused intense anti-American feelings among ordinary Mexicans. Pershing and his troops ended up occupying towns more than they went in search for Villa. This unstable environment, as American and Mexican forces were in a literal standoff, ultimately pushed Mexico toward Germany for assistance.

In the interim, Carranza had never approved Wilson's order to send in troops and protested Pershing's continued occupation. The two men, who at one time had generally agreed with each other, were now at odds.

Germany, however, waiting and watching from the sidelines, saw an opportunity. On January 16, 1917, German ambassador Arthur Zimmermann sent an encoded telegram—intercepted by British intelligence—to the German ambassador in Washington. In it, Zimmerman wrote:

We intend to begin on the first of February unrestricted submarine warfare. We shall endeavor in spite of this to keep the United States of America neutral. In the event of this not succeeding, we make Mexico a proposal or alliance on the following basis: make war together, make peace together, generous financial support and an understanding on our part that Mexico is to re-conquer the lost territory in Texas, New Mexico, and Arizona ... You will inform the president of the above most secretly as soon as the outbreak of war

COMMANDER JOHN J. PERSHING LED OVER 11,000 U.S. MILITARY TROOPS AND CIVILIANS INTO MEXICO TO TRACK AND KILL FRANCISCO PANCHO VILLA AFTER THE BANDITO ATTACKED A SMALL VILLAGE IN NEW MEXICO AND KILLED INNOCENT AMERICANS.

with the United States of America is certain and add the suggestion that he should, on his own initiative, invite Japan to immediate adherence and at the same time mediate between Japan and ourselves. Please call the president's attention to the fact that the ruthless employment of our submarines now offers the prospect of compelling England in a few months to make peace.

CURTISS JN4S ATTACK PANCHO VILLA'S MEN DURING THE "PUNITIVE EXPEDITION" INTO MEXICO LED BY COMMANDER JOHN J. PERSHING, ONE OF THE EARLIEST MILITARY USES OF THE RECENTLY INVENTED "AEROPLANES."

No longer was Pershing's mission a "punitive expedition" for Villa's head on a platter, nor was it a small military incursion between Mexico and the United States. Germany was proposing a possible alliance with Mexico *against* the United States, which could mean a world war.

Pershing and his American forces departed on February 5, 1917—without a drop of Villa's blood on their swords.

The infamous Zimmerman telegram helped provoke American public opinion against Germany and generate support for joining Britain and France when Wilson went before Congress on April 2, 1917, to ask for a declaration of war. In that war message, Wilson was clear about Germany's disloyalty, saying at one point, "But they have played their part in serving to convince us at last that that government entertains no real friendship for us and means to act against our peace and security at its convenience—that it means to stir up enemies against us at our very doors, [and] the intercepted [Zimmermann] note to the German Minister at Mexico City is eloquent evidence."

In April of that year America entered World War I.

On June 20, 1923, after Villa cut a deal with the Mexican government to disband his revolution, he was murdered.

CHAPTER 11

THE BONUS ARMY

HERBERT HOOVER

IN THE SWELTERING HEAT OF A JULY NIGHT IN 1932, 600 CRACK TROOPS OF THE U.S. Army, supported by a detachment of cavalry and five Renault tanks— ungainly, seven-ton dinosaurs left over from World War I—stood at attention with bayonets fixed on one side of Washington, D.C.'s, Eleventh Street Bridge. On the other side of the river lay Anacostia Flats, where hundreds of men, women, and children—underfed, poorly clothed, and unemployed—ran about frantically, trying to pack up their pitiful possessions and get away before the military moved in to destroy the ramshackle camp known as Bonus City. Major General Douglas MacArthur had granted the camp's inhabitants an hour to get the women and children to safety.

Back in the White House, President Herbert Hoover, who had ordered MacArthur to clear out the squatters, was having second thoughts about unleashing American troops against unarmed, impoverished American veterans and their families. Hoover sent new instructions to MacArthur, ordering him not to cross the bridge. The president's messenger returned to the White House to say that the general showed no signs of pulling back. Once again Hoover sent MacArthur a direct order: He was not to cross the Eleventh Street Bridge. MacArthur scoffed. He would not waste time, he said, listening to couriers who pretended to bring fresh orders from the president.

TO THE END OF HIS LIFE, HERBERT HOOVER BELIEVED THAT THE BONUS ARMY HAD BEEN ORGANIZED "BY THE COMMUNISTS AND INCLUDED A LARGE NUMBER OF HOODLUMS AND EX-CONVICTS DETERMINED TO RAISE A PUBLIC DISTURBANCE."

When the hour's grace was up, in defiance of two explicit commands from his commander-in-chief, MacArthur ordered his men across the bridge. They pulled on their gas masks first, fired tear gas grenades into the camp, then moved in. In spite of the hour's reprieve, there were still people in the camp, men who thought to put up some form of resistance, and even families who tried to hide in the makeshift huts that had become their homes. The mother of one such family recalled, "One of the soldiers threw a [tear gas] bomb … we all began to cry. We got wet towels and put them over the faces of the children. About a half hour later, my baby began to vomit. I took her outside in the air, and she vomited again. Next day she began to turn black and blue, and we took her to the hospital."

As methodically as possible under the circumstances, the troopers drove the last inhabitants of Bonus City out of the camp. It was a terrible scene—women and children crying in fear; men, tears streaming down their cheeks from the gas, cursing their brother soldiers. And then the fire started. From a window of the White House, President Hoover saw the flames as Bonus City erupted into an enormous bonfire. The next day, the body of a baby was found amid the ashes of the camp.

"EYES FRONT—NOT LEFT!" The Great Depression was in its third year in 1932. Somewhere between fifteen and seventeen million Americans were

unemployed. In September 1932, *Fortune* magazine estimated that thirty-four million men, women, and children—about 28 percent of the population—were living without any income at all. (That figure did not include the nation's eleven million farm families.) Two million Americans—about a quarter million of them between the ages of sixteen and twenty-one—were homeless wanderers, most of them sharecroppers or farmers who had lost their land, or members of the lower middle class who had lost their jobs and could no longer pay rent.

It is impossible to estimate how many Americans suffered from malnutrition or whose health was seriously impaired because they could not afford doctors, much less a stay in a hospital. (According to historian William Manchester, nine years later, when America was gearing up for World War II, John Kelly, Roosevelt's national physical fitness director, found that about 40 percent of all men of draft age suffered from some kind of physical impairment, such as stunted growth or rotten teeth.) President Hoover was not blind or insensitive to the crisis, but he rejected the idea that direct financial assistance from the federal government would be helpful. And the men he turned to for advice only reinforced the president's disinclination. Former president Calvin Coolidge proclaimed that America was a country of businessmen and it must conduct itself in a businesslike manner. Automobile tycoon Henry Ford said that if the government started paying unemployment insurance, loafers would quit their jobs to collect the checks and the level of unemployment would rise. Silas Strawn, president of the United States Chamber of Commerce, warned everyone that "the dole" would undermine the enterprising, can-do spirit of America. "If this country ever votes the dole," Strawn said, "we've hit the toboggan as a nation." Hoover believed these men, and so when the Democratic Congress passed a $2 billion relief bill, he vetoed it.

The arrival in Washington of perhaps as many as 20,000 (estimates vary) Bonus Army veterans and their families in spring 1932 was an embarrassment to Hoover and his administration, but it was not a conversion experience. The president remained unmoved by the veterans' plight, but Congress was more receptive. On June 15, the House passed a bill to pay them the promised bonus immediately. The bill was sent to the Senate, and on June 17, 10,000 veterans and their families gathered around the Capitol building as the senators debated the question. After hours of tense anticipation, Walter Waters, a former army sergeant from Oregon and the leader of the Bonus Army, announced to a stunned, silent crowd that the Senate had defeated the bill by a vote of sixty-two to eighteen. "Sing *America*," Waters said, "and go back to your billets." And that's what the 10,000 did.

Even the marchers' response to this crushing disappointment did not persuade President Hoover that these thousands were peaceful, patriotic

PRESIDENTIAL BRIEFING
(1874–1964)

• THIRTY-FIRST PRESIDENT OF THE UNITED STATES (1929–33)

• BORN AUGUST 10, 1874, IN WEST BRANCH, IOWA

• DIED OCTOBER 20, 1964, IN NEW YORK, NEW YORK

• AN INTERNATIONAL HERO AS RELIEF ADMINISTRATOR OVERSEEING MONUMENTAL DISTRIBUTION OF FOOD AFTER WORLD WAR I

• SECRETARY OF COMMERCE TO WARREN G. HARDING AND CALVIN COOLIDGE (1921–28)

• DIRECTED RELIEF AFTER THE GREAT MISSISSIPPI RIVER FLOOD OF 1927

• ELECTED IN 1928, WITH PROGRESSIVE PLANS, JUST IN TIME FOR THE STOCK MARKET CRASH OF OCTOBER 1929, AND THE GREAT DEPRESSION

• THE LAST REPUBLICAN PRESIDENT UNTIL EISENHOWER (1952)

Americans. He was convinced that the Bonus Army was not a grassroots movement of impoverished veterans but a mass of Communist agitators plotting a Bolshevik-style revolution. In fact, there were some Communists in the camps, led by John T. Pace from Michigan. But if Pace believed that the Bonus Army was a ready-made revolutionary cadre, he was mistaken. The marchers routinely expelled avowed Communists from the camps. They destroyed Communist leaflets and other literature. And among their slogans the veterans adopted a motto directed at the Communists, "Eyes front—not left!"

THE KINDNESS OF STRANGERS
There were several camps in Washington, but most of the people who left Capitol Hill that afternoon returned to the largest camp on the other side of the Anacostia River, to the southeast of the capital, toward Maryland. A newspaper described the veterans'

housing as "tented huts made of tattered cloth fixed up on old boards with packing boxes serving as props." Some of the huts had straw mattresses for the women and children—the gift of District of Columbia Police Superintendent Pelham D. Glassford. And everywhere there were faded American flags. These were, after all, veterans of World War I who had come to the capital to ask their government for help.

Moderately more comfortable housing was found for about 1,000 veterans and their families just three blocks from the U.S. Capitol on Pennsylvania Avenue in a row of derelict red-brick buildings that had once been warehouses and a few shabby businesses. Police Superintendent Glassford knew he should evict the squatters, but he hadn't the heart to do it. An article in the *Baltimore Sun* had described the men of the Bonus Army as "ragged, weary, and apathetic, [with] no hope in their faces." And besides, there were women and children in there. So Glassford let them be.

Food for so many was a problem, of course. One Washington baker supplied a hundred loaves of bread, free, every day. Another baker sent in 1,000 pies. Shipments of food arrived in a haphazard, unpredictable way, from as far off as Des Moines, Iowa. The Washington police, moved to pity, distributed free coffee, bread, and stew. But the veterans and their families had not traveled all the way to Washington for handouts. They wanted the government to give them now the bonus they were scheduled to receive in another thirteen years.

In 1924, Congress had passed the Adjusted Compensation Act—as demanded by the American Legion, and over President Coolidge's veto—which promised World War I veterans a bonus of about $500 apiece (approximately $7,400 in modern money). The legislation stipulated, however, that the payment would not be made until 1945 because the bonus was structured as a kind of insurance policy that would be "paid up" in twenty years. The thousands who had come to Washington in summer 1932—out of work, out of luck, hungry, and in many cases homeless—wanted Congress to dispense the bonus at once. (The way things were going, they might not live to 1945.) Newspaper writers christened the veterans "the Bonus Army," although they called themselves "the Bonus Expeditionary Force" (after the American Expeditionary Force, the name of the U.S. forces in World War I).

President Hoover was highly displeased by the arrival of a horde of hungry, worn-out families in his capital. Waters and other BEF leaders petitioned the president to receive a delegation; he refused. Instead, Hoover hunkered down in the White House as if he were besieged. He brought in police officers to patrol the White House grounds twenty-four hours a day. He had barricades erected across streets so no vehicle could come within a city block of the Executive Mansion. Finally, he ordered the gates of the White House chained shut.

"Hoover Locks Self in White House" proclaimed the *New York Daily News*. When a one-armed veteran bearing a picket sign walked through the barricades toward the White House, patrolmen beat him up, then hauled him off to jail.

As the sweltering summer dragged on and the Bonus Army showed no signs of leaving town, Hoover decided to act.

MACARTHUR GOES TO WAR By ten o'clock on the morning of July 28, 1932, the heat and humidity in downtown Washington were already stifling. That morning, two agents of the Treasury Department came to the veterans' encampment inside the derelict buildings on Pennsylvania Avenue to inform the community's leaders that they would have to move out. The veterans refused to go. An hour later, Police Superintendent Glassford arrived in front of the buildings on his blue motorcycle leading a large detachment of police officers. Slowly, even gently, they began to move the veterans and their families out of the buildings.

Some of the veterans must have brought word of the eviction to the main camp at Anacostia because around noon hundreds of veterans poured across the Eleventh Street Bridge into the center of the city. When they reached the Pennsylvania Avenue "camp," some of the angry veterans began hurling rocks and broken bricks, one of which struck Glassford on the side of the face. At the sight of his chief hurt and bleeding, a police officer drew his revolver and fired at a veteran. The man, William Hrushka, an out-of-work butcher from Chicago, fell dead, shot through the heart.

Immediately other police officers began firing into the crowd. As Glassford shouted, "Stop the shooting!" another veteran, Eric Carlson of Oakland, California, dropped to the ground, mortally wounded. The shooting stopped, and some of the veterans began to fall back to Anacostia while others milled about in the street. Meanwhile, word of the melee was brought to the White House. Hoover, who was having lunch, instructed Secretary of War Patrick J. Hurley to use troops to clear out the veterans, and Hurley passed on the president's order to the Army's chief of staff, Douglas MacArthur.

Against the advice of his assistant, Major Dwight D. Eisenhower, MacArthur made up his mind to lead the troops himself. "MacArthur," he declared of himself, "has decided to go into active command in the field." (The general had a peculiar habit of referring to himself in the third person.) "There is incipient revolution in the air," he informed Eisenhower. "We are going to break the back of the BEF."

About 4:45 that afternoon, just as thousands of civil service workers were leaving their offices for the commute home, the troops MacArthur had called up arrived. They were a magnificent sight: 600 infantrymen in starched uniforms, bayonets fixed, steel helmets glinting in the late afternoon sun, all marching in perfect order down the broad boulevard. There was a machine gun

detachment and five rumbling tanks, but most splendid of all were the cavalry-men, trotting down the street with their sabers drawn, under the command of Major George S. Patton. It is a sign of the naïveté of the Bonus Army—and a tribute to their sincerity—that they thought this was a parade in their honor. They began to applaud, and the thousands of spectators lining the street joined them. Suddenly the horsemen wheeled about and charged into the crowd. They rode down men and women, including Senator Hiram Bingham of Connecticut, beating anyone who defied them with the flat of their sabers.

"Clear out!" the cavalrymen ordered.

"Shame! Shame!" answered the crowd of office workers.

The veterans formed a cordon across Pennsylvania Avenue. Their leaders waved American flags, and these banners became the new targets of the cavalry-men. They galloped into the ranks of veterans, yanking the flags from their hands. One young cavalryman tore a flag from the hands of a veteran, called

STREET BRAWLS ERUPTED WHEN THE WASHINGTON, D.C., POLICE FORCED MEMBERS OF THE BONUS ARMY OUT OF DERELICT BUILDINGS THEY HAD BEEN OCCUPYING.

him "a crummy old bum," and spat on him. MacArthur sat in his limousine with the top down for an unobstructed view of the proceedings. A civilian who stood nearby shouted at the general, "The American flag means nothing to me after this!" Furious, MacArthur ordered his staff, "Put that man under arrest if he opens his mouth again!"

Now the infantry advanced, throwing tear gas grenades into the crowd of veterans and into the buildings that had been their homes. A huge crowd of women and children staggered out of the buildings, gasping for breath, as they retreated with the men across the bridge to Anacostia. At the entrance to the bridge, MacArthur and his men stopped. A mess tent was sent up and everyone had dinner. Then, after darkness had fallen over Washington, sometime between nine and ten in the evening, MacArthur climbed out of his limo, and, with Major Eisenhower at his side, led his troops across the Eleventh Street Bridge and into the ramshackle camp of the Bonus Army.

The infantry and cavalry charged through the camp, rousting out the inhabitants, then setting fire to the shacks. Seven-year-old Eugene King taxed a soldier's patience when he stopped to rescue his pet rabbit. The trooper plunged his bayonet through the child's leg. It was not an isolated incident; there would be more than a hundred casualties that night.

Shortly after midnight, with the veterans and their families in full flight and the camp a raging inferno that six city fire companies could not contain, Secretary of War Hurley declared to an assembly of reporters, "It was a great victory. Mac did a great job; he's the man of the hour."

FEELINGS OF HORROR It appears that Hoover as well as MacArthur

believed in their hearts that the men in the camps were not destitute, desperate veterans of the U.S. armed forces but subversives. It was a case of paranoia. In June 1932 the intelligence division of MacArthur's General Staff reported that of the twenty-six leaders of the Bonus Army only three were Communists, and that among the veterans and their families in the camps, the feeling was overwhelmingly anti-Communist. MacArthur and Hoover dismissed the report; to their mind, the Bonus Army was a dangerous, subversive mob, and driving them out of Washington was imperative for national security.

Shortly after the expulsion of the Bonus Army, President Hoover declared that the men who had been cleared out of the abandoned buildings along Pennsylvania Avenue and the shantytown at Anacostia Flats were not veterans but "Communists and persons with criminal records." MacArthur claimed that 90 percent of the Bonus Army had never served in the U.S. military, while Secretary of War Hurley made a more conservative estimate that 33 percent were non-veterans. The Veterans Administration, however, weighed in with

A WORLD WAR I RECRUITING
POSTER RECALLS THE DAYS
WHEN THE VETERANS WERE
REGARDED AS HEROES.

The Doughboys Make Good

an entirely different figure. The VA staff had conducted an exhaustive survey of the men of the Bonus Army, then compared the information they gathered in the camps with their own records and found that 94 percent of the Bonus Army men had served in the army or navy, 67 percent had served overseas, and 20 percent were listed as disabled. Very few newspapers picked up the VA report, however. Most believed what the White House, the War Department, and MacArthur were telling them. The *New York Times* derided the veterans as "ordinary trespassers." The *Boston Herald* asserted that the American public had "had enough of holdups by the undeserving." The *Chicago Tribune* condemned the "unreasonable demands by ex-servicemen [that] inflamed their mistaken sense of judgment."

PRESIDENT HOOVER DECLARED THAT THE MEN WHO HAD BEEN CLEARED OUT OF THE ABANDONED BUILDINGS ALONG PENNSYLVANIA AVENUE AND THE SHANTYTOWN AT ANACOSTIA FLATS WERE NOT VETERANS BUT "COMMUNISTS AND PERSONS WITH CRIMINAL RECORDS."

Nonetheless, some people took the side of the now-scattered Bonus Army. Alabama Senator Hugo Black (a future justice of the U.S. Supreme Court) went on record saying, "As one citizen, I want to make my public protest against this militaristic way of handling a condition which has been brought about by wide-spread unemployment and hunger." And in New York, the governor and first lady, Franklin and Eleanor Roosevelt, read with "a feeling of horror," as Mrs. Roosevelt put it, the newspaper accounts of the attack on the Bonus Army. "Why didn't Hoover offer the men coffee and sandwiches," FDR asked a friend, "instead of turning Pat Hurley and Doug MacArthur loose?"

Hoover never abandoned his belief that the Bonus Army was a fraud. Thirty years later when he published his memoirs, he wrote bitterly about the incident:

> The march was in considerable part organized and promoted by the Communists and included a large number of hoodlums and ex-convicts determined to raise a public disturbance. They were frequently addressed by Democratic Congressmen seeking to inflame them against me for my opposition to the bonus legislation. They were given financial support by some of the publishers of the sensational press. It was of interest to learn in after years from the Communist confessions that they also had put on a special battery of speakers to help Roosevelt in his campaign, by the use of the incident.

The year 1932 was a presidential election year, and for millions of American voters—those in terrible straits, those barely hanging on, those frightened that they would lose what little they had left—Hoover's treatment of the Bonus Army was the last straw. There are accounts of theater audiences booing as the projectors played newsreel footage of the expulsion of the Bonus Army. As Election Day drew near, one resident of Washington sent a letter to the editor of the *Washington Daily News*. "I voted for Herbert Hoover in 1928," she wrote. "God forgive me and keep me alive at least until the polls open!" It was people like her and the booing crowds in the theaters who elected Franklin D. Roosevelt, a man who projected confidence, optimism, and sympathy. When the votes were counted, FDR had carried forty-two states, taking 472 electoral votes, while Herbert Hoover garnered only fifty-nine electoral votes. As for the congressional contests in 1932, the Republicans lost 101 seats in the House of Representatives and twelve seats in the Senate, giving the Democrats control of both houses of Congress. MacArthur's reputation also suffered. After the Bonus Army episode, he came to be seen as a bully at the very least, although it wasn't unusual to hear the word "fascist" applied to him. In 1937, MacArthur left the country to accept an assignment from Manuel Quezon, president of the Philippines, to prepare the island nation's defenses against a possible invasion from Japan.

As for Hoover, by sending infantry, cavalry, and even tanks against ragged, hungry veterans and their wives and children, he confirmed a suspicion among ordinary Americans that he was heartless and out of touch with humanity. Hoover became a political pariah. For decades, even his own party, the Republicans, kept Hoover at arm's length. Twenty years would pass before another Republican president lived in the White House. And as for the Communists and other leftist organizations in the United States, the attack on the Bonus Army gave them propaganda material for years.

CHAPTER 12

INTERNMENT OF JAPANESE-AMERICANS IN WORLD WAR II

FRANKLIN D. ROOSEVELT

PRESIDENT FRANKLIN D. ROOSEVELT, MORE CONCERNED WITH THEATERS OF WAR THAN WITH THE CIVIL RIGHTS OF JAPANESE AMERICANS ON THE WEST COAST, INSTRUCTED HIS ATTORNEY GENERAL AND WAR SECRETARY TO DO AS THEY THOUGHT BEST, BUT TO TREAT THEM HUMANELY AND "BE AS REASONABLE AS YOU CAN."

FOUR-YEAR-OLD JOHN TATEISHI WOULD OFTEN STAND AT THE BARBED-WIRE fence beneath the guard towers and feel the dry desert wind across his face. He was too young to recall what life had been like before he and his family were sent with thousands of others to this camp in a desolate wasteland where the wind blew endlessly down into the Owens Valley from snowcapped Mount Whitney and the Sierra Nevada. John had just turned three the day they were forced from their home in Los Angeles. He was told later that he had come down with German measles and was taken from his mother and placed in quarantine at Los Angeles General Hospital with armed guards posted at his door. About three weeks later, he was placed on a bus and sent with other internees from Los Angeles to the Manzanar Relocation Center, where his parents were waiting.

Armed guards were everywhere, carrying guns, shining searchlights across the camp at night. All the adults were silent, depressed, and guilt-ridden for being suspected of disloyalty to the United States—a stigma worse than being sent to the camps—and shamed by their inability to protect themselves or their children from the humiliation of losing their homes and livelihoods. They had no idea when or whether they would ever be allowed to return to their former lives. Little John Tateishi had not seen his father in more than a year, since the night of a riot in the relocation center when the guards took him away, and he was sure his father was going to be shot.

LOOK

ROOSEVELT, CHURCHILL and HITLER
by Dorothy Thompson

NORTH

AMERICA

AT WILL HAPPEN TO
SCIENTIOUS OBJECTORS?

SOUTH

ry 14, 1941 . . .

PRESIDENT ROOSEVELT

THE *SAN FRANCISCO EXAMINER*, A HEARST PUBLICATION, WAS AMONG THE WEST COAST NEWSPAPERS MOST EAGER TO SEE AMERICANS OF JAPANESE DESCENT ROUNDED UP IN THE INTEREST OF NATIONAL SECURITY.

John and his family were among about 120,000 Japanese Americans—more than two-thirds of them native-born American citizens—quarantined in ten federally operated military internment camps from early 1942 until early 1945, when it was clear that the Allies would win the war and the federal government determined that the Japanese Americans were no longer a security risk.

What prompted the roundup and internment of law-abiding civilians? On December 7, 1941, in what President Franklin D. Roosevelt described as "a day which will live in infamy" in his address to Congress the following day, an attack force of Japanese emperor Tojo's warplanes blitzed the American naval base at Pearl Harbor, Hawaii. The assault destroyed nineteen naval vessels and 188 aircraft and killed 2,280, nearly eliminating the entire U.S. Pacific Fleet in a single morning. The attack was unprovoked, and it took the American public completely by surprise. In recent years, the nation's attention had been focused on the worsening war in Europe, where German forces were advancing almost unopposed. Americans were already worried that the United States might be drawn once again into a great European war.

The morning after Pearl Harbor, California Governor Culbert L. Olson and State Attorney General Earl Warren (later chief justice of the U.S.

Supreme Court) worked with sheriffs and district attorneys to dismiss from civil service positions all first-generation Japanese Americans (*Issei*) and their U.S.-born children (*Nisei*). Licenses to practice law and medicine were revoked, and commercial fishermen were barred from their boats. The civil authorities' drive to round up Japanese Americans was loudly seconded by the West Coast press, especially the excitable San Francisco–based Hearst newspapers.

There had long been a strong intolerance of Asians on the West Coast, especially in California, dating back to the 1860s, when Chinese laborers (called coolies) were imported as essentially slave labor to build the Transcontinental Railroad and for other projects. Japanese and Chinese immigrants were targeted for exclusion by state laws and by such federal legislation as the Chinese Exclusion Act of 1882 and the Immigration Act of 1924, which limited Japanese immigration. Other discriminatory laws prevented immigrants from becoming citizens, thereby enforcing an alien status on people who would willingly have sought citizenship.

Although Japanese constituted only 1 percent of California's population, their contributions to the state's economy were substantial. Japanese farmers occupied only 1 percent of the state's cultivated land, but they supplied about 40 percent of its fruits and vegetables. They mainly kept to themselves in ethnic enclaves. After Pearl Harbor, old prejudices were inflamed against all Japanese in the Golden State. Attorney General Warren had frozen their assets, so banks would not honor their checks. Insurance companies canceled policies, grocers refused to sell them food, and so on.

The state of California demanded that the federal government do something about the internal threat to domestic security, the so-called Yellow Peril. After Pearl Harbor, Californians feared the next attack would be on their shores. In congressional testimony on February 4, 1942, General Mark Clark, the deputy chief of staff, and Admiral Harold R. Stark, chief of naval operations, said people on the Pacific coast were unduly alarmed. General Clark said the chances of an invasion were "nil."

But their assurances calmed no one. On January 24, the commission appointed by Roosevelt to investigate the attack on Pearl Harbor reported, among other findings, that the Japanese air force had been aided by espionage agents based in Hawaii, including Japanese Americans, though that assertion was not substantiated by any evidence. Only days earlier the *Los Angeles Times* had been urging calm and moderation; now the *Times* called for relocation of all Japanese Americans in California, whether they were citizens or not.

Lieutenant General John De Witt, army commander of the West Coast, asked his superiors for permission to evacuate all Japanese from the Coast, but the army was not inclined to grant his request. In a memorable demonstration

PRESIDENTIAL BRIEFING
(1882-1945)
• THIRTY-SECOND PRESIDENT OF THE UNITED STATES (1933-45) AND GOVERNOR OF NEW YORK (1929-33)
• BORN JANUARY 30, 1882, IN HYDE PARK, NEW YORK
• DIED APRIL 12, 1945, AT WARM SPRINGS, GEORGIA
• INHERITED THE GREAT DEPRESSION FROM HERBERT HOOVER; INITIATED MASSIVE RECOVERY EFFORT THROUGH NEW DEAL LEGISLATION, INCLUDING NATIONAL RECOVERY ADMINISTRATION, WORKS PROGRESS ADMINISTRATION, AND CIVILIAN CONSERVATION CORPS
• ESTABLISHED SECURITIES AND EXCHANGE COMMISSION (1934) AND SOCIAL SECURITY (1935)
• ELECTED TO UNPRECEDENTED THIRD AND FOURTH TERMS (1940, 1944); LED THE NATION THROUGH THE GREAT DEPRESSION AND WORLD WAR II
• MET WITH WINSTON CHURCHILL AND JOSEPH STALIN AT TEHERAN (1943) AND AT YALTA (1945) TO PLAN POSTWAR GLOBAL SECURITY THROUGH THE UNITED NATIONS, A GLOBAL SECURITY COLLECTIVE
• WIDELY REGARDED AS THE MOST INFLUENTIAL PRESIDENT OF THE TWENTIETH CENTURY

The President has signed the following Executive Order:

AUTHORIZING THE SECRETARY OF WAR TO PRESCRIBE MILITARY AREAS

9066

WHEREAS the successful prosecution of the war requires every possible protection against espionage and against sabotage to national-defense material, national-defense premises, and national-defense utilities as defined in Section 4, Act of April 20, 1918, 40 Stat. 533, as amended by the Act of November 30, 1940, 54 Stat. 1220, and the Act of August 21, 1941, 55 Stat. 655 (U.S.C., Title 50, Sec. 104):

NOW, THEREFORE, by virtue of the authority vested in me as President of the United States, and Commander in Chief of the Army and Navy, I hereby authorize and direct the Secretary of War, and the Military Commanders whom he may from time to time designate, whenever he or any designated Commander deems such action necessary or desirable, to prescribe military areas in such places and of such extent as he or the appropriate Military Commander may determine, from which any or all persons may be excluded, and with respect to which, the right of any person to enter, remain in, or leave shall be subject to whatever restrictions the Secretary of War or the appropriate Military Commander may impose in his discretion. The Secretary of War is hereby authorized to provide for residents of any such area who are excluded therefrom, such transportation, food, shelter, and other accommodations as may be necessary, in the judgment of the Secretary of War or the said Military Commander, and until other arrangements are made, to accomplish the purpose of this order. The designation of military areas in any region or locality shall supersede designations of prohibited and restricted areas by the Attorney General under the Proclamations of December 7 and 8, 1941, and shall supersede the responsibility and authority of the Attorney General under the said Proclamations in respect of such prohibited and restricted areas.

I hereby further authorize and direct the Secretary of War and the said Military Commanders to take such other steps as he or the appropriate Military Commander may deem advisable to enforce compliance with the restrictions applicable to each Military area hereinabove authorized to be designated, including the use of Federal troops and other Federal Agencies, with authority to accept assistance of state and local agencies.

I hereby further authorize and direct all Executive Departments, independent establishments and other Federal Agencies, to assist the Secretary of War or the said Military Commanders in carrying out this Executive Order, including the furnishing of medical aid, hospitalization, food, clothing, transportation, use of land, shelter, and other supplies, equipment, utilities, facilities, and services.

This order shall not be construed as modifying or limiting in any way the authority heretofore granted under Executive Order No. 8972, dated December 12, 1941, nor shall it be construed as limiting or modifying the duty and responsibility of the Federal Bureau of Investigation, with respect to the investigation of alleged acts of sabotage or the duty and responsibility of the Attorney General and the Department of Justice under the Proclamations of December 7 and 8, 1941, prescribing regulations for the conduct and control of alien enemies, except as such duty and responsibility is superseded by the designation of military areas hereunder.

FRANKLIN D. ROOSEVELT

THE WHITE HOUSE,

February 19, 1942.

- - - - - - -

of wartime logic, De Witt insisted, "The very fact that no sabotage has taken place [in California] is a disturbing and confirming indication that such action *will* be taken."

After an interview with General De Witt, the influential liberal columnist Walter Lippmann published a column in the February 12, 1942, *Herald Tribune* titled, "Fifth Column on the West Coast." Lippmann declared the whole Pacific coast a battle zone and asserted, "Nobody's constitutional rights include the right to reside and do business on a battlefield." The widely read conservative columnist Westbrook Pegler opined, "The Japanese in California should be under armed guard to the last man and woman right now. And to hell with habeas corpus until the danger is over."

War Secretary Henry L. Stimson believed an invasion on the West Coast was a possibility, though he had doubts about the necessity for a mass relocation of civilians. Stimson had the authority to deny General De Witt and the California officials' requests, but before doing that he consulted the president. Roosevelt was weary of the issue and trying to concentrate on larger concerns such as theaters of war and arms production. When Stimson called on February 11, the president expressed no opinion on the evacuation question, but, according to Stimson's diary, "told me to go ahead on the line that I thought the best." After being taken by surprise at Pearl Harbor, Roosevelt was inclined to play it safe. He would have preferred voluntary relocation, but, logistically and practically, it was unrealistic to expect that 120,000 citizens with businesses and jobs embedded in close-knit communities would willingly relocate, or that people in the rural West and Midwest would accept them. The president urged Stimson to be as humane as possible.

Stimson's assistant secretary for domestic security, John J. McCloy, viewed relocation as a military necessity: "If it is a question of the safety of the country or the Constitution of the United States, why the Constitution is just a scrap of paper to me." After Stimson's talk with the president, McCloy wrote to Fourth Army headquarters in San Francisco, "We have carte blanche to do what we want to as far as the president is concerned … He states there will probably be some repercussions, and it has got to be dictated by military necessity, but as he puts it, 'Be as reasonable as you can.' "

AFTER PEARL HARBOR, OLD PREJUDICES WERE INFLAMED AGAINST ALL JAPANESE IN THE GOLDEN STATE. ATTORNEY GENERAL WARREN HAD FROZEN THEIR ASSETS, SO BANKS WOULD NOT HONOR THEIR CHECKS. INSURANCE COMPANIES CANCELED POLICIES, GROCERS REFUSED TO SELL THEM FOOD, AND SO ON.

U.S. Attorney General Francis B. Biddle, however, recommended caution. He regarded relocation as "ill-advised, unnecessary, and unnecessarily cruel," and advised the president that the army had not yet advised him of its conclusions on the question. Federal Bureau of Investigation (FBI) director J. Edgar Hoover agreed, calling the evacuation "utterly unwarranted." Biddle sought the views of three trusted New Deal legal thinkers, hoping their opinions would help him make the case against relocation, but they surprised him by returning a seven-page brief that affirmed the constitutionality of removing citizens on the basis of race in case of military necessity.

Further, Biddle was at odds with War Secretary Stimson, the strong man of the Roosevelt cabinet who was being pushed toward relocation by De Witt and McCloy. The attorney general recalled twenty years later, "If Stimson had insisted, had stood firm, as he apparently suspected that this wholesale evacuation was needless, the president would have followed his advice. And if … I had urged the Secretary to resist the pressure of his subordinates, the result might have been different. But I was new to the cabinet and disinclined to insist on my view to an elder statesman."

On February 19, 1942, three months after Pearl Harbor, Roosevelt issued Executive Order 9066, which suspended the civil rights of Japanese Americans and authorized Stimson to designate military exclusion zones from which the United States could exclude "any or all persons," without having to prove disloyalty or ill intent, for the duration of the war. Then, in March, Roosevelt's Executive Order 9012 established the War Relocation Authority (WRA). On March 21, at the request of the War Department, Congress unanimously passed

THREE MONTHS AFTER PEARL HARBOR, PRESIDENT ROOSEVELT'S EXECUTIVE ORDER 9066 SUSPENDED THE CIVIL RIGHTS OF JAPANESE AMERICANS AND AUTHORIZED WAR SECRETARY HENRY L. STIMSON TO DESIGNATE MILITARY EXCLUSION ZONES FROM WHICH THE U.S. COULD EXCLUDE "ANY OR ALL PERSONS" WITHOUT NEEDING TO PROVE DISLOYALTY OR ILL INTENT.

THE PUBLIC NOTICE ON THE RIGHT INSTRUCTS ALL SAN FRANCISCO-AREA "PERSONS OF JAPANESE ANCESTRY" TO REPORT TO CIVIL CONTROL STATIONS FOR PROCESSING. OF THE 120,000 INCARCERATED, MOST WERE GIVEN NO MORE THAN TEN DAYS TO STORE OR SELL THEIR PERSONAL POSSESSIONS AND ARRANGE TO RENT HOMES, FARMS, AND BUSINESSES.

legislation authorizing removal of Japanese Americans from the West Coast.

Lost amid all the official concern and press hysteria was the quiet fact that there had not been a single reported instance of disloyalty, sabotage, or plotting against the United States by a Japanese American.

"OUT, JAPS!" Abruptly, between March and June 1942, all Japanese Americans on the West Coast were ordered to sell their homes, liquidate their businesses, pull their children out of school, and report to civil control stations for processing. The residents of Terminal Island in Los Angeles Harbor had less than three days to store or sell their personal possessions and arrange to rent homes, farms, and businesses, while Japanese in other areas were allowed up to ten days. In a brisk military operation beginning at dawn on March 30, copies of General De Witt's Civilian Exclusion Order No. 20 directed at "persons of Japanese ancestry" were nailed to doors, toddlers were issued I.D. tags like pieces of luggage in case they

were accidentally separated from their parents, and truck convoys pulled up as soldiers shouted, "Out, Japs!" The internees were allowed to bring only the bags they could carry.

Trucks drove the internees to fifteen processing centers and assembly areas, including Pasadena's Rose Bowl and the race tracks at Santa Anita and Tanforan, where families were housed in horse stalls. In the summer and fall of 1942, families were assigned to one of ten barracks-like internment camps established in the wastelands of California and Arizona, Utah, Colorado, and Wyoming and administered by the WRA. Because the main impetus for the roundups in the first place came from the demands of California state officials, the roundups involved mainly the Japanese Americans in the Pacific coast states of California, Oregon, and Washington. The large Japanese population in Hawaii and those in the rest of the United States were for the most part not affected by the executive orders. The general public was told that the Japanese Americans were being gathered into the relocation centers to assure their protection.

The camp where John Tateishi and his family were settled, at Manzanar, California, was, at 813 acres, one of the largest incarceration centers, and one of the first to be settled. Manzanar, which means "apple orchard" in Spanish, was a desolate spot in the Owens Valley in the shadow of the Sierra Nevada, about halfway between Los Angeles (to the south) and Reno, Nevada. Once watered by the nearby Owens River, the area by the early 1900s had grown into a thriving agricultural settlement of about 200 European immigrant farmers and ranchers. But in 1919, Manzanar was bought by the government so that the river could be diverted to the Los Angeles aqueduct. The apple orchards turned to desert.

Busloads of internees began arriving at Manzanar on March 21, 1942, and within six months, more than 10,000 people were settled in 504 barracks measuring 120 feet by 20 feet and divided into six one-room apartments that ranged in size from 320 to 480 square feet. The rooms were furnished with army cots, straw mattresses, and electricity. The camps provided an infirmary and each block of fifteen barracks shared bath, latrine, mess (dining), and laundry buildings. Temperatures in the Owens Valley varied between extremes. Even in late spring the temperature could dip below freezing, and in summer the heat would rise to hotter than 110 °F (43 °C).

WRA administrators living at the camps tried to establish conditions approximating normal life, and the internees did their best to adapt. Girls could join a choir, boys could join the Boy Scouts and play in a basketball league and in physical education programs, and there were churches— Buddhist (the largest congregation), Catholic, and Protestant. Adults took courses in the English language and American history. Internees were also

ON THIS PAGE AND THE NEXT, PHOTOGRAPHS SHOW THE RELOCATION CENTER AT MANZANAR, CALIFORNIA, ABOUT HALFWAY BETWEEN LOS ANGELES AND RENO. ABOUT 10,000 PEOPLE WERE HELD HERE IN 504 BARRACKS HASTILY BUILT ON LAND WHERE TEMPERATURES DIPPED BELOW FREEZING IN WINTER AND SOARED TO 110°F (43°C) IN SUMMER.

employed in the camp's infirmary and mess hall and were kept busy planting trees and painting Army recruiting posters. Chemists and doctors assisted in the infirmaries and in conducting experiments making artificial rubber, among other tasks. Determined to show their loyalty to the United States, internees at Tule Lake in northern California assembled each morning to raise the flag while their Boy Scout drum and bugle corps played "The Star-Spangled Banner." In the three years the ten relocation camps were in operation, from early 1942 through 1944, there were 2,120 marriages, 5,981 christenings, and 1,862 funerals.

Despite the WRA's efforts, however, camp life strained relationships and upset the social order within the community. Most families lived in one-room apartments, and privacy was impossible. Children often stayed away from the dwelling and refused to eat with their families. Parents complained that they could not discipline their children. Working women received the same amount of pay as men, and the traditional patterns of arranged marriages disintegrated. At first the WRA, to the embitterment of many internees, deprived the older

men of power within the community, but eventually traditional community leaders were allowed to participate in camp "self-government."

The Japanese Americans showed incredible stoicism and personal discipline, but not everyone took the internment submissively. Japanese Americans who had been born in the United States but were educated or partly raised in Japan, known as *Kibei,* tended to be the most outspoken in protesting the mass incarceration. The authorities regarded them as troublemakers. John Tateishi's father was a Kibei, and so was his father's friend, Harry Ueno. Ueno had discovered that shipments of meat, flour, and sugar to the Manzanar mess hall were being shorted: Someone was skimming goods off the top. When Ueno complained to camp administrators, he was arrested. Tateishi confronted the authorities and demanded his friend's release, and he, too, was arrested.

MANZANAR BARRACKS
BEFORE THE MOUNTAINSCAPE
OF THE SIERRA NEVADA,
HOME OF MOUNT WHITNEY.
MANZANAR MEANS "APPLE
ORCHARD" IN SPANISH. UNTIL
THE NEARBY OWENS RIVER
WAS DIVERTED TO THE LOS
ANGELES AQUEDUCT ABOUT
1920, THIS AREA IN THE
OWENS VALLEY WAS A
THRIVING AGRICULTURAL
SETTLEMENT.

It was about that time, as Ueno and Tateishi were being handcuffed and taken away to jail at Independence, California, that a riot broke out across the camp, prompted mainly by fellow Kibei. While guards shot at the crowd of rioters—two internees were killed—in other parts of the camp Japanese were attacking Japanese, accusing them of snitching and collaborating with the administrators, betraying their own people. All night long, the prisoners heard gunshots and shouts and barking guard dogs, and the searchlights swept across the grounds until daybreak.

On January 28, 1943, War Secretary Stimson announced that the U.S. Army would accept Nisei (second-generation, American-born) volunteers. Before the end of the war, more than 17,000 Japanese had joined the army, taking the oath of allegiance to the United States while still behind barbed wire. The 442nd Infantry and the 100th Infantry, for example, served with great distinction; their bravery was legendary in the European theater. The 442nd, the most celebrated all-Japanese unit, fought in the Italian campaign, suffering massive losses but still winning 3,000 Purple Hearts, 500 oak-leaf clusters, 810 Bronze Stars, and 47 Distinguished Service Crosses, among many other honors.

Driving the soldiers' valor, of course, was the hope that by proving their loyalty to their country they could win their families' freedom. In late 1944, the U.S. Supreme Court ruled that the government could not continue to impound people and exclude them from the Pacific coast without proof of disloyalty. The army rescinded the exclusion order on January 1, 1945, and Japanese Americans were allowed to return to the coastal areas of California, Washington, and Oregon. The internees came home, if it could be called that, only to find that in many cases their stored possessions had been stolen and their homes, farms, and businesses were now being run by the white Californians who had bought the properties at fire-sale prices and would not sell them back. Returning Nisei soldiers still in uniform were refused haircuts and service at restaurants. The *San Francisco Examiner*, a Hearst publication, printed a headline "Soldiers of Nip Ancestry Allowed to Roam on Coast," and a soldier who had lost a leg in Europe was publicly beaten.

Gradually the most brazen acts of intolerance subsided as the War Department launched a public relations campaign in which non–Japanese American soldiers toured West Coast towns and attested to their Nisei comrades' bravery and loyalty.

BEFORE THE END OF THE WAR, MORE THAN 17,000 JAPANESE HAD JOINED THE ARMY, TAKING THE OATH OF ALLEGIANCE TO THE UNITED STATES WHILE STILL BEHIND BARBED WIRE.

The loss of property, however, was irreparable. The Japanese Americans had been forced to liquidate their homes and businesses at pennies on the dollar, and the federal government had provided no assistance in securing fair prices, guaranteeing land values, or securing goods in storage. "I am not concerned about that," Roosevelt had said to Treasury Secretary Henry Morgenthau Jr. in March 1942. Some Japanese Americans stored their belongings in churches or community organization buildings, but many of these storage facilities were looted during the war. Estimated property losses were more than $400 million in 1942 dollars—about $5 billion today. In 1948, Congress passed the Evacuee Claims Act, awarding $37 million in reparations.

NATIONAL REGRET A movement for redress gathered force in the late 1960s and early 1970s and gradually, belatedly, won some concessions from the government. In 1976, President Gerald Ford rescinded Executive Order 9066 and issued a formal apology to Japanese Americans. Federal courts vacated opinions that had upheld the constitutionality of the internment. In 1988, Congress passed a bill authorizing a tax-free payment of $20,000 payable to some 60,000 survivors of the camps. In 1990, the reparations checks were sent along with a letter of apology on White House stationery signed by President George H. W. Bush. The letter conveys a sense of the nation's guilt and awkwardness half a century after the roundups began:

A monetary sum and words alone cannot restore lost years or erase painful memories; neither can they fully convey our Nation's resolve to rectify injustice and to uphold the rights of individuals. We can never fully right the wrongs of the past. But we can take a clear stand for justice and recognize that serious injustices were done to Japanese Americans during World War II.

In enacting a law calling for restitution and offering a sincere apology, your fellow Americans have, in a very real sense, renewed their traditional commitment to the ideals of freedom, equality, and justice. You and your family have our best wishes for the future.

During the 1980s, while searching for official records to assist the redress movement, researcher Aiko Herzig-Yoshinaga came across a document showing that in 1942 the federal government had deliberately suppressed official reports from before the incarcerations began that found no evidence of disloyalty among the population about to be rounded up. And in all the years since, not a single case of sabotage or espionage by Japanese Americans was ever proved.

California Attorney General Warren wrote in his memoirs that he had been wrong to push for internment of Japanese Americans. "I have since deeply regretted the removal order and my own testimony advocating it," Warren wrote. "Whenever I thought of the innocent little children who were torn from home, school friends, and congenial surroundings, I was conscience-stricken. It was wrong to act so impulsively ... even though we had a good motive."

Attorney General Biddle later wrote in his memoir, *In Brief Authority*, "I do not think [Roosevelt] was much concerned with the gravity or the implications of this step ... What must be done to defend the country must be done ... Nor do I think that the constitutional difficulty plagued him—the Constitution has never greatly bothered any wartime president."

The political consequences of the internments for the Roosevelt administration were slight to nil. The nation's attention was wholly centered on the war, and there was little sympathy for the rights of Japanese Americans. Roosevelt died in April 1945, just months before the end of the war, and he was succeeded by Harry S. Truman, who had his own Japanese remorse following the atomic bombings of Hiroshima and Nagasaki in August 1945. But like the atomic bombing, in which much greater force was used than was militarily necessary, the imprisonment of innocent, loyal Japanese Americans in what Roosevelt himself termed "concentration camps" has long been a stain on the nation's reputation for protecting civil rights. Today, few Americans even know the internments took place, and probably the majority who do hear of the camps are not greatly distressed.

Roosevelt and Stimson might have steered a different course, however, that could have set a precedent more helpful to Americans' civil liberties in later decades. With the incarceration and torture of "enemy combatants" at Guantánamo Bay, Cuba, in the years since September 11, 2001—including U.S. citizens suspected of collaborating with terrorist organizations—and little-known provisions in the U.S. Patriot Act that allow for warrantless wiretapping and arrests and confiscations without cause, many Americans worry that the internment camps of the 1940s might one day reappear. The revelation in late 2007 through declassified documents that former FBI director Hoover sent the White House a plan, shortly after the Korean War began in 1950, calling for the imprisonment of some 12,000 Americans he suspected of disloyalty, gives further reason for concern that the mass imprisonment of a group of Americans on the basis of suspected disloyalty may turn out not to be a unique incident in United States history.

JAPANESE-AMERICAN INTERNEES WERE ALLOWED TO BRING ONLY THE BAGS THEY COULD CARRY, AND CHILDREN WERE TAGGED LIKE PIECES OF LUGGAGE IN CASE THEY WERE SEPARATED FROM THEIR PARENTS.

The camps were certainly never far away for John Tateishi. In the 1970s, he returned to Manzanar for the first time in thirty years, and he wrote about the experience some twenty years later in "Memories from Behind Barbed Wire," a chapter in the collection *Last Witnesses: Reflections on the Wartime Internment of Japanese Americans*. He recalled that when he was there as a child, "I knew (and I can distinctly remember being aware of this) that my confinement was because I was Japanese. I knew, even at the early age of three or four, that I was different from the men who stood in the towers, different from the white faces that stared curiously at the camp and at us from the cars that passed by on the distant highway ... And somehow for me, in the strange logic of a child's mind, that represented America, riding off into the solitary distance away from this wasteland and this prison." In his return visit, when he stood where the barbed wire had been strung beneath the search towers, it struck him that he had never really left. "[S]tanding there, I realized that I have never been free of this place ... no one really leaves ..."

EARL WARREN, 1948, THREE-TERM GOVERNOR OF CALIFORNIA, LATER CHIEF JUSTICE OF THE SUPREME COURT. MANY OF THE OFFICIALS PUSHING MOST AGGRESSIVELY FOR THE INTERNMENTS WERE DEMOCRATS, OFTEN NEW DEAL LIBERALS. FBI DIRECTOR J. EDGAR HOOVER, HOWEVER, CALLED THE INCARCERATIONS "UTTERLY UNWARRANTED."

CHAPTER 13

THE BAY OF PIGS INVASION

JOHN F. KENNEDY

THE UNITED STATES-BACKED INVASION OF CUBA AT THE BAY OF PIGS IN APRIL
1961 was conceived as a covert operation that couldn't miss, but it was a disaster
from the start. Nothing went right for the Cuban exiles and their American
backers. Central Intelligence Agency (CIA) Director Allen W. Dulles assured
President John F. Kennedy, only three months in office, that the invasion would
prompt a massive, widespread anti–Fidel Castro uprising across the island. (In
1960, Castro was prime minister of Cuba.) Planning had started back in
Dwight D. Eisenhower's administration, but the idea made Kennedy nervous.
It sounded too risky, and he did not want the United States being seen
meddling heavy-handedly in a weaker neighboring country. Aside from some
CIA-run B-26 bombers used to strike Cuba's air bases and failing to knock out
the Cuban air force, Kennedy refused to commit air support or involve any part
of the U.S. military in the invasion.

IN THE EYES OF
SOVIET PREMIER, NIKITA
KHRUSCHEV, THE FAILURE OF
THE BAY OF PIGS INVASION
SUGGESTED THAT PRESIDENT
JOHN F. KENNEDY WAS
WEAK, INEXPERIENCED, AND
INDECISIVE. KHRUSCHEV'S
ASSESSMENT PAVED THE
WAY FOR THE CUBAN
MISSILE CRISIS.

The idea of training and equipping a brigade of Cuban exiles to topple
Castro had been formulated during the last year of Eisenhower's presidency,
but Kennedy adopted it and put it into action. It was a decision with long-
lasting, tragic, and almost disastrous consequences. The Bay of Pigs debacle
made the United States and Cuba permanent enemies—at least as long as
Castro is alive. The fiasco humiliated the United States and its new president, who was a serious student of diplomacy and history who usually prided

WEARING COMBAT FATIGUES
AND WIELDING SEMI-
AUTOMATIC JOHNSON M1941
RIFLES, CIA-TRAINED CUBAN
EXILES PREPARED TO LEAD A
COUNTER-REVOLUTION
AGAINST FIDEL CASTRO.

himself on being a cool, dispassionate realist. The failure of the Bay of Pigs invasion made the United States look incompetent and Kennedy soft, inexperienced, and indecisive—weaknesses that Soviet Premier Nikita Khrushchev intended to exploit. Four months after the Bay of Pigs, Khrushchev began building a large concrete wall through Berlin to divide Soviet-controlled East Berlin from West, recently administered by the United States, Britain, and France following the end of World War II in 1945. And in October 1962, Khrushchev and Castro were caught installing ballistic missiles in Cuba—only ninety miles south of the United States. When Kennedy was shown U-2 reconnaissance photos of the missile sites being built, he confronted the Soviets with a naval blockade around the island of Cuba and negotiated with them in high-level, back-channel diplomacy. Over the course of thirteen nerve-racking days, the Kennedy administration and Moscow managed to pull back from the brink of possible nuclear war.

John Kennedy is often—and justly—praised for his handling of the missile crisis, for pulling the world back from the brink of destruction. Mentioned less often is that the crisis would not have arisen had he not approved the scheme to send a Cuban paramilitary force into Cuba to overthrow Castro.

THE SECRET LEAKS OUT The day after the fiasco, April 18, Soviet Premier
Khrushchev sent a message to Kennedy:

> "It is not a secret to anyone that the armed bands which invaded [Cuba] have been trained, equipped, and armed in the United States of America … We shall render to the Cuban people and their government all necessary assistance in beating back the armed attack on Cuba."

Khrushchev had not had to turn to Soviet intelligence agencies for information about the American-backed invasion of Cuba. Plans for such an incursion had been reported in the *New York Times* on January 10, 1961, when the *Times* ran a front-page story titled, "U.S. Helps Train an Anti-Castro Force at Secret Guatemalan Base." The *Times's* story reported, "In the Cordillera foothills a few miles from the Pacific, commando-like forces are being drilled in guerrilla warfare tactics by foreign personnel, mostly from the United States." In fact, the *Times* had been scooped about ten weeks earlier by a Guatemalan paper, *La Hora*, which reported on October 30, 1960, that the CIA was operating military training camps in Guatemala, preparing anti-Castro Cubans to invade and overthrow the island's Communist regime.

Not only the press, but military slip-ups too exposed the United States' involvement in anti-Castro maneuvers. Air attacks on Cuba had been going on for more than a year before the Bay of Pigs invasion. On February 18, 1960, a plane on a bombing run over the central España, Matanzas, province of Cuba exploded in midair. The pilot was identified as Robert Ellis Frost, and a U.S. military I.D. card was found on his body.

The *Times* and other papers exposed the mission's cover, and it was very likely that Castro's military would be waiting for any invasion force, but Kennedy gave the go-ahead anyway. Shortly after midnight on Monday, April 17, 1961, approximately 1,300 American-trained Cuban exiles who called themselves Brigade 2506 stormed ashore at a place called Bahía de Cochinos, the Bay of Pigs, a stretch of beach at the edge of a large swamp along the south central coast of Cuba. The name Brigade 2506 came from the personnel number of their

PRESIDENTIAL BRIEFING
(1917–1963)

• THIRTY-FIFTH PRESIDENT OF THE UNITED STATES (1961–63), CONGRESSMAN (1946–53), SENATOR (1953–60)

• BORN MAY 29, 1917, IN BROOKLINE, MASSACHUSETTS

• DIED (ASSASSINATED) NOVEMBER 22, 1963, IN DALLAS, TEXAS

• WINNER OF THE 1957 PULITZER PRIZE FOR *PROFILES IN COURAGE*

• ELECTED THE FIRST ROMAN CATHOLIC PRESIDENT

• APPROVED AND WAS EMBARRASSED BY BOTCHED, CENTRAL INTELLIGENCE AGENCY-SPONSORED BAY OF PIGS INVASION OF CUBA (1961)

• IN THE CUBAN MISSILE CRISIS (1962), FORCED THE REMOVAL OF SOVIET MISSILES; ESTABLISHED THE WASHINGTON-MOSCOW HOTLINE AND SIGNED THE NUCLEAR TEST-BAN TREATY (1963)

• ESCALATED U.S. INVOLVEMENT IN VIETNAM TO 16,000 AMERICAN "ADVISERS"

comrade, Carlos Rodriguez Santana, who had died in an accident at the training camp in Guatemala.

The Brigade was told that air strikes had crippled Castro's air force, that anti-Castro dissidents on the island would rise up against the regime, and that they could expect massive defections from the Cuban army and boundless support from a popular uprising of the Cuban people. None of it was true.

Like Kennedy and Khrushchev, Castro read the newspapers. Long before the launch of the invasion, while members of Brigade 2506 were still training in Guatemala, Castro had ordered the arrest of thousands of dissidents who might join the invasion force or provoke an uprising in Cuba. (In the aftermath of the invasion, about a hundred of these dissidents were executed.) As for the air strikes, the CIA claimed its pilots had destroyed at least half of Castro's thirty-six-plane air force. The truth was, some Cuban aircraft had been destroyed, but not nearly as many as the CIA had hoped. As for the defections from Castro's army, they never happened.

At 1:30 A.M., Monday April 17, 1961, the commander of Brigade 2506, José Pérez San Román, was on the beach of the Bay of Pigs supervising the unloading of troops and supplies when the local militia appeared on the scene. The militia and the brigade skirmished while some militia scouts ran back to their head-quarters with news that the invasion had begun. At 6:30 A.M. Cuban fighter planes—the planes San Román had thought were destroyed—strafed the beach.

OPERATION SUCCESS: A TEST-RUN IN GUATEMALA
The plan to invade Cuba had begun more than a year earlier. Eisenhower, like every U.S. president after him, chafed at having a Communist regime just ninety miles from the continental United States. On St. Patrick's Day, March 17, 1960, after discussing the proposed invasion with his national security advisors, President Eisenhower approved the CIA's plan to oust Castro. The program included opening a radio station on Swan Island in the Caribbean to broadcast anti-Castro programming to Cuba, supplying anti-Castro resistance groups within Cuba, and training a paramilitary force for the eventual infiltration of Cuba. Eisenhower approved the whole package, saying he knew of "no better plan" to eliminate Castro.

Eisenhower and the CIA had already experienced success in promoting regime change in the Americas as well as in Iran. In Guatemala in 1954, the CIA launched a program it named "Operation Success" to instigate a coup against Jacobo Árbenz Guzmán, Guatemala's popular, democratically elected president. Shortly after Árbenz's inauguration in 1952, he had begun a program of land reform, expropriating property that was not under cultivation and giving it to impoverished landless families. The goal was to create what Guatemala had never had—a class of prosperous farmers. Landowners whose property was expropriated received compensation from the government in the form of twenty-five-year bonds with a 3 percent interest rate. Nonetheless, in Washington the Eisenhower administration and CIA worried that Árbenz's land redistribution program was Communist-inspired and a hint that Guatemala was entering the orbit of the Soviet Union.

The most vocal critics of Árbenz's land program were the outraged executives of the U.S.-based United Fruit Company. The corporation, which grew tropical fruit on vast plantations throughout the Caribbean and Latin America, was one of the largest landowners in Guatemala. Because a large percentage of United Fruit's holdings were not under cultivation, the company stood to lose a great deal of its property.

The United Fruit Company had long been represented by Sullivan & Cromwell, the law firm where Allen Dulles and his older brother, John Foster Dulles, worked for many years. In 1952, Allen was director of the CIA, and John was President Eisenhower's secretary of state. In meetings with the Dulles brothers, United Fruit executives claimed that Árbenz was planning to make Guatemala a Soviet satellite. That claim was probably an exaggeration, yet it was true that Árbenz was tolerant of the Communist Party and Communist organizations in Guatemala. Árbenz even had Communists serving in his government. When the White House learned that Árbenz had concluded a deal to purchase arms from Czechoslovakia (a member of the Soviet Bloc), Eisenhower decided it was time to act before Guatemala fell to the Communists. At a meeting of the National Security Council on June 15, 1954, Eisenhower declared that the United States was committed to the overthrow of Árbenz.

To lead the coup, the CIA recruited Colonel Carlos Castillo Armas, an officer in the Guatemalan army who opposed Árbenz's drift to the left. On June 18, Castillo led 200 anti-Árbenz rebels from their camp in Honduras across the border into Guatemala. The CIA supplied three P-47 fighter planes and two Cessnas to cover the invasion from the air. Meanwhile, CIA-operated radio stations in the Caribbean barraged the Guatemalan airwaves with reports that Castillo was leading a massive army of Guatemalan patriots into the country and that Árbenz's government was on the verge of collapse. High-ranking officers in the Guatemalan army, fearful that Árbenz would summon leftist militia units to defend him, called out the army and seized the government. Árbenz took refuge in the Mexican Embassy.

In the aftermath of the Guatemalan coup, President Eisenhower signed off on a new National Security Council (NSC) statement of U.S. policy: To keep Soviet influence out of the Americas, the United States would take any "economic or military action deemed appropriate." This NSC statement paved the way for the invasion of Cuba.

"AN ILLITERATE AND IGNORANT MILLIONAIRE" Fourteen stories tall and built of dazzling white brick, the Hotel Theresa was known as the "Waldorf-Astoria of Harlem." Over the years, the hotel's list of distinguished guests included Louis Armstrong, Josephine Baker, Dorothy Dandridge, Little Richard, Lena Horne, and Ray Charles.

In September 1960, Castro checked into the Theresa; he had come to New York for the opening session of the United Nations. A day or two after Castro's arrival, a bald, burly man entered the hotel's lobby, surrounded by security personnel and trailed by a crowd of reporters. A member of the man's entourage informed the Theresa's manager that Soviet Premier Khrushchev had come to see his comrade, the prime minister of Cuba, Fidel Castro.

While Castro and Khrushchev held their meticulously publicized tête-à-tête in Harlem, in Tennessee, Kennedy, the Democrats' handsome, forty-three-year-old candidate for president, told an audience that he was "not satisfied to see a Communist satellite ninety miles off the coast of Florida, eight minutes by jet." Kennedy returned to the theme of Cuba two days later when he asserted that Cubans who were fighting to overthrow Castro, whether in Cuba or elsewhere in the world, deserved every kind of assistance until the island was free from Communist rule. While the candidate continued on the campaign trail, Castro took the podium before the United Nations General Assembly to deride Kennedy as "an illiterate and ignorant millionaire … [lacking] political brains."

Kennedy and many other Americans had good reason to be anxious about a Communist regime so close to home. During the previous fifteen years, the Soviet Union had absorbed into its empire all of Eastern Europe and the eastern part of Germany. China had fallen to the Communists. North Korea and North Vietnam had fallen to the Communists. It appeared to many foreign policy experts as well as ordinary American voters that the Domino Theory was correct—once one country was taken over by the Communists, it was almost a sure thing that its neighbors would fall, too.

The thought of Communist infiltrators toppling one Caribbean and Latin American nation after another was a source of tremendous apprehension in Washington, as well as to corporate interests such as United Fruit, but even more frightening was the prospect that Castro would permit Khrushchev to install missiles in Cuba—missiles that could reach major cities in the southern half of the United States within minutes.

Kennedy knew about the CIA plan to send a U.S.-trained paramilitary force into Cuba. On July 23, 1960, CIA Director Dulles visited Kennedy at his family's home at Hyannisport on Cape Cod to brief the candidate about the anti-Castro operation. But a few weeks later, the plan changed. The CIA abandoned the idea of infiltrating the island in favor of an invasion by exiles trained as a paramilitary force, complete with air support, to drive Castro from power. Eisenhower had approved a budget of $13 million for the operation, but he had stipulated that no U.S. military personnel could be part of the combat force.

POISONED ICE CREAM

On March 11, 1961, President John F. Kennedy invited to the White House CIA Director Allen Dulles and Richard Bissell, the CIA's chief of operations. Now that the *New York Times* had spilled the story, the president wanted to know, in detail, the CIA's plans for the invasion of Cuba. Kennedy knew already that the clandestine services were devising various schemes to assassinate Fidel Castro. Presidential historian Michael Beschloss has surmised that the president may have expected that the Cuban leader might be dead by the time of the invasion, in which case the anticipated popular uprising would more easily overthrow the remains of the regime.

Dulles and Bissell explained that the small city of Trinidad on the southern coast of Cuba had been chosen as the target for the invasion. After aircraft had run bombing missions over the city and the surrounding region, 750 Cubans recruited from exiles living in Miami would take the beach. The CIA men expected that the invasion would inspire anti-Castro Cubans to rise up and overthrow the dictator. With any luck, Castro would be dead before a single Cuban exile stepped ashore outside Trinidad.

The CIA supplied a man named Tony Varona, a member of the anti-Castro Democratic Revolutionary Front, with poison pills and several thousand dollars. The deadly pills would be slipped into a bowl of ice cream that would be served to Castro. Unfortunately, the assassins, perhaps for convenience sake, stored the poison pills in the freezer. When the moment came to lace Castro's ice cream, the pills were found frozen to the freezer's coils. They were unusable.

Kennedy didn't like the idea of beginning the invasion with air strikes. "Too spectacular," he said. "It sounds like D-Day. You have to reduce the noise level of the this thing." The president would have preferred that the invasion and overthrow of Castro appear to be the work entirely of the Cuban exile community, with no links to the United States. The United States needed "plausible deniability." But Dulles and Bissell believed that "noise" was essential

to this mission: If U.S. aircraft would not support Brigade 2506, and if there were no U.S. battleships offshore full of American troops ready to back up the exiled fighters, then the invasion was likely to fail. The presence of the U.S. military was the key to a successful invasion and an uprising of Cubans disenchanted with the Castro regime.

Yet neither Dulles nor Bissell revealed their worries to the president. Instead, Bissell, in an attempt to be reassuring, said that if Castro's army pinned down the exiles, they could always run into the Escambray Mountains and join up with a large army of anti-Castro guerrillas based there. Unfortunately, Bissell's sense of Cuban geography was poor. The Escambray Mountains were eighty miles from Trinidad, much too far away for a quick strategic retreat on foot. And there was one more point that Bissell failed to mention and that Kennedy may not have known: With 200,000 troops and militia at his disposal, Castro would have no trouble disposing of 750 exiles—most of whom had no battlefield experience.

FLEEING FROM FIDEL
The Cubans who were preparing to invade their old homeland dated their exile to the early hours of New Year's Day 1959, when General Fulgencio Batista, president of Cuba, fled the island and sought refuge in the Dominican Republic. Since August 1958, Batista's army had been defeated time and again by the revolutionary forces led by Castro and his second-in-command, Che Guevara.

The rebels proclaimed they would end Batista's corrupt and brutal rule, restore the rights guaranteed under the Cuban constitution (which Batista had effectively abolished), and restore democracy to the island (in the last presidential election, Batista had been the only "legal" candidate). However, given the large number of Communists serving in Che Guevara's army and entourage, many Cubans feared that the revolution would merely replace one dictatorship with another: the corrupt Batista with the Communist Castro.

Once word got out that Batista had left the country, thousands of upper-class Cubans followed his example, most of them heading to the United States, where they settled in large numbers in Miami. In many cases these Cubans—largely the elite, professional class—expected their exile to be brief. Either Castro would be defeated, or the revolutionary spirit of his uprising would be tamed and life would return to normal on the island. These Cubans were so optimistic that when they left, many of them had asked relatives and friends to look after their properties, fully expecting they would return home shortly.

By 1961, all of the Cuban exiles understood that Castro's revolution was a national cataclysm, and he wasn't going away. Within weeks after seizing power, Castro's agents paraded hundreds of captured policemen (who had

IN 1957, WHEN THIS PHOTO WAS TAKEN, FIDEL CASTRO (SEATED) WAS HOLED UP IN CUBA'S SIERRA MAESTRA MOUNTAINS. TWO YEARS LATER HE MOVED INTO THE PRESIDENTIAL PALACE IN HAVANA.

worked for the Batista regime) and soldiers (who had served in Batista's armed forces) before military tribunals as a prelude to taking the prisoners outside for summary execution by firing squad. Castro's government seized farmland and organized agricultural cooperatives for poor peasants, and nationalized companies and businesses. By the end of 1960, more than $25 billion worth of private property was in government hands, ostensibly for the good of the Cuban people. Cubans in the United States looked on in horror and disbelief as all their wealth was expropriated and their homeland turned into a Communist state.

The exiles' loathing for Castro was in line with the U.S. government's worries about having an ally of the Soviet Union so close by—and the bad example of a leftist, anti-imperialist revolution overthrowing a U.S.-backed regime that was friendly to American firms doing business there. Washington could not let another domino fall. When the CIA formulated a plan to topple Castro, the Cuban exile community provided a fertile recruiting ground.

A TOTAL FAILURE Many of the men of Brigade 2506 believed fervently that they were the first wave of Cuban freedom fighters who would liberate their homeland from Castro. They were convinced as they stormed ashore that they would be supported overhead by some of the finest fighter pilots of the U.S. Air Force, and they thought that as they advanced into Cuba, the U.S. Marines would be right behind them. Whether the insurgents had talked themselves into this conviction or the trainers from the United States had made such a promise is still a subject of debate.

The air support promised by the CIA consisted of sixteen B-26 twin-engine light attack bombers. From an airstrip in Nicaragua to the Bay of Pigs was a journey of 1,000 miles, round-trip, which left a B-26 with enough fuel to provide less than forty minutes of air cover for the Brigade. Anything longer than forty minutes and the pilots risked running out of gas somewhere over the Caribbean.

On April 14, 1961, just three days from the invasion, Kennedy called CIA Operations Chief Bissell to ask how many planes he planned to use in the operation. Bissell told the president the CIA planned to use all sixteen of their B-26s. "Well, I don't want it on that scale," Kennedy replied. "I want it minimal." So Bissell cut the number of planes for the invasion to eight. The next day, those eight planes attacked the three airfields of the Cuban air force, knocking out some of the aircraft, but not enough to cripple the fleet.

On the morning of April 17, as the Cuban militia pinned down the men of Brigade 2506, the Cuban planes that had survived the air strikes attacked the exiles from the air. Meanwhile, the B-26s, their fuel low and their forty minutes up, veered away from the beach for the flight home. The Brigade's commander,

San Román, radioed his CIA handlers for help. "We are under attack by two Sea Fury aircraft and heavy artillery," he reported. "Do not see any friendly air cover as you promised. Need jet support immediately." When San Román's request was denied, he replied, "You, sir, are a son of a bitch."

With the sea at their backs, no means of retreat, and no chance of advancing into the interior of Cuba, the Brigade was in a desperate position. Back in Washington, the CIA and the Kennedy administration concluded that the invasion would fail. In a conversation with his brother, Robert Kennedy, the president said he wished he had permitted the use of U.S. ships to back up the Cuban exiles. "I'd rather be an aggressor," he said, "than a bum."

WITH THE SEA AT THEIR BACKS, NO MEANS OF RETREAT, AND NO CHANCE OF ADVANCING INTO THE INTERIOR OF CUBA, THE BRIGADE WAS IN A DESPERATE POSITION.

On April 18, Kennedy authorized six fighter jets from the aircraft carrier Essex to provide one hour of air cover for the CIA's attacking B-26s over the beach at the Bay of Pigs. But the jets from the Essex and the B-26s missed their rendezvous because the Pentagon forgot to factor in the one-hour difference in time zones between the B-26s' base in Nicaragua and the beach in Cuba.

That same day, Kennedy's national security advisor, McGeorge Bundy, gave the president a status report on the invasion. "The Cuban armed forces are stronger, the popular response [is] weaker, and our tactical position is feebler than we had hoped," Bundy said. That was perhaps the kindest possible description of the Bay of Pigs operation.

As a humanitarian concession, the president permitted U.S. destroyers to approach the Cuban coast to pick up survivors. The ships were authorized to get within two miles of shore after dark, but no closer than five miles during daylight hours. The directive meant the rescue mission was beyond the reach of almost every man in Brigade 2506. A handful who had managed to swim to one or another of the bay's outlying cays were picked up, but the rest lay dead on the beach or were captured by Castro's forces.

At 2 P.M. on April 19, after two days of being pounded by militia, tanks, and the Cuban air force, Commander San Román and Brigade 2506 surrendered. "Everything is lost," Allen Dulles told former vice president Richard Nixon. "The Cuban invasion is a total failure."

Sixty-eight Cuban exiles were killed in the Bay of Pigs debacle; 1,209 were captured, and nine of them died of asphyxiation in a windowless sealed truck that took them from the beach to prison in Havana. After twenty days of interrogation, the prisoners were given show trials and sentenced to life in prison.

Soon after the conviction of the men of Brigade 2506, Castro made a public offer to exchange the prisoners for farm machinery. Kennedy leapt at the proposal. Immediately he formed the Tractors for Freedom Committee, chaired by former first lady Eleanor Roosevelt, with the purpose of collecting donations to purchase farm equipment for Cuba. But the group was not able to meet Castro's exorbitant demand of $30 million worth of capital relief, and it disbanded. The tractor deal fell through.

Negotiations between the two governments went on sporadically over the next twenty months. Finally, on December 24, 1962, Castro announced that he was releasing the Brigade 2506 prisoners in exchange for $53 million in medicine and food from the United States. He also promised, "as a Christmas bonus," to permit 1,000 of the prisoners' relatives to emigrate to the United States.

The animosity between Cuba and the United States intensified after the Bay of Pigs debacle. Cuba allied itself with the Soviet Union, while America continued its policy of isolating Cuba economically and diplomatically. Soviet Premier Nikita Khrushchev viewed America's failure at the Bay of Pigs as a sign of Kennedy's weakness and inexperience, an assessment he felt was confirmed after meeting Kennedy at the Vienna Summit of April 1962, where it appeared to some that Kennedy was sandbagged by Khrushchev's threat to cut off West Berlin from the Western powers. Within six months, Khrushchev was placing nuclear missiles in Cuba, an action that brought the world as close as it has ever come to all-out nuclear war.

In the face of the missile crisis, Kennedy held firm. The Soviets backed down, removing the nuclear weapons from Cuba, but the tension between Cuba and the United States has dragged on for more than forty years. During that time, political observers and historians have argued that the failed invasion actually strengthened Castro's grip on Cuba. Certainly Che Guevara thought so. In August 1961, at a meeting of the Organization of American States in Uruguay, he sent a note to Kennedy saying, "Thanks for Playa Giron [another name for the site of the invasion]. Before the invasion, the revolution was weak. Now it is stronger than ever."

THE BAY OF PIGS DEBACLE COST THE LIVES OF SEVENTY-SEVEN CUBAN EXILES. ANOTHER 1,209 WERE CAPTURED BY THE CUBANS, GIVEN SHOW TRIALS, AND SENTENCED TO LIFE IN PRISON.

CHAPTER 14

THE TONKIN GULF RESOLUTION

LYNDON B. JOHNSON

ON MONDAY, AUGUST 3, 1964, AT 10:30 A.M., PRESIDENT LYNDON B. JOHNSON was on the telephone with the secretary of defense, Robert S. McNamara. The president vascillated between defensive and somewhat confused, then confident and in command of the situation.

McNamara had called to discuss increasing hostilities with the North Vietnamese in the Gulf of Tonkin, an area in the South China Sea directly east of Laos and Hanoi, the capital of North Vietnam. McNamara wanted to know what to do about a recent military action in which the USS *Maddox* had been engaged with three North Vietnamese Soviet-built P-4 motor torpedo boats. According to reports, a standoff had turned into a firefight between the two sides. Most of the shots fired from the P-4s had missed the *Maddox*, but there were reports that at least of two bullet fragments hit the destroyer.

"Now, I wonder if you don't think it'd be wise for you to call a group… together from the Armed Services and Foreign Relations to tell them what happened," the president told McNamara that morning.

"Right," McNamara said. As was normal in their close personal relationship, the two men routinely talked over each other. While McNamara tried to finish his thought, Johnson interrupted with a rather sobering realization.

"They're going to start an investigation," the president said. "They," of course, meant Congress and the press.

The massive, 2,200-ton warship *Maddox* had been in the Gulf of Tonkin since July 1964 to keep an eye on the North Vietnamese's activities in Laos and South Vietnam. On August 2, about twenty-four hours before this historic telephone call, the ship and its crew had gotten into what was their first altercation with the North Vietnamese. As details funneled into the White House, McNamara learned that the large destroyer had been able to avoid a direct hit, yet McNamara confirmed that one of the P-4s had damaged the *Maddox* with a 14.5-millimeter machine gun slug. All was well with the *Maddox* and its crew. But that wasn't the point. Although the *Maddox* had not suffered major damage, the *Maddox's* captain John Herrick felt war with North Vietnam was on.

The *Maddox* struck all three torpedo boats, but it had not disarmed any of them. Captain Herrick was certain the North Vietnamese were planning a second, possibly even more significant, attack. In lieu of striking first and fast, Herrick called in air support, which President Johnson authorized. The USS *Ticonderoga*, an aircraft carrier cruising in the South China Sea just outside the Gulf of Tonkin, dispatched several F-8 Crusader fighters, which quickly fired

UNDER THE DIRECTION AND ADVICE OF SECRETARY OF DEFENSE ROBERT STRANGE MCNAMARA, PRESIDENT LYNDON JOHNSON UNKNOWINGLY LIED TO CONGRESS ABOUT A SUPPOSED ATTACK BY NORTH VIETNAMESE PATROL BOATS CRUISING IN THE TONKIN GULF IN 1964, THUS FACILITATING THE START OF THE VIETNAM WAR.

rounds at the three torpedo boats, leaving one of them burning in the water; the other two escaped without any major damage.

At the time, Johnson and McNamara were looking to Congress to support a full-scale war against Ho Chi Minh, the Vietnamese Communist leader, but they needed something big to happen to justify escalating the conflict. It needed to be something menacing and antagonizing. Could this dust-up in the Gulf of Tonkin be it? U.S. Pacific Fleet Commander Admiral Thomas Moorer, told the president that Ho Chi Minh had challenged the United States. The two nations were, in effect, standing nose to nose. The way the admiral saw it, America could not back down now.

The USS *Turner Joy* was dispatched to the Gulf to support the *Maddox*. Several Johnson administration representatives had explained to the American public late in the day on August 2 that the *Maddox* had been in the Gulf, just minding its own business, when it was attacked, and a battle ensued between the *Maddox* and several North Vietnamese torpedo boats.

FOR THE PAST YEAR, HE HAD BEEN PUSHING A RELUCTANT PRESIDENT INTO A WAR WITH THE NORTH VIETNAMESE—AND HERE THEY WERE, NOW ON A DIRECT COLLISION COURSE WITH HO CHI MINH, OVER WHAT SEEMED TO BE NOTHING MORE THAN A PETTY SKIRMISH.

As that August 3 telephone call continued, McNamara agreed with the president that surely an investigation would be launched into the Tonkin Gulf situation. McNamara and Johnson were looking to get a resolution for war passed by Congress, which had been discussed two months prior, according to the Pentagon Papers, by U.S. government leaders meeting in Honolulu. The *Maddox* incident was a possible tipping point—just what McNamara had been hoping for.

Johnson instructed McNamara what to say, ordering him to put all the blame on the North Vietnamese. "Say to [Senator Mike] Mansfield 'Now the President wants us—you—to get the proper people.' And we come in and you say, 'They fired at us. We responded immediately. And we took out one of their boats… and… we're not running on in.'"

McNamara felt uneasy about how the public relations end of the situation would be handled. He was in a terrible squeeze. For the past year, he had been pushing a reluctant president into a war with the North Vietnamese—and here they were, now on a direct collision course with Ho Chi Minh, over what seemed to be nothing more than a petty skirmish.

"On Friday night," McNamara continued at one point, "as you probably know, we had four PT boats from Vietnam manned by Vietnamese or other nationals, attack two islands. And we expended a thousand rounds of ammunition… against them. We probably shot up a radar station… And… with this destroyer in that same area, undoubtedly led them to connect the two events."

"Well, say that to Dirksen," the president responded, referring to Minority Leader Everett M. Dirksen, a Republican from Minnesota. The president asked McNamara to choose his words carefully when talking to these key congressional figures. Many of them would likely be heading an investigation into the Tonkin Gulf incident, but also, perhaps more important, they would be voting on any war resolution presented, which would give Johnson and McNamara the authority they needed to go ahead with a full-scale military effort against Ho Chi Minh.

"That's what I know he'll like," McNamara said confidently.

"You notice Dirksen says this morning that, 'We got to reassess the situation. Do something about it.' I'd tell him that we're *doing* what he's *talking* about."

A few minutes later, President Johnson concluded, "Now, I wish that you'd give me some guidance on what we ought to say. I want to leave an impression … that we're going to be firm as hell without saying something that's dangerous…." Johnson said he had spoken to a few constituents, telling them "the Navy responded wonderfully…. But they want to be *damned* sure I don't pull 'em out and run. And they want to be *damned* sure that we're firm. That's what all the country wants… [that] we sure ought to always leave the impression that if you shoot at us, you're going to get hit."

McNamara encouraged Johnson to tell White House Press Secretary George Reedy to explain to the media that the White House ordered the navy to "carry on the routine patrols off the coast of North Vietnam." He said Reedy should inform reporters straightforwardly that the president had issued "instructions to the commanders to destroy any force that attacks our force in international waters."

McNamara knew the American public needed to be spoon-fed this notion that the war was going to start "officially" any moment now. The administration couldn't appear too eager for a fight, bragging how it had finally managed to get the North Vietnamese to shoot first. Nor could the administration send a message to the global community monitoring the situation that the United States would back down before an outright threat and unprovoked attack.

Later that day, at 1:21 P.M., McNamara called and told the president he had assembled the players the president wanted. Then McNamara added, "I thought if it was agreeable with you, I would say to them that some months ago you asked us to be prepared for any eventuality in the Southeast Asia area, and as a result… we just completed target analyses of the targets of North Vietnam." McNamara said he had taken it upon himself to arrange to have

PRESIDENTIAL BRIEFING
(1908–1973)

• THIRTY-SIXTH PRESIDENT OF THE UNITED STATES (1963–69)

• BORN AUGUST 27, 1908, NEAR STONEWALL, TEXAS

• DIED JANUARY 22, 1973, IN JOHNSON CITY, TEXAS

• ELECTED VICE PRESIDENT ON THE DEMOCRATIC TICKET WITH JOHN F. KENNEDY (1960); TOOK OFFICE UPON JFK'S ASSASSINATION (1963)

• REELECTED IN 1964 WITH MORE THAN 61 PERCENT OF THE POPULAR VOTE, WHICH WAS A RECORD PLURALITY

• WON THE PASSAGE OF MASSIVE SOCIAL WELFARE AGENDA (THE GREAT SOCIETY): CIVIL RIGHTS ACT (1964), 1965 VOTING RIGHTS BILL, MEDICARE, MEDICAID, EQUAL OPPORTUNITY ACT, ETC.

• IN MARCH 1968, AFTER THE TONKIN GULF INCIDENT (1964), ORDERED A MASSIVE BUILDUP TO MORE THAN 500,000 U.S. TROOPS IN VIETNAM BY 1968

• AFTER STUNNING LOSSES IN THE TET OFFENSIVE (JANUARY 1968) AND WIDESPREAD DOMESTIC UNREST FOR MANAGEMENT OF THE WAR, DECLINED A SECOND RUN FOR REELECTION

A PHOTOGRAPH PROVIDED BY THE U.S. NAVY PURPORTEDLY SHOWS A NORTH VIETNAMESE MOTOR TORPEDO BOAT ATTACKING THE USS *MADDOX*, AUGUST 2, 1964, IN THE GULF OF TONKIN, EAST OF NORTH VIETNAM.

"pictures, analyses, numbers of sorties, bomb loadings [and] everything prepared for all the target systems of North Vietnam—and I would describe this to the leaders, simply indicating your desire that we be fully prepared for whatever may develop."

The president paused. How does one respond to such an obvious fabrication of events?

As McNamara had spun it, the ideal situation had presented itself in the Gulf, and it was time to take advantage of it.

As Johnson and McNamara fine-tuned their strategy, events out of their control—which would eventually help the administration's cause for war—were taking shape in the Gulf of Tonkin. The *Maddox* reported that on the night of August 4, 1964, as she and the *Turner Joy* made their way around the coast near

North Vietnam, the *Maddox*'s radar indicated an attack in the works by several North Vietnamese naval vessels out at sea. The report was based on "special intelligence" the *Maddox* had obtained. A cable sent by Captain Herrick explained that "two mysterious dots" had appeared on one of the ship's radar screens. In response to the report, during a meeting that day with Johnson and his advisers, McNamara asserted, "We *cannot* sit still as a nation and let them attack us on the high seas and get away with it."

Captain Herrick's cable, although sent with good intention, turned out to be erroneous. The only threat the *Maddox* and *Turner Joy* faced at sea was a violent thunderstorm, which Herrick's radar men had misread as the enemy heading toward them.

Several hours after Herrick sent the first cable, he sent a second cable that explained the mistake. Herrick reported that "freak weather had effects on radar and over-eager sonar men..." There had been "no actual sightings. Suggest complete evaluation before any further action taken."

Herrick went on to say it was all a "confusing picture," but he made it clear that there had not been an attack. The North Vietnamese were not engaging U.S. forces on the high seas, a fact McNamara and the president were well aware of as they headed into Congress to lobby for the Tonkin Gulf Resolution.

In spite of Captain Herrick's second cable, McNamara told Secretary of State Dean Rusk a deliberate lie. MacNamara said he had a cable from the *Maddox* "reporting three unidentified boats and three unidentified aircraft approaching the destroyers"; the destroyer was "under torpedo attack." Later, when Rusk knew that McNamara had lied to him he stood by his colleague, pushing the blame onto the North Vietnamese, saying there was a "great gulf of understanding between that world [North Vietnam] and our world, ideological in character." The North Vietnamese, he added, "see what we think of as the real world in wholly different terms" and "their very process of logic is different."

THE DOMINO EFFECT

At the time, the American people didn't understand how unpredictable and intimidating the situation in Asia was for the 16,000 American soldiers stationed in and around Vietnam. War with North Vietnam had been on the minds of Americans since the mid-1950s, but even more so since Johnson took office after President John F. Kennedy was assassinated. According to what McNamara later wrote in his book, *Argument Without End*, the Johnson administration's major concern was that if North Vietnam took over South Vietnam, a domino effect would occur. Hanoi, McNamara explained, "was seeking to make South Vietnam the next domino to fall in Southeast Asia." The other countries McNamara named were Thailand, Malaya, Indonesia, the

"FROM THIS NETTLE, DANGER, WE PLUCK THIS FLOWER, SAFETY."
(Shakespeare, Henry IV)

Philippines, and even Japan. And if all those countries fell, McNamara suggested, the West was also at risk.

In that same book, however, McNamara admitted that he and his White House colleagues, who included members of the Kennedy administration, "failed to ask the necessary hard questions about our U.S. mindset." Two of the questions McNamara later posed were: "Could we win it with U.S. troops fighting alongside the South Vietnamese?" and, "Was it true that the fall of South Vietnam would trigger the fall of all South Asia?"

Those valid questions were certainly not being discussed in the White House during those crucial moments leading up to what the administration would soon term the "Vietnam War" and Ho Chi Minh would refer to as the "American War."

At 11:37 P.M. on August 4, President Johnson went live from the Oval Office to address the nation about the recent developments in the Tonkin Gulf. It was a solemn message, tinged with Johnson's familiar Texas drawl and earnest sincerity. "[A]s President... it is my duty... to report that renewed hostile actions against United States ships on the high seas in the Gulf of Tonkin have today required me to order the military forces of the United States to take action in reply. The initial attack on the destroyer *Maddox*, on August 2, was repeated today by a number of hostile vessels attacking two U.S. destroyers with torpedoes...."

A short while into the address came a telltale sign—for those who understood the blurry line between politics, rhetoric, and reality—that a full-scale war with North Vietnam was undoubtedly in the works.

Johnson continued, "In the larger sense this new act of aggression, aimed directly at our own forces, again brings home to all of us... the importance of the struggle for peace and security in Southeast Asia. Aggression by terror against the peaceful villagers of South Vietnam has now been joined by open aggression on the high seas against the United States of America."

Further into the message, Johnson said, "I shall immediately request the Congress to pass a resolution making it clear that our government is united in its determination to take all necessary measures in support of freedom and in defense of peace in Southeast Asia."

When Congress debated the Tonkin Gulf Resolution, Johnson had the respect of his colleagues and the momentum of ten months in office as president behind him. Just a month before the Tonkin Gulf crisis, Johnson had signed the Civil Rights Act of 1964, a bill his predecessor, JFK, had encouraged the nation to embrace with open arms. It was a piece of legislation that changed America. The bill required that hotels, restaurants, swimming pools, and all other public places be open to all people regardless of race, color, or creed. The

A 1965 EDITORIAL CARTOON BY BILL MAULDIN OF THE *CHICAGO SUN-TIMES* DEPICTING AN ALREADY SCRATCHED AND SCARRED PRESIDENT JOHNSON FORETELLS THE PERILS OF ESCALATING THE U.S. MILITARY PRESENCE IN SOUTHEAST ASIA.

bill was Johnson's innovation; he had fought assiduously because he believed that all Americans must be treated equally.

But now Johnson was faced with this escalating crisis in North Vietnam, a military impasse that would not go away on its own. The Tonkin Gulf Resolution had been initiated and written that August to, in part, "promote the maintenance of international peace and security in Southeast Asia." Over the course of just a few days, however, things had changed dramatically in the Gulf region, and the resolution had been tidied up to incorporate the changing policies and growing animosity between the United States and North Vietnamese. It was clear by the language in the document that "the Communist Regime in Vietnam" was now in violation of key Charter principles endorsed by the United Nations and established in international law governing the world during a time of war. According to the resolution, the regime of North Vietnam had "deliberately and repeatedly attacked the United States' naval vessels lawfully present on international waters." The major cause of concern on Congress's part was that in doing so, the North Vietnamese had "created a serious threat to international peace." If the United States didn't stand up to this new threat, what sort of message would it send to an unstable world community?

IF THE UNITED STATES DIDN'T STAND UP TO THIS NEW THREAT, WHAT SORT OF MESSAGE WOULD IT SEND TO AN UNSTABLE WORLD COMMUNITY?

The events leading up to the signing of the Tonkin Gulf Resolution were, unmistakably, "thought up by the U.S. government," according to historian Walter LaFeber writing his book *The Deadly Bet*. McNamara would in fact explain to the Fulbright Committee, a group of senators headed by J. William Fulbright, chairman of the foreign relations committee, who held hearings on the Johnson administration's handling of the Vietnam War, that the attacks by the North Vietnamese in the Gulf had "been provoked." Former defense analyst Daniel Ellsberg, a special assistant to an assistant secretary of defense at the time (and later famous for leaking the documents that became known as the Pentagon Papers), wrote in *Harper's* magazine in 2006 that "the alleged attack ... had not, in fact, occurred at all."

Johnson addressed Congress on August 5, 1964, giving his—or, rather, McNamara's—assessment of what had transpired in the Gulf, making sure Congress understood the dangerous circumstances America faced. After his opening remarks, the president said, "I had therefore directed air action against gunboats and supporting facilities used in these hostile operations. This air action has now been carried out with substantial damage to the boats and facilities."

Johnson was clear about the United States' commitment in Vietnam. "Our policy in Southeast Asia has been consistent and unchanged since 1954." It was President Eisenhower and then-Vice President Richard Nixon, who in 1954, after France withdrew from its former colonies in Indochina following its defeat by Ho Chi Minh's nationalist Viet Minh at Dien Bien Phu, had first resolved to defend America's commitments in the region. Their proclamation of U.S. commitment was further sustained by and defined in the Southeast Asia Collective Defense Treaty (SEATO), which had been approved by the Senate almost ten years before the problems in the Tonkin Gulf. The SEATO group included the United States, France, Great Britain, New Zealand, Australia, the Philippines, Thailand, and Pakistan, countries whose chief purpose was to prevent Communism from gaining ground and spreading.

Johnson summarized America's role back on June 2, "In four simple propositions: America keeps her word… The issue is the future of southeast Asia as a whole. A threat to any nation in that region is a threat to all, and a threat to us. Our purpose is peace… This is not just a jungle war, but a struggle for freedom on every front of human activity."

Citing the 1962 Geneva International Agreement, Johnson asked that the Tonkin Gulf Resolution be passed, asserting, "The United States will continue in its basic policy of assisting the free nations of the area to defend their freedom."

After Johnson's appeal to Congress, the Tonkin Gulf Resolution took a 416 to 0 vote in the House after only forty minutes of discussion. The Senate debated for nine hours, then voted eighty-eight to two in favor of the resolution. The only senators voting against the Tonkin Gulf Resolution were Wayne Morse of Oregon and Ernest Gruening of Alaska.

The swift signing of the resolution on August 7, 1964, was exactly what McNamara and Johnson needed. Three days before, Johnson had dispatched fighter planes to defend the *Maddox*. Now, one could argue, he was appealing to Congress to authorize that decision and the choices he and McNamara had already made. With the resolution in hand, Johnson was free to use any means necessary to provoke the North Vietnamese into war—and free to send approximately 500,000 additional American soldiers into a battle that would arguably

SENATOR WAYNE L. MORSE OF OREGON WAS ONE OF ONLY TWO SENATORS TO VOTE AGAINST THE TONKIN RESOLUTION. HE LATER TOLD DANIEL ELLSBERG, WHO LEAKED THE PENTAGON PAPERS, "IF YOU HAD GIVEN THOSE DOCUMENTS TO ME AT THE TIME, THE TONKIN GULF RESOLUTION WOULD NEVER HAVE GOTTEN OUT OF COMMITTEE."

have no end—a perpetual fight. As for McNamara, he got what he had wanted all along: Congressional support for any military action he and the president of the United States wanted to take.

THE BUILDUP Robert McNamara was a numbers man. In his early twenties, McNamara left the University of California, Berkeley, with a degree in economics and philosophy and went on to earn his master's degree from the Harvard Graduate School of Business. After graduate school, McNamara joined what is today known as PriceWaterhouseCoopers, an accounting firm in San Francisco. He taught business at Harvard before entering the Air Force in 1943, departing from active duty just three years later as a lieutenant colonel. It was at this time that "Mac" entered the private sector as Ford Motor Company's manager of planning and financial analysis, a dream job for a man whose life was built around facts and figures. At Ford, McNamara was one of the "Whiz Kids," a group of ten management science officers who had served in the Air Force's Statistical Control group to coordinate logistics during the war. The automaker hired the men after the war to revitalize the company. Thus, when McNamara was later chosen as secretary of defense by John F. Kennedy, he walked into the White House a pure statistics man: someone who collected data and made decisions based on what that data proved.

McNamara's background was one of the reasons why the Special National Intelligence Estimate, put together by the CIA in May 1964 as part of what would become known as the Pentagon Papers, was so vital to him in his resolve to wage war with the North Vietnamese. It is a remarkable top secret document, which has been made available to the public only since June 2004. Titled "Probable Consequences of Certain US Actions with Respect to Vietnam and Laos," the fifteen-page report primarily focuses on what would happen throughout the world if the United States became actively involved in Vietnam—the results of which, we can now clearly see, had little to do with McNamara's domino theory.

1964 WAS AN ELECTION YEAR, AND HE WANTED TO SHOW HIMSELF AS A STAUNCH ANTI-COMMUNIST AGAINST THE CHALLENGES OF THE HAWKISH, ARCH-CONSERVATIVE REPUBLICAN PRESIDENTIAL CANDIDATE SENATOR BARRY GOLDWATER.

The CIA insisted that air and naval actions had to be considered first in Communist-held Laos, which had been the scene of a rebellion, or as the CIA put it, an insurrection, which violated the 1962 Geneva International Agreement regarding the neutrality of Laos. Further along, the CIA insisted that, "In the absence of all-out attacks by the [North Vietnamese] or

Communist China, the measures foreseen would not involve attacks on population centers or resort to nuclear weapons."

AGREE TO DISAGREE In Hanoi on a clear day in November 1995, more than three decades after the Gulf of Tonkin crisis, two elderly men, both nearly eighty, wrinkled with age, and still resentful after years of disagreement, sat down to take a critical look at history and, with any luck, learn a lesson from it. Retired Vietnamese General Vo Nguyen Giap sat with McNamara. After exchanging forced smiles, McNamara told the general he believed the attack by the North Vietnamese on August 4, 1964, was "probable but not certain."

General Giap listened intently to his interpreter, then replied, "There had been *no* attack on August 4. [Furthermore,] the attack on August 2 had been ordered not from Hanoi"—which was something the Johnson administration steadfastly believed—"but by a local commander."

In his book, *Argument Without End*, McNamara detailed what he believed were the most important moments of this conversation. At one point he said, "General, I want us to examine our mindsets and to look at the specific instances where we—Hanoi and Washington—may each have been mistaken, have misunderstood each other, such as in the Tonkin Gulf episode."

McNamara was eager to split the blame. He was trying to say, in so many words, that the buildup and start of actual combat in Vietnam should be on the conscience of both nations. But General Giap was not willing to share blame with McNamara. He was annoyed with the former secretary, and unhappy about sitting across from the man whom he believed fanned the flames of an extremely volatile situation in Vietnam and provoked the North Vietnamese into war.

"I don't believe we misunderstood you," General Giap said irritably. "You were the enemy. You wished to defeat us—to destroy us. So we were forced to fight you, to fight a 'people's war' to reclaim our country from your neo-imperialist ally in Saigon—we used the word 'puppet,' of course, back then—and to reunify our country."

They went back and forth: McNamara insisting that America "misunderstood" North Vietnam and what it was doing in the Gulf, and Giap insisting that the United States carried out "sabotage activities to create a pretext that would allow [it] to take over the war from the Saigon government, which was incompetent."

Although the former general and the former defense secretary could not agree, it is now generally accepted among historians that the incident in the Tonkin Gulf—which probably did not involve the actual firing of weapons—was seized by a president and a secretary of defense seeking an excuse to escalate the conflict, or at least to show American resolve against a Communist insurgency.

An additional motive for Johnson was political: 1964 was an election year, and he wanted to show himself as a staunch anti-Communist against the challenges of the hawkish, arch-conservative Republican presidential candidate, Senator Barry Goldwater. As time passed, such close advisers to the president as National Security Advisor McGeorge Bundy, and even McNamara, publicly voiced doubts about continuing the war. The Vietcong's stunning Tet Offensive in January 1968 demolished any illusions that the war could be won conclusively, or at all. Public opposition to the war and criticism from within the Democratic Party reached such intensity that in March 1968, the president gave a televised address in which he announced, "I will not seek, nor will I accept, the nomination of my party." Just weeks before, antiwar candidate Senator Eugene McCarthy had won 42 percent of the vote in the New Hampshire primary; almost immediately afterward, New York Senator Robert F. Kennedy entered the race.

Many members of Congress later concluded that they had been misled by the administration about what, if anything, happened at the Gulf of Tonkin in August 1964. The Senate voted in June 1970 to terminate the resolution, and in 1973 the War Powers Act was passed to curb the ability of a president to wage war without congressional authorization. By that time, of approximately 2.1 million American servicemen and women sent to the war, more than 58,000 soldiers had died, over 150,000 were wounded, and 2,000 were missing in action. Between 1.5 million and possibly as many as five million Vietnamese combatants and civilians died.

THE BOMBING OF CAMBODIA

RICHARD NIXON

IT WAS A NEW YEAR, AND HENRY KISSINGER WAS ABOUT TO BEGIN HIS NEW JOB as national security advisor to newly elected President Richard M. Nixon. Having made final arrangements for his departure from Harvard's Center for International Affairs Department, Kissinger was busy gathering a team of foreign affairs experts to help the president remake American policy in Vietnam. Sitting in his office on January 8, 1969, Kissinger read a note from his soon-to-be boss. "In making your study of Vietnam, I want a precise report on what the enemy has in Cambodia and what, if anything, we are doing to destroy the buildup [of enemy forces] there," Nixon wrote. "I think a very definite change of policy toward Cambodia probably should be one of the first orders of business when we get in." It was two weeks before the inauguration, and Nixon was planning to make some drastic changes in the execution of the Vietnam War. Namely, he wanted to make good on his campaign promise to withdraw U.S. troops completely.

Two very long years later, in December 1970, Kissinger received a call from Nixon regarding the same subject: Cambodia. The president had launched a major offensive against the Communists in that "neutral" country less than three months into office, and in his opinion it wasn't going well. Nixon fumed over the phone that U.S. pilots were "farting around doing nothing." Kissinger listened calmly. "It's a disgraceful performance," Nixon groused. "I want

gunships in there. That means armed helicopters, DC-3s, anything else that can destroy personnel that can fly. I want it done!"

The marked change in tone in Nixon's communiqués is indicative of the direction his presidency had taken in two years. His reasoned request for a "precise report" on the state of Cambodia was soon followed by vast carpet-bombing operations and a subsequent incursion into the territory of South Vietnam's neighbor to the west. Nixon went through great pains to keep the initial bombings secret, not so much to ensure that the enemy was taken by surprise, but rather to keep the operations secret from the American public, press, and even some members of the air crews flying the missions! Although these bombings inarguably harmed the Communist forces taking refuge in Cambodia, the strategic value of the raids was limited. Yet hundreds of thousands of Cambodian citizens lost their lives during the incessant and often imprecise bombing runs. It was "collateral damage" that, once revealed, horrified many Americans and provided the antiwar movement with the cause célèbre that its war- and protest-weary members needed to take the offensive once again. And when the public learned that the bombings were conducted in an explicitly secretive manner, Nixon, already suspect to many, became firmly established in the public mind as a president not to be trusted. It can even be argued that this perception of Nixon is what inspired members of the press and others to conduct the Watergate investigation with such energy.

Nixon's presidency was supposed to be defined by ending America's involvement in the Vietnam War. Instead, his legacy (like that of his predecessor) was swallowed by it.

COMMUNIST SANCTUARY It was no great secret that Communist forces, numbering in the tens of thousands, had been operating with relative impunity in Cambodia long before Nixon had a chance to send B-52s after them. While maintaining his nation's official stance of neutrality in the Vietnam War, Cambodia's head of state, Norodom Sihanouk, tacitly supported America's enemies.

Born into a line of Cambodian royalty dating back more than 1,000 years, Sihanouk was a master of realpolitik. After World War II, a wave of independent spirit washed through the nations of Indochina. As Cambodians' desire for freedom from colonial French rule grew during the 1950s, Sihanouk began lobbying Paris on behalf of his people. Initially, the French ignored him. They were busy fighting a war in Vietnam, which was a much more valuable commodity to them than Cambodia. But when Sihanouk went into voluntary exile, declaring that he would never return home as long as it was colonized, the French gave in and declared Cambodia a free state. Under the Geneva Peace Accord, Cambodia maintained official neutrality in the French-Indochina War.

The problem for Sihanouk was that Cambodia would also have free elections, and people wanted the monarchy out.

Characteristically, Sihanouk went with the flow. He abdicated the throne and went on record as a bona fide politician, promising to establish a truly democratic society. To that end, he created the People's Socialist Party and was easily elected head of state.

By the time the Viet Minh had expelled the French from Vietnam in 1954, Sihanouk had become convinced that the Communists would achieve ultimate victory in the contentious fight for Indochina. Plus, he had begun developing close ties with China, which later agreed to purchase rice at inflated prices in exchange for Sihanouk's tolerance of Communist military forces operating near the Vietnam border. Officially straddling the line of neutrality but obviously siding with the Communists, Sihanouk allowed the North Vietnamese Army (NVA) and the Vietcong (VC) to receive weapons and armaments shipments into Sihanoukville Harbor and transport them up and down the Sihanouk Trail (the southern equivalent of the Ho Chi Minh Trail). From here they would launch hit-and-run attacks on American and Army of the Republic of Vietnam (ARVN) troops stationed near the Cambodian border in the 1960s.

BOMBS AWAY
One of Lyndon B. Johnson's last acts as president was to initiate peace negotiations with Hanoi by agreeing to temporarily end the Air Force's bombing of North Vietnam. The agreement was shaky at best. Neither side ever quite agreed about whether the cessation of bombing would be "unconditional" or not. Nevertheless, an "understanding" existed among all those involved. When Nixon entered office, he and his administration planned to pursue these public peace talks, but they also opened up a channel to Xuân Thuy, head negotiator for North Vietnam, in order to hold separate, secret talks. Out of the public eye, political niceties would not impede the negotiations. It was an early example of Nixon's preference for secrecy.

If the leaders in Hanoi hoped that the new president might take some time to establish himself in his new position, they were disappointed. Nixon made it clear from the outset that he was a military hawk, and he even attempted to imply that he was a little bit crazy. "I call it the Madman Theory, Bob," he told Chief of Staff H.R. Haldeman. "I want the North Vietnamese to believe I've reached the point where I might do anything to stop the war. We'll just slip the word to them that, 'for God's sake, you know Nixon is obsessed about Communism. We can't restrain him when he's angry, and he has his hand on the nuclear button'— and Ho Chi Minh himself will be in Paris in two days begging for peace."

Even to a madman, however, Cambodia posed a particular problem for American withdrawal. In order for troops to safely depart without giving up

PRESIDENTIAL BRIEFING

(1913-1994)
• THIRTY-SEVENTH PRESIDENT OF THE UNITED STATES (1969-74)
• BORN JANUARY 9, 1913, IN YORBA LINDA, CALIFORNIA
• DIED APRIL 22, 1994, IN NEW YORK, NEW YORK
• VICE PRESIDENT OF THE UNITED STATES UNDER DWIGHT D. EISENHOWER (1952-61)
• IN 1960, LOST THE PRESIDENTIAL ELECTION TO JOHN F. KENNEDY BY A RAZOR-THIN MARGIN
• ELECTED IN 1968 WITH THE PROMISE OF A "SECRET PLAN" TO END THE VIETNAM WAR; BEGAN U.S. TROOP WITHDRAWALS; REELECTED IN 1972 IN A LANDSLIDE, CARRYING FORTY-NINE STATES
• ORDERED A MASSIVE BOMBING OF NORTH VIETNAM AND CAMBODIA TO FORCE AN END TO THE WAR; ANNOUNCED "PEACE WITH HONOR" AND AN END TO U.S. FIGHTING IN VIETNAM (1973)
• FACING IMPEACHMENT, IN 1974 BECAME THE FIRST U.S. PRESIDENT TO RESIGN FROM OFFICE

South Vietnam to the Communist forces, the United States would need to reinforce the South's military, economy, government, and social infrastructure. American ambassador Ellsworth Bunker called it the "three selfs": self-defense, self-government, and self-development. Often termed Vietnamization, it was a massive task. And guerilla assaults and rocket attacks from the Cambodian border country made Vietnamization, in essence, impossible. Those enemy forces would have to be pacified.

Within days of beginning his term, Nixon ordered the Pentagon to provide suggestions on how to proceed with Cambodia. Proposals ranged from breaking the "understanding" and resuming bombing in the North to using the navy to cut off the Cambodian coast, thus depriving the Communists and the Khmer Rouge of weapons and supplies from China. (The Khmer Rouge was a radical Marxist group intent on transforming Cambodia into an agrarian utopia. The name, coined by Sihanouk, means 'red Khmer' in French. The Khmer people are the predominant ethnic group in Cambodia.) Because a negotiated peace was the final goal, Nixon decided against bombing the North. He was leaning toward the naval blockade, but he was talked out of it by his Joint Chiefs of Staff. Sihanouk, they told the president, could probably be pressured into allowing air strikes in his territory. At the end of January 1969, General Earl Wheeler, chairman of the Joint Chiefs of Staff, and General Creighton Abrams, the American commander in Vietnam, urged Nixon to seriously consider bombing the Communist bases in Cambodia. The president balked. Cambodia's neutrality introduced numerous legal and political issues.

But less than a month later, following the Tet holidays, NVA and VC forces launched the "mini-Tet" offensive, using mortars and rockets to attack 115 targets from across the border. The cities of Saigon, Da Nang, and Hue were hit, as well as a U.S. base at Bien Hoa. Whether Nixon was prompted by indignation that the enemy had violated the "understanding" brokered by Johnson or wheather he considered this a direct attempt to discredit his new administration, as some historians have claimed, Nixon made the decision to violate Cambodia's sovereignty and launch air strikes against the enemy.

(Note: In fact, Operation Menu was not the first time American forces had crossed the border or bombed targets inside Cambodia. Throughout Johnson's term [1963–1969], various special forces units had run reconnaissance and sabotage missions in Cambodia. The Pentagon had urged Johnson to use B-52s against larger enemy targets, but to no avail. Smaller air strikes were used, though, in support of ground operations.)

The Nixon administration was in general agreement that the decision to bomb was justified, especially after the Cambodia-based Communists attacked once again three weeks later. Whether it was a practical decision was another matter. At least two high-ranking figures held strong reservations. Defense Secretary Melvin Laird and Secretary of State William Rogers feared major domestic outrage at what would be perceived as an expansion of the war, rather than the drawdown that Nixon had promised in the campaign. Furthermore, they feared it would uproot the ongoing peace process. Richard Sneider, a national security aide to Kissinger, questioned the use of B-52s. Using such heavy ordnance, he believed, would likely send enemy forces deeper into Cambodia, adding to the problems of a nation already beleaguered by anti-Western forces—namely, the Khmer Rouge.

But the detractors were outnumbered. A Communist defector had recently provided the exact location of the Central Office for South Vietnam (COSVN)—headquarters for all VC and NVA operations into South Vietnam. His information matched the military's interpretation of aerial reconnaissance photos, so the plan to take out COSVN went ahead. The opportunity was simply too good to pass up. General Wheeler suggested deploying B-52s for an intense, contained bombing of the area. A Communist offensive was expected

very soon. Even if the aerial assault didn't destroy COSVN, it would cause enough damage and confusion to at least prevent the attack.

Although Nixon did not heed the warnings of Laird and Rogers, he did agree with them on one thing: The bombings would create a firestorm at home. Nixon and Kissinger went to work creating a plan to prevent this. Because the air strikes would take place thirty miles, at the most, into Cambodian territory, it would be possible to make it *seem* like they were occurring in South Vietnam. They came up with a combat reporting system that would circumvent protocol, ensuring that exact target information would be handled by the fewest people possible. Only a handful of officers and men with the highest levels of clearance would be provided with the actual, top-secret coordinates of the Cambodian targets. The rest would be briefed that they were bombing enemy strongholds in South Vietnam. Certain pilots and navigators, however, would be taken aside just prior to the mission, informed of their true destination, and advised that this was top-secret information.

When the B-52s were in the air, command and control would send orders that the planes were being diverted to another target. The crews were accustomed to this because coordinate changes often occurred during bombing missions. At that point, a high-tech computer system would take control of the plane, fly it over Cambodia, and drop the payload. After-reports would reflect successful bombing runs near the border, in South Vietnam.

One supervisor at the command and control center involved in diverting the planes, Air Force Major Hal Knight, testified before the Senate Armed Service Committee in 1973 about the secret missions. "The thing that disturbs me is the fact that ... I could have gone to the typewriter, picked me out a town, say, within a reasonable distance of the actual aiming point, changed the coordinates of the aiming point to those of the town ... and no one would have known the difference." Tampering with this level of command and control passed an extraordinary amount of power through the hands of any one of the individuals "inside" the system. When the dual-reporting plan was made public, critics pointed out that nuclear-armed B-52s had also been part of the same command and control system.

As for reporters, Nixon administration officials involved in the operation were given strict orders to "know nothing" about the bombing. If pressed by a tenacious journalist, they were to reveal that bombings did, in fact, take place near the border and that they would look into it. If the reporter presented proof that bombs had fallen into Cambodia, the member of the administration would get back to him or her and admit that some of the bombs did accidentally land on the western side of the border, and that the Cambodian government had already been informed and apologized to.

The bombing campaign—dubbed Operation Menu because its various missions were named after meals of the day: Breakfast, Lunch, Supper, etc.— began on March 18, 1969, and lasted for fourteen months, until May 26, 1970. It involved 3,800 B-52 carpet-bombing sorties that released 108,232 tons of ordnance. The first mission, Breakfast (named during an early morning Pentagon meeting), targeted Communist supply caches and staging areas close to the border. Forty-eight of the sixty B-52s that took off from a base in Guam were diverted to Cambodia, where they dropped 2,400 tons of bombs.

While the targets were specific, the tactics were not. Carpet bombing covers a wide swath of land, destroying the target along with everything around it. Similar bombings in Laos covered swaths of land six kilometers (about 3.7 miles) long and two kilometers (1.25 miles) wide. Furthermore, the Cambodian targets were often located in heavily populated areas. The U.S. chief of targets working out of Thailand characterized the target zones as "almost suburban in character with close-spaced villages throughout." At one point, as information about the bombings began leaking through White House channels, Secretary of State Rogers received a letter of protest signed by 250 State Department employees. Rogers refused to hand over the names when Kissinger demanded them.

The Breakfast mission was initially considered a resounding success. A small reconnaissance unit of two Green Berets and eleven South Vietnamese soldiers stationed near the border were immediately sent in to assess the damage and pick up anyone who happened to be alive. Randolph Harrison, one of the Green Berets, was told that everything had been demolished and that if there happened to be any survivors, there would be no fight left in them. But when the team entered the target zone, they were met with fierce resistance. "The visible effect [of the B-52 bombing] on the North Vietnamese who were there was the same as taking a beehive the size of a basketball and poking it with a stick," Harrison said. "They were mad." Nine of the thirteen on the reconnaissance team were killed. When a second Green Beret team was ordered in the next morning, the response was, "[Expletive] you."

COSVN, the North Vietnamese Army and the Vietcong's headquarters for operations against South Vietnam, remained intact. Much later it was learned that although the defector's information was likely accurate at the time he gave it, the Communist headquarters was a much smaller operation than military planners realized, allowing it to be constantly moved from one location to another. It never stayed in the same place more than ten days in a row.

On May 8, Nixon's greatest nightmare came true when the *New York Times* published a story about Operation Menu. Clearly, someone in the administration had leaked the information, and the president wanted to know who. He ordered Kissinger to recruit the FBI to find the source. J. Edgar Hoover told Kissinger that the informant was most likely Morton H. Halperin, one of Kissinger's own aides. They then tapped Halperin's phone for almost two years. It was the first of the administration's illegal wiretaps. Incredibly, only two publications followed up on the story—*Newsweek* and United Press International (UPI)—but only in relatively brief articles. The operation continued in secrecy.

One year to the day of the beginning of the Breakfast mission, March 18, 1970, Cambodia's National Congress ejected Sihanouk from power in a no-confidence vote. Sihanouk's prime minister, Lon Nol, took his place, and then Cambodia began falling apart in earnest. From Sihanouk's second exile (this time in Beijing), he formed a guerrilla resistance against the new government, and Cambodia plunged into civil war. The nation's economy collapsed, and the Khmer Rouge gained ground against the government. Highly superstitious Lon Nol's response was the murder of thousands of Vietnamese citizens, who he believed were evil spirits.

Adding to Cambodia's woes was the invasion in May of 50,000 ARVN (South Vietnamese) and 30,000 U.S. troops. Nixon had ordered an incursion into Cambodia to aid Lon Nol's army in the fight against the Communists and, thus, to ensure that the country remained neutral. Fighting continued for two months, with the ARVN, to everyone's surprise, performing well. Body counts were almost always vastly in their favor. Because South Vietnam's ability to provide its own security was the most important element for the success of Vietnamization, the Nixon administration touted the incursion as a huge success. However, the ARVN's true test came the following February, during an incursion into Laos without the support of the American military. It failed miserably. Military analysts pointed out that the importance of U.S. air support of the ARVN troops in Cambodia had been initially underestimated.

DAMAGE REPORT
The Cambodian bombings and subsequent incursion doubtless provided military benefits. Nixon called the incursion "the most successful operation of the war." North Vietnam's infrastructure in Cambodia had been damaged beyond repair, preventing countless enemy forays into South Vietnam. Indeed, the next Communist assault against South Vietnam, in 1972, was launched from North Vietnam and Laos, not from Cambodia. The operations' supporters also pointed out that the incursion bought enough time for the safe withdrawal of American forces.

Still, Operation Menu's objective—the destruction of COSVN—was not achieved, and ARVN (South Vietnamese) General Tran Dinh Tho said the incursion "proved, in the long run, to pose little more than a temporary disruption of North Vietnam's march toward domination of all of Laos, Cambodia, and South Vietnam."

RA SỨC RÈN LUYỆN QUÂN SỰ SẴN SÀNG BẢO VỆ TỔ QUỐC

A NORTH VIETNAMESE PROPAGANDA POSTER USED IN 1970. IT READS, "STRIVE TO TRAIN SOLDIERS TO DEFEND THE NATION."

Defense Secretary Laird's fears of domestic unrest as a direct result of the Cambodian campaign also came to fruition, full-blown. Protests on university campuses grew in number and intensity. It was at one of these demonstrations, at Kent State University in Ohio on May 4, 1970, that four students were shot dead and nine wounded by Ohio National Guardsmen. This was one of the darkest moments of Nixon's presidency and an event that galvanized the antiwar/anti-Nixon movements more than anything else up to that point. Hundreds of schools, from middle schools to universities, closed as some eight million American students struck in protest against the killings. Hundreds of thousands marched on Washington, campus ROTC buildings were burned or bombed, and instances of violence between students and National Guardsmen escalated. (It should be noted, however, that a sizeable pro-war rally of more than 100,000 supporters of President Nixon—a three-hour parade of flag-waving construction workers, teamsters, and longshoremen organized by the Building and Trades Council of Greater New York—took place in New York City during this time. The march came two weeks after "hardhats" assaulted "longhairs" in an antiwar demonstration.)

In 1970, directly following the incursion into Cambodia, Senator Jacob Javits of New York introduced the War Powers Act to Congress. Designed to limit the president's control over of all aspects of war-making, it requires the president to provide clear war aims to Congress within strictly defined time frames. The act was meant to give Congress a greater say in major military operations, such as in Korea and Vietnam. Nixon originally vetoed it, but it passed by an overwhelming vote in 1973.

In the end, Cambodia emerged the most brutalized nation in the war that killed millions. Largely as a result of the bombings and incursion, the Communists spread deeper into Cambodia, which was another of Laird's and Rogers's fears. Five days after U.S. troops withdrew, Lon Nol's army fell to Pol Pot's Khmer Rouge, which in its four-year reign of terror (1975–1979) murdered between 850,000 and two million Cambodians. The American bombing raids on Cambodia killed as many as 600,000 civilians between 1969 and 1973.

CONCLUSION

Some of President Nixon's decisions to commit troops to actions in Cambodia, both legally and illegally, can, at best, be viewed as military successes. But those achievements are isolated in time and space. As policy, they amounted to catastrophe. Vietnam marked the first time America faced a modern guerrilla army en masse. By war's end, the body count was hugely in our

THE AFTERMATH OF U.S. AIRSTRIKES AGAINST NORTH VIETNAMESE TROOPS—SUCH STRIKES DAMAGED ENEMY FORCES IN CAMBODIA BUT DID NOT DESTROY THEM.

favor. American bombs in Cambodia killed untold numbers of enemy troops. The war's outcome proved, however, that body counts do not matter much when facing such an enemy. Carpet bombing will not subdue a guerrilla army forever. John F. Kennedy had said in a Senate speech in 1954, when the United States was considering taking over France's fight against the Viet Minh, "I am frankly of the belief that no amount of American military assistance in Indo-China can conquer an enemy which is everywhere, and at the same time nowhere, an enemy of the people which has the sympathy and covert support of the people."

Perhaps Nixon was driven to expand the war into Cambodia by honest feelings that it was the best thing to do militarily. Maybe he truly believed it was in the average American citizen's best interest to remain ignorant of the Cambodia bombings. Or, perhaps, Nixon was, as some historians believe, simply a man out of control, and his "madman theory" was more accurate than he realized. Whatever his reasons, failed military strategies, massive civilian casualty numbers, and "collateral damage" as experienced in Cambodia (and, more recently, in Afghanistan and Iraq) can be forgiven and forgotten (or at least ignored) by the American public. Government conspiracies and abuse of power, however, cannot.

NEITHER CARPET-BOMBING NOR PRECISION STRIKES (AS SHOWN HERE) CAN SUBDUE A WELL-TRAINED GUERILLA FORCE FOREVER— A HARD LESSON THAT PRESIDENTS JOHNSON AND NIXON LEARNED IN THE VIETNAM WAR.

CHAPTER 16

WATERGATE

RICHARD NIXON

DOUGLAS CADDY'S TELEPHONE RANG HIM AWAKE DURING THE EARLY MORNING hours of June 17, 1972. Caddy opened his eyes and looked over at the alarm clock; it was a few minutes after 3:00 A.M.

"Doug," a man's voice said nervously, "I hate to wake you up. But I've got a tough situation, and I need to talk to you."

Educated at Georgetown University and New York University School of Law, Caddy was a Beltway conservative and committed Republican soldier. Caddy had worked as a corporate attorney for a division of General Foods, but he had left that well-paid job to join the Washington law firm Gall, Lane, Powell and Kilcullen, where he met former Central Intelligence Agency (CIA) spy E. Howard Hunt Jr., one of the firm's clients.

And it was Hunt on the telephone now, rustling Caddy out of bed. Hunt, the ultimate keeper of secrets himself, had been on President Richard Nixon's payroll for years as a plumber, one of many responsible for finding and plugging leaks in the administration. Caddy was someone Hunt could trust.

Something bad had happened at the Watergate Hotel with five guys Hunt later said he had recruited for a "special job." He didn't want to discuss it over the phone; he needed to speak privately with Caddy at once.

About a half hour before Hunt called Caddy, he was inside his White House Executive Office Building office, twisting the dial on his private safe.

Inside was Caddy's number in what Hunt later called his "operational note-book," a black book he shared with G. Gordon Liddy, another well-known Nixon plumber and former Federal Bureau of Investigation (FBI) agent. Years later, Hunt would write, referring to himself and Liddy, "Five of our guys had been arrested and presumably taken to a D.C. jail … and it was my responsibility to get them out."

What Hunt didn't say was that he and Liddy were in on the operation, monitoring every move of the five via walkie-talkie from their command post in a nearby Watergate Hotel room.

Hunt took $10,000 in cash from the safe and arrived at Caddy's home thirty minutes later. In the interim, he had called the wife of one of the men who had been arrested, fifty-five-year-old, Cuban-born, U.S. Army veteran Bernard Barker. In a hurried tone, Hunt told the woman that her husband was in trouble. Knowing she wasn't going to be happy, Hunt said at one point, "Things have gone wrong." He referred to Barker as "Macho" and told her he'd "been arrested."

She screamed.

AT A WHITE HOUSE NEWS CONFERENCE ON MARCH 15, 1972, PRESIDENT NIXON SAID HE WOULD NOT ALLOW HIS LEGAL COUNSEL, JOHN DEAN, TO TESTIFY ON CAPITOL HILL BEFORE THE SENATE WATERGATE COMMITTEE AND CHALLENGED THE SENATE TO TEST HIM IN THE SUPREME COURT.

"He's got bail money with him," Hunt assured her, as he recounted later in his book *American Spy*. "So maybe he'll be able to get out before dawn. I don't know how these things work, but I think he ought to have an attorney. I've already called one, and I want you to call him, too."

Mrs. Barker wanted to know what her husband was doing in Washington, D.C., a thousand miles from home. Hunt said he didn't have time to answer questions. "Just call Caddy. That's all you or anybody can do."

Barker had served under Fidel Castro's Cuban guerrilla movement in the 1950s. The *Washington Post* reported that he had become disillusioned and left Cuba for Miami in 1959 and that he was also one of the organizers of the Bay of Pigs invasion in 1961. Since that time, however, Barker had been doing free-lance jobs for the CIA.

Wired and manic, Hunt stumbled into Caddy's home. Caddy wanted answers. *What in the world is going on here, Howard?* Moreover, what could Caddy do? He wasn't a criminal attorney.

Hunt reached into his pocket and took out $8,500 (the additional $1,500 was in his briefcase, to be used for any emergencies that might arise) in cash, put it on the table, and asked, "Could you go down to police headquarters ... and see if you can bail them out?"

Hunt would later refer to these moments as the "beginning of Watergate," and what transpired in the coming days as "a scandal that would bring down a president and destroy my life in the process."

THE G-MEN

At forty-two, G. Gordon Liddy was a devoted soldier in President Nixon's "slush fund" army, acting as an attorney for the White House on campaign finance and contribution issues. Liddy and Hunt had known each other as White House plumbers and spent part of the night of June 17, 1972, together. Hunt was someone with connections and an intellect capable of taking on most any job the president's people asked of him. He had been CIA station chief in Mexico City in 1950, and he helped plan the overthrow of Guatemalan president Jacobo Árbenz in 1954. Liddy was the means and muscle. During the spring of 1972, Liddy and Hunt were in California recruiting for several jobs they needed done at Watergate. As Liddy recounted in his autobiography, *Will*, they were in the market for a locksmith and an electronics expert, people who could "get ... into campaign headquarters of Democratic candidates as soon as possible." To prove how dedicated Liddy was, he asked a woman he was interviewing to light her cigarette lighter and hold it out in front of herself. After she did, Liddy placed the palm of his hand over the flame. "Presently the flesh turned black," Liddy wrote, describing the moment, "and ... she smelled the scent of burning meat."

On the night of June 17, Liddy was sleeping when Hunt telephoned him from Caddy's house. Liddy had gotten home about an hour earlier. (Hunt had dropped him off.) Before the call, Caddy had recommended to Hunt that they hire criminal attorney Joe Rafferty.

Hunt agreed, and he explained the situation to Liddy, who replied, "If that's Caddy's judgment, that's fine with me."

Earlier that night, Liddy and Hunt had discussed how important Caddy was going to be, calling him the perfect lawyer "for emergency use."

Liddy and Hunt knew the Watergate break-in they had planned and supervised was crumbling. They were both deeply involved, and if they weren't careful, the evidence could point straight back to the president of the United States.

After they discussed the $8,500 retainer Caddy suggested, which Liddy later referred to as a "contingency fund," Hunt put Caddy on the phone with Liddy, who said, "Doug, the fee's fine, but I think it should include Howard *and* me." If he retained Caddy at that moment, Liddy knew that whatever was said between them would be considered covered under an attorney-client privilege agreement, essentially binding Caddy to his pledge of loyalty.

They agreed that Rafferty and Caddy would represent both Liddy and Hunt. Liddy then explained how he wanted Rafferty to bail "the five" out of jail immediately. Thus, by 10:30 A.M., Caddy and Rafferty were inside the cellblock of the Second Police Precinct in downtown Washington discussing the situation with their new clients.

Along with Barker, the Metropolitan Police had arrested Edward Martin (a.k.a. James W. McCord Jr.), the group's electronics expert and leader, who was also the security director for the Committee for the Reelection of the President, and had also worked for the CIA and FBI; Eugenio Martinez; Frank Sturgis; and Virgilio Gonzales (all Cuban-born hired hands). The five were charged with "felonious burglary," as well as "possession of implements [of a] crime."

The *Washington Post* was all over the story that morning, already reporting how the five had been caught. One of the five would later call the break-in "Mission Impossible." Still, it was a good bet that none of them—especially Liddy and Hunt—ever expected to be fingered by a twenty-four-year-old security guard.

Frank Willis was walking through the Watergate building when he noticed a door leading into the stairwell had a piece of tape over the locking mechanism. Willis took the piece of tape off and continued checking the building. On his way back through the same area, Willis saw that the door had been re-taped. He telephoned the Metropolitan Police. When officers arrived, they conducted a complete sweep of the building and found that every door leading up the stairwell to the sixth floor had been taped in the same fashion.

Because the taped doors had ended on the sixth floor, the three officers, weapons drawn, searched the Democratic National Committee (DNC) headquarters, which took up the entire sixth floor. As they slowly opened the door to Deputy Party Chairman Stanley Griegg's office, one of the five "jumped up from behind" Griegg's desk, raised his hands, and cried out, "Don't shoot, please ..."

Police ultimately took the five into custody and booked them. Afterward, investigators discovered that the break-in was only part of a more concerted plot to get into one specific office for two purposes: to bug the office of DNC National Chairman Lawrence O'Brien and to search through his filing cabinets for any documents that could help the Republicans. Later, police uncovered $5,000 in cash, additional burglary tools, and a small set of electronic bugging devices in six separate suitcases inside hotel suites the five had rented under fictitious names. What made the five men seem especially suspicious and well organized was that they all were wearing surgical gloves, plus police found all types of fancy, state-of-the-art electronics equipment in their hotel suites that strongly suggested CIA involvement.

TRICKY DICK The dilemma Hunt, Caddy, and Liddy had discussed during the early morning hours of June 17, which the *Washington Post* reported in the morning's newspaper as an "elaborate plan to bug the offices of the Democratic National Committee," was the culmination of a series of break-ins initiated the previous year, all of which were connected to the release of the Defense Department's "secret history of the Vietnam War," more widely known as the Pentagon Papers.

Nixon's legacy as a politician would ultimately be summed up in one word: Watergate. But his first presidential run began more than two decades before his presidential term of turmoil. It was 1950, and Nixon was running for Senate after four years in the House of Representatives, building a career as a Communist-hunter. During what was a nasty California Senate race, Nixon unfairly portrayed his opponent [Helen Douglas] as a Communist sympathizer. This was the year that introduced the true red baiting era into politics. It was that attack by Nixon's campaign on Douglas, along with an election ad the Democrats ran ("Look at 'Tricky Dick' Nixon's Republican Record"), that earned him the nickname he was never quite able to shake.

Dwight D. Eisenhower noticed how assertive and persistent Nixon was in getting State Department official Alger Hiss indicted on charges of perjury stemming from his alleged involvement in the Communist Party of the 1930s. Nixon used his connections in the media to reportedly expose Hiss, resulting in a jail sentence for perjury—which made Nixon admired by conservatives and hated by liberals. Impressed by Nixon's new national reputation, Eisenhower invited him onto his 1952 ticket as the Republican vice presidential nominee.

From the moment Dick Nixon entered politics, he was either ostensibly, directly, or indirectly involved in scandal. No sooner had Eisenhower taken Nixon under his wing than he tarnished the campaign with rumblings of an $18,000 slush fund and the gift of a dog named Checkers. In light of the charges, Nixon gave what would become his famous "Checkers" speech, saying, "I am sure that you have read the charge, and you've heard that I, Senator Nixon, took $18,000 from a group of my supporters." He sounded uncannily sincere, even apologetic, smiling at times, twiddling his thumbs, appearing innocent and naïve. These were the assets that made Nixon's political character so flush with riches: the ability to look Americans in the eye and lie through his large, very white teeth. Continuing, he carried on about how not only was taking money illegal, but it was also dishonest. He would never accept gifts of any kind, he implied. Then, after a long-winded interlude into his private life, he raged, "Not one cent of the $18,000 or any other money of that type ever went to me for my personal use."

Gifts were a politician's nightmare. In light of rumors floating that Nixon's daughter had been given a dog by a wealthy Texan Republican, he looked into the camera, twitched, and answered the allegation: "We did get something—a gift—after the election… It was a little cocker spaniel, Checkers. And you know, the kids, like all kids, love the dog. And I just want to say this right now, regardless of what they say about it, we're going to *keep* it."

Eisenhower and Nixon were elected in 1952 and reelected in 1956. Still, when Nixon tried a run himself in 1960, he was narrowly defeated by John F. Kennedy. In this tight race, particularly during the last days of it, Nixon might actually have won if not—it has been fairly widely accepted—not for some voting shenanigans in Illinois allegedly arranged by the candidate's father Joe Kennedy and Chicago's Mayor Richard J. Daley. In his book, *A Thousand Days*, Arthur Schlesinger said even JFK himself knew from the way the race was tightening that had the election gone on one more week, he might have been defeated.

It was at this time that one of Nixon's many celebrated catchphrases would begin to saturate popular culture. After he lost the 1962 California gubernatorial race and announced his retirement, he blamed reporters for the mess of his political life, saying, "You won't have Dick Nixon to kick around anymore!"

WOODWARD AND BERNSTEIN
On an average day in Washington during the 1970s, there were about fifty burglaries. During mid-June 1972, however, there was only one worth talking about. A D.C. reporter couldn't have asked for a more fascinating story: five men arrested inside the DNC headquarters, all wearing gloves and business suits, each with his own piece of bugging equipment. It was a drama straight out of a James Bond movie. Furthermore, the money the Watergate five had was in sequentially numbered $100 bills. Looking at it, the entire scenario spoke of an organized conspiracy.

After working their sources throughout the weekend of June 17 and 18, *Post* reporters Bob Woodward and Carl Bernstein were able to publish a devastating front-page story on Monday, June 19 which exposed the true identity of James McCord, the Watergate ringleader. The story identified McCord as a "salaried security coordinator for President Nixon's re-election's committee ... [who] also holds a separate contract to provide security services to the Republican National Committee ..." Major news. It tied McCord, who was one of the five, directly to Nixon. In addition to Woodward and Bernstein, the acting associate director of the FBI, W. Mark Felt, was on the trail of the McCord-Nixon connection, too. "In view of the headlines," Felt wrote in an interoffice, confidential memo, "I feel we should move immediately ... before somebody else gets the idea and has it done privately thereby complicating the evidence picture."

There was going to be a complete political meltdown, and everyone in Washington knew it. Felt was concerned that, as Woodward described in *All the President's Men*, "politics had infiltrated every corner of government—a strong-arm takeover of agencies by the Nixon White House." Not to mention that "junior White House aides," Felt continued in that same book, "were giving orders on the highest levels of the bureaucracy." The president's men all fought dirty, Felt told Woodward off the record, "and for keeps, regardless of what effect ... [it had] on the government and the nation."

In the weeks to come, Woodward would cultivate perhaps the most celebrated confidential source in journalism history, a government official in a position to know a great many secrets, whom Woodward usually met in discreet assignations at odd hours in an underground parking garage. The *Post's* managing editor, Howard Simons, nicknamed the mystery source "Deep Throat" after the title of an infamous pornographic movie at the time. The man was a top FBI agent and White House insider, feeding Woodward a series of leads that ultimately helped the *Post* break the Watergate story and trace a $25,000 check back to the five that were connected to the president's re-election committee. One *Post* story later reported:

> A $25,000 cashier's check apparently earmarked for President Nixon's re-election campaign was deposited in... a bank account of one of the five men arrested... The check was made out by a Florida bank to Kenneth H. Dahlberg, the president's campaign finance chairman.

Within that summer of reporting, Woodward and Bernstein had established the facts that Nixon had a slush fund controlled by the former attorney general, John Mitchell, who was also the head of Nixon's reelection campaign at one time—a bank account set up for the purpose of specifically financing break-ins and paying off Nixon's plumbers.

CAUGHT ON TAPE
H.R. "Bob" Haldeman and President Nixon sat in the Oval Office at 10:04 A.M. on June 23, 1972, discussing the very serious situa-

tion that had suddenly developed. The last thing the Nixon White House needed was the leaking of any more details of the break-in, or for the FBI to figure out what was actually going on. Haldeman was Nixon's chief of staff. A cocky man, whose dedication to the president could be defined as admirable. Haldeman once referred to himself as the president's "son of a bitch." During this meeting, Haldeman sounded nervous. There was a voice-activated tape recorder in the room picking up what both men were saying.

"Now, on the investigation, you know, the Democratic break-in thing," Haldeman said to the president, "we're back to the… problem area. Because the FBI is not under control. Because [interim FBI director L. Patrick] Gray doesn't exactly know how to control them. And they have, their investigation is now leading into some productive areas. Because they've been able to trace the *money*. Not through the money itself, but through the bank, you know, sources—the *banker* himself."

Nixon listened as Haldeman described several documents the media had uncovered that would ultimately shed light on what Nixon's reelection campaign had been up to.

"The way to handle this now," Haldeman continued, "is for us to have [someone] call Pat Gray and just say, 'Stay the hell out of this. This is, uh… business here. We don't want you to go any further on it.'"

"Uh-huh," the president agreed.

"And that would take care of it."

"What about Pat Gray? You mean he *doesn't* want to?" the president wondered.

"Pat *does* want to," Haldeman said confidently. "But he doesn't know *how* to. And he doesn't have any basis for doing it. Given this, he will then have the basis. He'll call Mark Felt in and the two of them… and Mark Felt wants to cooperate because… he's ambitious."

Neither man knew it, of course, but Felt, the number two man in the FBI, was more determined than anyone to expose the true nature of the break-in. As the world learned by Felt's own surprise announcement in 2005, he was "Deep Throat," Bob Woodward's clandestine source. In the summer of 1972, Felt realized that no matter what he and the FBI did, the Nixon administration would manage to cover it up. There was only one way for Felt, once he figured out what was going on, to expose the corrupt disease infecting the White House. "Follow the money," he told Woodward. It was good advice that always panned out.

For Nixon, the main failure in successfully seeing his plan through was trusting too many people. There were far too many hands involved in that $25,000 check. Sooner or later, Nixon implied to Haldeman, someone would talk.

"He'll call him in and say," Haldeman explained, "'We've got the signal from across the river to put the hold on this.'" Haldeman was talking about how Felt and the FBI should tone down the investigation and get off the trail of the money. "And that will fit rather well, because the FBI agents who are working the case, at this point, feel that this is CIA."

"But they've traced the money to *them*," Nixon said worriedly.

"Well, they have. They've traced a name. But they haven't gotten to the guy yet." That "guy" was Kenneth H. Dahlberg, a Minnesota Nixon campaign volunteer who gave Barker the $25,000 check.

"Who the hell is Ken Dahlberg?" Nixon wondered angrily.

Haldeman explained, noting cautiously, "He gave $25,000 in Minnesota and, ah, the check went directly to this—to this guy Barker."

"Maybe he's a bum?" Nixon lamented, insinuating that Dahlberg was going to crack under the first sign of pressure, or that he didn't even know how deep he was involved. Then, "He didn't get this from the committee …?"

"Yeah," Haldeman said. "It's *directly* traceable…."

"Well," Nixon said, "I mean, there's no way… if they don't cooperate, what do they say?" Then, answering himself, "That they were approached by the Cubans! That's what Dahlberg *has* to say…."

AN OFFICIAL WHITE HOUSE PHOTOGRAPH SHOWS JOHN D. EHRLICHMAN (LEFT), ASSISTANT TO THE PRESIDENT FOR DOMESTIC AFFAIRS, LISTENING TO CHIEF OF STAFF H. R. "BOB" HALDEMAN ONBOARD *AIR FORCE ONE* IN APRIL 1973, THREE DAYS BEFORE THEY WERE ASKED TO RESIGN.

Nixon and Haldeman spent the next several moments discussing how many plumbers were involved and how each could eventually be traced back to Nixon and his reelection committee. Nixon directed Haldeman to talk to everyone and make it clear how important it was to keep their mouths shut. If necessary, use intimidation. "When you get these people … say, 'Look, the problem is that this will open the whole Bay of Pigs thing, and the president just feels that'… without going into the details. Don't lie to them to the extent to say there is *no* involvement, but just say: 'This is sort of a comedy of errors, bizarre, without getting into it. The president believes that it's going to open the whole Bay of Pigs thing up again.' And because these people are playing for, for keeps, and that they should call the FBI in and say, '[We're] for the country. Don't go any further into this case, period!'"

Many conspiracy theorists later speculated that Nixon's use of "the whole Bay of Pigs thing" was code for the assassination of JFK and a possible Washington cover-up, but, of course, this is all conjecture, as it was never proven. Nixon could have just as well been referring to the four Cuban-born Watergate burglars and any possible connection to the Bay of Pigs each of them might have had.

A FISH-EYE LENS VIEW OF THE SENATE WATERGATE COMMITTEE HEARING ROOM IN THE UNITED STATES CAPITOL BUILDING. THE COMMITTEE'S TELEVISED HEARINGS RAN FROM MAY TO AUGUST 1973 AND WERE SEEN BY AN ESTIMATED 85 PERCENT OF AMERICANS WITH TELEVISION SETS.

Nonetheless, Haldeman said, "Okay."

Nixon and Haldeman spoke for a few more moments. In the end, both were comfortable in knowing that they had just made a decision to force the CIA, who were essentially in the president's back pocket and deeply involved in the Pentagon Papers, into pressuring the FBI to back off of what the White House was publicly referring to as nothing more than a third-rate burglary.

"I AM NOT A CROOK" In April 1973, as pressure surrounding the Watergate scandal mounted, Nixon forced H.R. Haldeman to resign. Haldeman admitted immediately that he had been involved in the Watergate cover-up from the beginning and had pulled Nixon back onto what was a rapidly sinking ship. One of Nixon's other senior top advisers, John Dean, then issued a statement after Nixon—no doubt trying to cling to any sort of life raft he could find—began cleaning house and fired even more of his staff. In that statement Dean indicated he was disinclined to be a "scapegoat" for Nixon's crumbling White House.

On June 25, the Senate committee investigating the Watergate break-in called Dean in to testify. Within a few moments of being behind the microphone, Dean gave it up, testifying that his former boss, the President of the United States, was indeed involved in the cover-up. Then he confirmed that Nixon had tape-recordings of meetings in which the very issue of a cover-up had been openly discussed. In one of his more famous statements during the Senate committee hearings, Dean said, "I began by telling the president that there was a cancer growing on the presidency—and if the cancer was not removed, the president himself would be killed by it."

Later, during the same inquiry, the deputy assistant to Nixon, Alexander Butterfield, was asked if he had been aware of a recording system inside the Oval Office. The Senate committee was, of course, interested in those tape recordings.

Butterfield replied, "I was aware of listening devices. Yes, sir."

In fact, as Butterfield and Dean would further explain, Nixon had a White House recording system, activated by sound, which documented on audio tape everything and anything said in the Oval Office, the Executive Office Building office, and the Lincoln Room. According to U.S District Court Judge John J. Sirica, in his book *To Set the Record Straight*, which detailed his experiences at the "center of this storm," the microphones "[i]n the president's main office… had been concealed in small holes drilled in the wood of his mahogany desk."

The question no one could answer later however, became, *Why in the world would Nixon allow his administration to be recorded while committing crimes?*

The Senate committee demanded access to the tape recordings. Nixon fought the request, but when members of the Senate screamed impeachment, Nixon gave in—although many of the tapes were now missing, while others had important portions, or "gaps," erased.

With the evidence against him mounting, on November 17, 1973, Nixon stood in front of 400 managing editors of the Associated Press in a televised press conference in Florida. He looked distracted and discouraged. As Nixon answered questions, he stumbled through his words and consistently proclaimed his innocence. He said more than once that he was preparing to release documents and those now-popular tape recordings that would prove he did not know about the Watergate break-in beforehand. At one point, after saying several times that he had never personally "profited from public service," he raged, "I have earned *every* cent. In all of my years of public life, I have *never* obstructed justice. People have got to know whether or not their president is a *crook*. Well, I am *not* a crook. I've earned *everything* I've got."

Eight months after that press conference, Nixon announced his resignation. Halfway into Nixon's second term, he resigned the office of the president of the United States, the first time a president had done so in the nation's history. "By taking this action, I hope that I will have hastened the start of the process of healing, which is so desperately needed in America…" Weeping, Nixon added near the end of the speech, "Those who hate you don't win unless you *hate* them. Then you destroy yourself."

It was soon proven that Howard Hunt and G. Gordon Liddy had directed the Watergate break-in via walkie-talkies from a hotel room adjacent to the Watergate Hotel. Both men were indicted. Hunt was convicted of burglary, conspiracy, and wiretapping, and he served thirty-three months in jail. Liddy was convicted of burglary, conspiracy, and contempt of court, but he ended up doing four and a half years in jail. In all, forty government officials were indicted and/or jailed. Haldeman was subsequently convicted of conspiracy and obstruction of justice. McCord, who would later make the claim that the White House had been behind the break-in all along, was convicted of six counts of conspiracy, burglary, and wiretapping. In 1973, he was sentenced to one to five years, and he was released in 1975.

In 1972, Nixon won his reelection bid against Democrat George McGovern, destroying him with an extraordinary 520 electoral votes to 17, but less than two years after that stunning victory, the House of Representatives was passing articles of impeachment against Nixon.

This was one of the motivating factors behind Watergate: Nixon's decision to win the election by the largest margin possible—which amounted to a type of electoral greed Richard Nixon's legacy epitomized.

Gerald R. Ford was sworn into office the day after Nixon resigned. Ford announced to a traumatized nation, exhausted by Nixon's troubles, "Our long national nightmare is over." Thirty days after Ford took over, he granted his former boss an unprecedented "absolute pardon" for all the crimes Nixon "committed or may have committed." It was a broad-brush pardon, exonerating Nixon from any further prosecution. Nixon could fall back into civilian life without worry, perhaps in search of the reasons that led to his many failures.

In his closing remarks to his staff on August 9, 1974, Nixon held fast to his old Tricky Dick way of escaping blame, at one point saying, "I am proud of this Cabinet. I am proud of all the members who have served in our Cabinet… I am proud of our White House Staff. As I pointed out… sure, we have done some things wrong in this Administration, and the top man always takes the responsibility—and I have never ducked it. But I want to say one thing. We can be proud of it—five-and-a-half years… Mistakes, yes. But for personal gain, never. You did what you believed in. Sometimes right, sometimes wrong…."

Nixon's failures as president had a lasting—and perhaps corrosive—effect on American culture and the future of politics. His health care, education, and job training cutbacks kicked the stilts out from underneath what were essential social programs for the poor. The country was also overwhelmed and burdened by both inflation and recession as the year 1974 came to an end—both of which could be attributed to Nixon's unsuccessful domestic and foreign policies. More devastating and dangerous to the well-being of Americans at that time was not Nixon's unsuccessful effort to secure arms control agreements with Russia, but to continue the Vietnam War for what was four additional, unnecessary years, on top of bombing Cambodia.

But Nixon was, right up until his death on April 22, 1994, beyond anything else, a politician—albeit one in total denial of his obvious failures. Well into his late seventies, struggling to get the words to flow just right, the former president was asked by Larry King if it bothered him to hear people talk about Watergate, or if he had any anxiety whenever he was in Washington and had to travel by the Watergate Hotel. "Well, I've never been in the Watergate, so it is not a hard thing, no," Nixon said stoically, trying to muster up that signature confident tone that had served him well for so many years. Regarding his years of political trouble, Nixon explained, "No, I don't live in the past. As a matter of fact, one of the problems older people have is when you get together and they always want to reminisce about the past. I don't do that. I like to think about the future."

CHAPTER 17

THE IRANIAN HOSTAGE CRISIS

JIMMY CARTER

THE BOEING 707 SCREAMED DOWN THE RUNWAY, ITS MASSIVE JETS ROARING LOUDER as it gained speed. It lifted lightly off the ground and began climbing on a steep angle toward the sun. As the pilot began banking the plane, he looked away from his controls to see the city below. From 3,000 feet, it looked like a toy village. The plane climbed higher. From 8,000, it was a mosaic of tiny tiles, all earth tones—browns, grays, whites, tans—with thick, dark lines cutting through at different angles. Disordered and imbalanced as the composition was, the pilot thought it was beautiful.

And from the air, the city was absolutely silent.

Now, at 20,000 feet, the pilot couldn't see, even if he had wanted to, the people—his subjects—marching through the street by the millions, holding placards, shouting slogans, burning flags, and chanting for his death. The pilot wondered if he would ever return. Yes, very likely. He had ruled the nation for nearly forty years, personally transforming it from a backward pawn of international power brokers into a modern, self-sufficient state with an exciting future. This was his country.

Mohammad Reza Shah Pahlavi, the shah of Iran, set his airplane to autopilot and leaned back in his seat. His destination was Egypt. In a few hours, his good friend Anwar el-Sadat would welcome him on the tarmac like a brother. Together, they would figure out a solution to his recent problems. Sadat had made peace

with Israel and shared the 1978 Nobel Prize for Peace with Israeli prime minister Menachem Begin, so perhaps he could give some good advice on pacifying Iran.

Half a world away, President Jimmy Carter was trying to figure things out, too. Two years into his term, he felt besieged from all fronts. Up until now, Carter had enjoyed some major domestic and foreign policy successes—the Panama Canal Treaty, the Camp David Accords between Israel and Egypt, and congressional approval of his energy plan—but as quickly as he built things up, it seemed, they came crumbling down.

SEEDS OF REVOLUTION
Carter and the shah of Iran had their differences. Carter had won the 1976 election by presenting himself as an honest public servant. "I will never lie to you," he promised voters, who were disaffected by years of government mendacity in the Vietnam War and Watergate scandal. Carter is a man who cares deeply about basic human rights, the poor, and the infirm. He had made a powerful point in his inaugural parade when he and his wife, Roslyn, walked down Pennsylvania Avenue, rather than riding in a

JIMMY CARTER SPENT 444 DAYS ATTEMPTING TO SECURE THE RELEASE OF AMERICAN HOSTAGES IN IRAN. HIS EFFORTS WERE FUTILE, FOR WHICH THE VOTING PUBLIC DEPRIVED HIM OF A SECOND TERM.

limousine, to the site of his inauguration. Carter was one of the people. In a departure from the trappings of the "imperial presidency" of Richard Nixon, Carter even refused to have "Hail to the Chief" play every time he entered a room.

The shah of Iran, on the other hand, was not known for holding similar concerns regarding human rights. One of the wealthiest people in the world, he had a fortune that totaled well over a billion dollars, and he ruled Iran sternly. His infamous secret police force, SAVAK, was one of the most feared security forces in the world, on par with the Soviet Union's KGB. With 5,000 members, the SAVAK was notorious for its unlimited powers to arrest, interrogate, torture, and execute anyone speaking out against Pahlavi (or, as he liked to specify, against *Iran*). In a 1978 *Time* magazine interview, a top official of SAVAK offered a morbidly frank defense against "misperceptions" about his organization. Demonstrators, he explained, had recently paraded an armless man through the streets, a supposed victim of SAVAK. "In fact, [that man] was a terrorist who ... was maimed when a bomb he was making exploded," said the official, who granted the interview on the condition of anonymity. Perhaps revealing more about the secret police force than he intended, the official explained, "If SAVAK had been responsible for his injuries, we could easily have got rid of him. We would not have let him live as a document of his torture." Although the shah was a staunch ally of the West, an avid purchaser of U.S. military hardware, a despiser of Communism, and a capitalist to the core, he seemed to take his lessons on state security from the totalitarian regime sharing a northern border with his country, the Soviet Union. In addition, the courts of Iran were packed with cronies of the shah, and political corruption was rampant.

Pahlavi didn't preach what he practiced, though. At a formal reception on New Year's Eve 1977, he hosted Jimmy and Roslyn Carter at one of his palaces. Before midnight, he lifted his Champagne and toasted America's "high ideals of right and justice, moral beliefs and human value." When it was time for Carter to talk, he recited lines from an ancient Persian poem about human dignity and compassion and proposed a toast: "Iran, because of the great leadership of the shah, is an island of stability in one of the more troubled areas of the world."

While the shah, Carter, and the other guests dined in elegant luxury, in the basements, apartments, and cafes of Iran, members of every type of political group imaginable—religious fundamentalists, Russian-funded Communists, European-style socialists, Marxists, nationalists—were busy plotting the shah's overthrow. Despite differences in ideology, they had formed loose alliances with one another and were beginning to bring the middle and working classes into the fold.

Earlier that year, Carter had spoken frankly with the shah about the simmering discontent in Iran. During one of Pahlavi's many visits to the

United States (he was always given a royal reception), he met with the president and his aides in the White House. After the meeting, Carter took him into a private room and asked if he had any plans to deal pragmatically with the situation at home, namely by acceding to at least some of the people's demands. Carter explained that the public gesture of reining in SAVAK a bit might go a long way in alleviating some of the dissident groups' discontent.

"No, there is nothing I can do," Pahlavi responded. "I must enforce Iranian laws, which are designed to combat communism ... [The troublemakers] are really just a tiny minority, and have no support among the vast majority of Iranian people." Carter had a choice at this point either to let the shah continue running things as he saw fit, or begin a campaign of diplomatic arm-twisting. He chose the former. Since World War II, when Pahlavi's Nazi-sympathizing father was chased out of Iran by Russian and British forces, Pahlavi, placed in power at the age of twenty-two, had been a steady ally. And, over the years, he had done an impressive job building up Iran's economy and infrastructure using the vast wealth gained from oil production. But to his people's distress, the shah spent far more of Iran's wealth on the armed forces than was necessary for the nation's security needs.

Carter's special assistant for national security affairs, Zbigniew Brzezinski, was an unwavering supporter of the shah, and he believed that America should support him at any cost. Brzezinski was the president's most experienced foreign policy expert. He was one of the very few members of Carter's inside circle who wasn't part of the so-called "Georgia Mafia"—the group of relatively inexperienced but fiercely loyal friends with whom the former governor of Georgia surrounded himself. Carter placed great value on the wisdom of his Polish-born adviser, considered the Democrats' answer to Henry Kissinger: a hawkish practitioner of realpolitik who distrusted the Soviets and counterbalanced the president's idealism while sharing his valuation of human rights.

In early 1977, soon after the beginning of Carter's presidency, the shah had begun a half-hearted attempt at liberalization by releasing some political prisoners, easing censorship laws, and forming commissions to hear people's grievances, but it was already too late. Nine days after those New Year's Eve toasts, dozens of students were killed by government forces at a demonstration in the city of Qum. Subsequently, the masses of demonstrators swelled to unprecedented proportions and became more vitriolic, and Pahlavi's tactics for dealing with them turned more draconian. By the end of 1978, more than 3,000 demonstrators would be gunned down in the streets.

Yet, in a sixty-page briefing titled "Iran in the 1980s," the Central Intelligence Agency (CIA) told Carter that "[Iran] is not in a revolutionary or even 'prerevolutionary' situation." This complete misreading of portents of revolution was a stark example of errors to come. During the next two years,

PRESIDENTIAL BRIEFING
(1924-)
• THIRTY-NINTH PRESIDENT
OF THE UNITED STATES
(1977-81), GOVERNOR OF
GEORGIA (1970-74)
• BORN ON OCTOBER 1, 1924,
IN PLAINS, GEORGIA
• OBTAINED PANAMA CANAL
TREATIES (1977), SIGNED
SALT II TREATY WITH SOVIET
UNION (1979), ANNOUNCED
CARTER DOCTRINE,
ASSERTING U.S. PROTECTION
OF PERSIAN GULF
• MEDIATED CAMP DAVID
PEACE ACCORDS BETWEEN
ISRAEL AND EGYPT (1979)
• INITIATIVES INCLUDED
TRANSPORTATION
DEREGULATION,
ENVIRONMENTAL PROTECTION,
NEW DEPARTMENTS OF
ENERGY AND EDUCATION
• PARALYZED BY IRAN
HOSTAGE CRISIS (1979-81)
• CHALLENGED BY SENATOR
EDWARD KENNEDY FOR
DEMOCRATIC NOMINATION IN
1980; DEFEATED BY RONALD
REAGAN IN LANDSLIDE

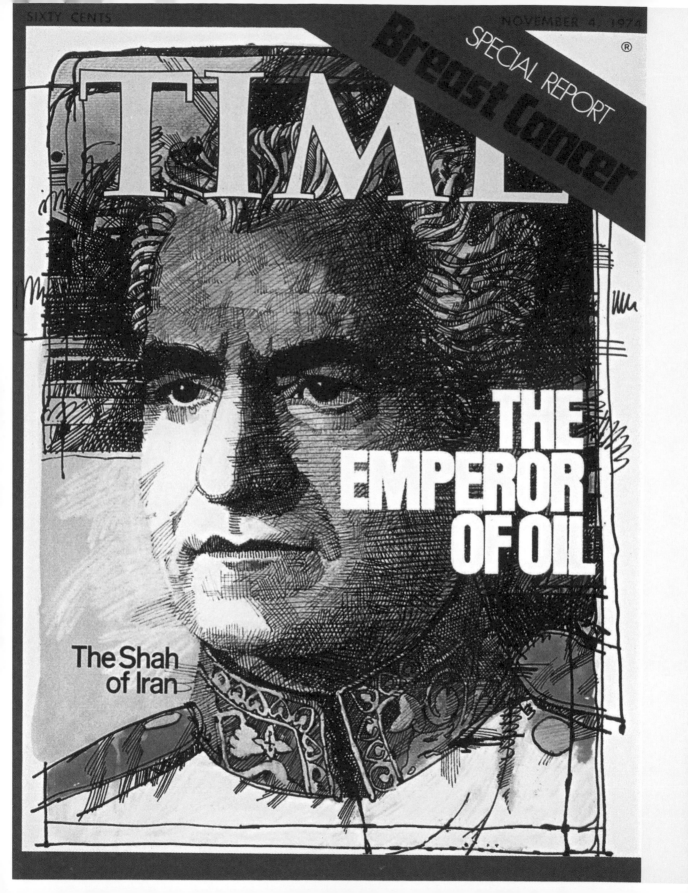

partly because of inaccurate intelligence and poor advice, but also because of his own tendency to act before consulting experts, Carter would take one misstep after another, with serious consequences for the nation, the Middle East, and his own political career.

Brzezinski's advice to Carter concerning the shah was to unconditionally "back him to the hilt," even if he wanted to create a military government—which is precisely what Pahlavi did on November 5, 1978, almost exactly a year before the American embassy was taken over. This was around the time that Ambassador William Sullivan, stationed at the Tehran embassy, began sending strong messages to the administration painting a very different picture of Iran's political situation from the CIA's view, and providing advice directly contradicting that of Brzezinski. Sullivan's opinion was that the situation was much graver than the administration realized, and he passionately urged Carter to broker a deal that would involve the military, moderates, and some of the less radical Shi'ite mullahs in a new government. In order to do so, they would have to deal directly with all the powers involved, including the Grand Ayatollah Ruhollah Khomeini.

CHARISMATIC, PIOUS, AND AN EXTRAORDINARY POLITICIAN, KHOMEINI HAD NEVER LOST POPULARITY IN IRAN, AND HE WAS CONSIDERED SOMETHING OF A MARTYR.

The ayatollah (the title means "gift of God") had been exiled in 1963 for vociferous opposition to the shah's social reforms, which included increasing women's rights and granting special legal rights to U.S. soldiers based in Iran. A popular Shi'ite cleric, Khomeini spent most of his exile in the southern Iraqi city of Al-Najaf, but he moved to France in 1978 when then Iraqi vice president Saddam Hussein, a Sunni, expelled him from the country. Charismatic, pious, and an extraordinary politician, Khomeini had never lost popularity in Iran, and he was considered something of a martyr. Although exiled, Khomeini was able to pull strings to help foment the revolution against the shah. Iranians had never forgiven the United States for its role in the coup that restored the shah to power in 1953 over the nationalist Mohammad Mosaddeq, and devout Muslims resented the Westernizing influences the shah imposed on the country. While Iranians assumed that, when the time came, the United States would try to replace the shah with another despot like him, the Grand Ayatollah gave hope of a purified, holier Iran.

Through cables and secret channels, Sullivan called so strongly for forceful action that Carter began considering him insubordinate. In Carter's memoirs, he wrote that Sullivan "seemed unable to present an objective analysis of the complicated situation in Iran." The president, whose ear belonged largely to his

THE IMAGE OF MOHAMMAD REZA SHAH PAHLAVI ADORNS THE COVER OF A 1974 ISSUE OF *TIME* MAGAZINE. THE SHAH OF IRAN WAS A GREAT ALLY OF AMERICA, BUT CAME TO BE DETESTED BY HIS OWN PEOPLE.

national security advisor, began generally ignoring Sullivan's communiqués. Brzezinski believed that the shah—a man who had weathered an incredible amount of friction during his thirty-seven-year reign, including two assassination attempts—was Iran's only hope. His contacts in Iran were informing him that the Iranian military and the provisional government were still loyal to the shah and could no doubt maintain order.

Secretary of State Cyrus Vance advised Carter to take an approach that was more cautious, albeit more active. He argued the importance of forming relationships with other leaders and groups in Iran to help smooth the transition and avoid all-out revolution. America would be inserting itself more directly into Iran's troubles, but in the end, Vance believed, this tactic would result in a more peaceful resolution and the formation of a government more sympathetic to the United States.

Carter took two paths of least resistance. Although he didn't throw his support fully behind the shah, as Brzezinski had advised, he did not abandon him. By keeping the shah at arm's length, he was taking Vance's approach of general caution (which was most likely his own instinct, anyway), but he did not reach out to the opposition. It was a recipe for disaster. Khomeini's supporters read Carter's actions as a complete backing of their enemy, and in the West the president appeared as indecisive and weak.

Had intelligence coming out of Iran been more accurate, the president might have received different advice. But almost everyone in the U.S. government had completely underestimated Khomeini's power and influence. And they didn't yet understand how weak the shah's position in Iran was at this point. There were more CIA agents in Iran per capita than in any other nation on earth, yet the superpower that the Ayatollah would call "the Great Satan" somehow missed the signs of incipient revolution, the people's hatred of the shah and of the United States.

THE WANDERING SHAH
By the end of 1978, President Carter, notwithstanding the influence of Brzezinski, was not passionately supportive of the shah—and the world knew it. When Carter was asked in a December press conference if he thought the shah would return to power, he replied, "I don't know, I hope so … We personally prefer that the shah maintain a major role in the government, but that's a decision for the Iranian people to make." Carter simply was not going to take a lead role to help solve Iran's problems.

Whether this emboldened the Iranian revolutionaries and Khomeini, who was now living in France, is up for speculation, but in 1979, Iran exploded. Anti-shah/anti-American demonstrations attracted millions, and Khomeini's rhetoric became ever more aggressive. In addition to calling for the shah's overthrow, he

urged his followers to attack American targets as well. He wouldn't budge from his position that the shah had to face justice; there was no place for Pahlavi in Iran beyond swinging from a Tehran light pole. Khomeini knew he had no reason to negotiate with anyone. He alone understood the extent of his own power.

President Carter remained passive. He would not give up the shah, yet he would not commit America fully to diffusing the situation in Iran. Sullivan sent his warnings, but they fell on deaf ears. The president was firmly in Brzezinski's camp. Pahlavi, at the urging of his military government, fled Iran on January 16, 1979. A trained pilot, he flew the plane himself. Two weeks later, Khomeini returned to Iran and was greeted by millions of adoring followers. Khomeini laid down the law: The shah's government would be dissolved, he (Khomeini) would appoint a new one, Iran would become an Islamic theocracy, and the shah would return to meet his maker. He made good on all promises, except the last.

Throughout most of 1979, as the ayatollah brought order and organization to Iran, which included the executions of many hundreds of "sinners," the staff employees in the American embassy scrambled to figure out their role in this new nation—as did the approximately 800 military personnel stationed throughout the country, which Carter did not deploy back to the States. Many soldiers lived on C-rations in apartments with no heat because the bills simply couldn't be paid; the country was basically shut down for business. Three days prior to the ayatollah's return, an air force major was shot in the street by radicals. (He survived.) Two weeks later, the embassy was overrun and the staff held captive, but Sullivan was able to negotiate their freedom after a day. Still, Khomeini's followers maintained an "occupying force" inside for months.

RATHER THAN CONDEMN THE ENEMIES OF THE "ISLAND OF STABILITY," CARTER SENT A MESSAGE TO THE BURGEONING THEOCRACY: THE UNITED STATES WOULD LIKE TO BE YOUR FRIEND.

With Iran firmly in the hands of the religious fundamentalists, the Carter administration had something to sink its teeth into. At least America had one thing in common with the ayatollah that the Russians didn't: religion. In the hope that Khomeini would soon understand that ayatollahs are meant for religion and that bureaucrats are meant for politics, the administration was confident that he would soon give in to more moderate political factions. Accommodation was the most easily defined course of action. Rather than condemn the enemies of the "island of stability," Carter sent a message to the burgeoning theocracy: The United States would like to be your friend. However, he did decide to bring the majority of the 1,000 embassy staffers home, leaving a skeleton force of seventy.

Carter had positioned himself between Khomeini and the shah, but he began feeling the pressure to make a choice between one or the other. He received phone calls from Henry Kissinger and David Rockefeller, both friends of the shah, asking him to offer sanctuary to Pahlavi. They had arranged for him to live at the palatial Annenberg Estate in Palm Springs, California. This Carter could not do, and, in saying so, basically abandoned the shah. Critics railed that this was a bigger blunder than the president's handling of the crisis to begin with. The political battle in Iran was all but lost. Once the damage had been done, wouldn't it be better to at least send the message that America is loyal to its allies?

In the fall of 1979, Shah Pahlavi was living in Mexico, where he was being treated for cancer. (He had flown from Egypt to Morocco, but when the Moroccan president's family was threatened by Khomeini supporters, Pahlavi decided to move to the Bahamas. The billionaire considered it "too expensive" there and moved to Mexico.) The Mexican facilities were inadequate for treating his ailment, malignant lymphoma, and the shah's friends, including Kissinger and Rockefeller, began lobbying Carter to allow him entry into the country on humanitarian reasons. They had hit the president's soft spot. After consulting with Vance, Carter consented and the shah arrived in New York on October 22, 1979. Thirteen days later, on November 4, the American embassy was overrun.

"AMERICA CANNOT DO A DAMN THING" The students' original plan was to occupy the embassy for three days. The international incident would attract cameras and reporters from around the world. The students would use the press to air their many grievances against the West, most of all, America's harboring of the hated shah.

In the weeks and months leading up to the takeover, huge crowds had gathered outside the embassy. Spray-painted slogans and posters of the ayatollah decorated the embassy's surrounding wall, now capped with steel spikes. By and large, though, the marchers were peaceful. But this Sunday, November 4, the remaining staff inside the compound saw thousands of Iranians breaking open the security gate and pouring into the compound. Looking out the bullet-proof windows, they wished the embassy had been closed in response to the planned "Students Day" march, as a few people had suggested.

CIA Station Chief Thomas Ahern immediately ran downstairs to the furnace and began feeding it with sensitive files. There were additional CIA files, though, in other areas of the compound, the discovery of which would lead the ayatollah to call the embassy a "nest of spies." In reality, most embassies have CIA agents on staff, and they're usually more active in the spying business than the ones in Tehran had been. None of the agents there spoke Farsi. The students didn't know this, however, and they were completely taken in by the ayatollah's words. They believed they had stumbled onto a mountain of evidence against America. Largely due to Khomeini's rhetoric, the situation went from a brief publicity stunt to a 444-day ordeal. (Ambassador Sullivan had been replaced by this point, and he was not one of the hostages.)

There is no evidence that Khomeini was directly involved in the planning of the embassy takeover, but there is no doubt that once it happened, it suited his purposes. So popular and powerful was the ayatollah that he could make or break the standoff with one sentence, and his words would reveal what he had in mind for the future of Iran. Would he join the civilized world and react with moderation, or was he planning to found a nation that held Islamic sha'ria law higher than Western standards of international law?

Khomeini wasted no time stoking the fire. During the first days of the crisis, he praised the hostage-takers as "expressing the will of the people," referred to America as "the Great Satan," and double-dared Carter with the now-famous words, "Our youth should be confident that America cannot do a damn thing." And Carter blinked ... for almost six months.

On November 19, the hostage-takers allowed fourteen embassy staffers free: women (Khomeini claimed that Muslims don't commit violence against women), African Americans (the hostage-takers considered them victims of American domestic policy), and one person diagnosed with multiple sclerosis.

So far, no military operation had been undertaken. But plans were in the works.

In February 1980, Carter authorized secret negotiations with the Iranian provisional government. They were carried out by one of the most loyal and influential members of Carter's aides, Chief of Staff Hamilton Jordan, who would leave Washington with undercover CIA escorts and dressed in disguise. Jordan met in Paris with Iranian foreign minister Sadegh Ghotbzadeh, one of the ayatollah's closest advisors, who conveyed Khomeini's desire for a resolution to the crisis. After two meetings, the second of which occurred on April 18, neither side would accede completely to the other's demands. It ended with Ghotbzadeh saying sadly, "My friend, I'm afraid it will be a long time before your people come home."

Carter's patience was at an end. He had taken some early steps not so much to get the hostages out of Tehran—that was completely out of the realm of possibility for the time being—but to cushion the beating America's image as a world power was taking. Carter had called for an embargo of Iranian oil and froze its assets in the U.S. Then he deported all Iranian students without proper papers. The Democratic president even went so far as to ban pro-Iranian demonstrations on federal property.

With the failure of the negotiations, though, Carter needed to take more direct measures. It was an election year, and Massachusetts senator Ted Kennedy was running a strong campaign against him for the nomination. In November, Carter had led in the polls, widely attributed to a "rally around the flag" effect after the Americans were taken hostage. But as the crisis wore on, and the public's patience dissipated, Kennedy began making strong gains, and the president began listening more and more to Brzezinski's advice to launch a covert rescue operation that had been in the training stages since November.

Vance vocalized his opposition to military action by threatening to resign if the mission were launched. Carter's final decision was made in a meeting with Brzezinski and other members of the National Security Council in April. Vance happened to be on vacation at the time and had sent his deputy, Warren Christopher, in his place. When Vance found out about the decision, he rushed back to the White House to change Carter's mind, but it was too late. The president wanted immediate action. (Critics of Brzezinski claim that he used Vance's absence as a means to influence the president on the military decision; Brzezinski refutes this charge, arguing that Vance had previously joined him in

THE APRIL 1980 HOSTAGE RESCUE MISSION IN ENDED IN FAILURE OF THE OBJECTIVE, EIGHT MILITARY PERSONNEL KILLED, AND AMERICAN IRE DIRECTED AT CARTER. HERE YOU SEE THE SCORCHED WRECKAGE OF A C-130 AFTER ITS MIDAIR COLLISION WITH A U.S. HELICOPTER.

recommending risky reconnaissance missions in preparation for the operation, and that when Vance raised objections, another meeting was held for him to do so among all members of the National Security Council.) Vance made good on his threat and submitted his resignation three days after the mission. He was replaced by Christopher.

The audacious two-day mission, named Operation Eagle Claw, called for the secret establishment of an airstrip in the Iranian desert (Desert One). From there, special operations teams would fly six helicopters to a second location near Tehran (Desert Two), where they would link up with CIA contacts in the city. In the dead of night, the team would overpower the hostage-takers and escort the hostages to a soccer stadium nearby, where they would be airlifted out by helicopter, flown to Desert One to board C-130 transport planes, and then flown out of Iran. That was the plan.

Operation Eagle Claw ended soon after it was launched on April 24. A small, surprise sandstorm malfunctioned the Sea Stallion helicopters' instruments, forcing two of the helicopters to return to the USS *Nimitz* in the Indian Ocean and one of the helicopters to be abandoned in the desert. Because the mission required a minimum of six helicopters, it was aborted at Desert One. As one helicopter repositioned itself to allow another one to refuel, it struck a C-130 transport plane packed with fuel. Both aircraft exploded, and eight crew members were killed. The next day, Iranians took footage of the smoldering wrecks and aired the images for the world to see.

Although Carter had no control over the events of the operation, he felt the full brunt of the mission's failure. Until this point, he had appeared weak and indecisive in the standoff against the Iranian revolutionaries. Now, right or wrong, many people saw him as wholly ineffectual, a ridiculous president. In *Prophet from Plains*, Frye Gaillard wrote:

> For a nation searching for images to explain Jimmy Carter, to account, somehow, for the mounting sense of things out of control, the chaos in the desert became a brutal symbol. Even years later it was the very way many Americans—and certainly the most cynical and unforgiving members of the news media—interpreted not only Carter's effectiveness as a president but also, it seemed, the very essence of his manhood.

By autumn 1980, as the year anniversary of the as-planned three-day embassy takeover approached, Khomeini and the hostage-takers had had enough. They had succeeded in their political aims (the revolution was complete), and the shah had died from cancer in July.

Khomeini began to learn, as have so many radicals and revolutionaries before him, that running a country is vastly more difficult than running a revolution. On September 22, Iraq's president Saddam Hussein invaded Iran, beginning a protracted eight-year war, with the United States favoring Iraq. If the Iranians had felt the pinch of economic embargoes and frozen assets before, they felt the effects tenfold during the war. The hostages had become a burden.

Khomeini offered a deal for the release of the hostages, which required the return of the shah's fortune to Iran, the freeing up of Iranian assets in the United States, and a promise not to interfere in Iranian affairs. Iran's parliament backed the measure. Carter accepted the offer, except for returning the shah's money. By January 19, 1981, the two sides finally agreed to a deal. After 444 days in captivity, the hostages were flown to Algiers and from there traveled to a U.S. air base in Germany, where Carter, now an ex-president, met them on the tarmac.

CONCLUSION Hamilton Jordan, Jimmy Carter's chief of staff in 1979, was perhaps the most loyal member of the president's inner circle. Jordan was so devoted to Carter that he was working harder than ever during the final moments of his tenure—Inauguration Day, 1981. Ronald Reagan had crushed Carter in the November election for a number of reasons, probably the most public and prominent of which was Carter's handling of the hostage crisis. Watching the inauguration ceremony on television, Jordan held a phone receiver to each ear, trying desperately to learn whether the hostages had been released. Reagan's right hand went up, and he took the oath. Jordan's hope that his friend might enjoy one bright moment vanished as the final seconds of his presidency ticked away. (Many people claimed afterward that in October Ronald Reagan and George H. W. Bush had made a secret deal with Iranians, including Khomeini himself, to delay the hostages' release until after the election, thus preventing a sudden surge of support for Carter when the hostages were released. A great deal of circumstantial evidence supports the theory, but a 1984 congressional investigation concluded that the "October surprise" charge was groundless.)

As a leader, Carter had many strengths. Neither Republicans nor Democrats questioned his exceptional intelligence and uncanny ability to quickly develop a deep understanding of any issue put before him. Carter was able to see all sides of an issue without bias, and he had brilliant foresight when it came to the future of America. His ideas about America's energy use were far ahead of his time. And his ability to develop trusting rapports with world leaders were borne out during the Sadat-Begin talks.

But Carter lacked the decision-making abilities needed to deal with the hostage crisis. To be fair, it would have been a legacy-breaker for most presidents, but Carter was particularly ill-equipped to handle it. Sol Linowitz, a lawyer who aided the president in the return of the Panama Canal to Panama in 1977, once said of Carter, "He learned by gathering details and putting them together, but there wasn't always the time to learn that way … He had an unusually strong grasp of what he wanted to accomplish but an uncertain hold on how to go about it." This approach impeded Carter's success in many of his objectives. His failure to move his energy plan through the Democratic Congress was the most blatant example of the president's inability to form a coherent plan of action. (As one historian said, "He seemed to think that if a decision were correct, it would sell itself.") In the case of the hostage crisis, it resulted in utter disaster.

During the crisis, Carter made each decision as it came and never quite formed a clear strategy to secure the release of the embassy staff. As historian Stephen E. Ambrose observed in his book *Rise to Globalism: American Foreign Policy Since 1938*:

> The President was widely perceived, by [mid-1980], as having gone from blunder to blunder. In an admittedly difficult situation, his decisions had been consistently wrong—his failure to support the shah

when the revolution began, his failure to open lines of communication with Khomeini, his recognition of a government in Iran that could not govern, his decision to allow the shah into the United States, his highly emotional response to the taking of the hostages, his long-delayed and then botched use of the military rescue option.

By failing to take a firm position on America's relationship with the shah, Carter lost the battle with Khomeini from the get-go. Gaillard points out that prior to the dramatic embassy takeover, "Carter was committed to both imperatives of his Iranian policy—support for the shah and support for human rights—and he was determined to avoid the necessity of a choice." After the embassy takeover, he faced crisis upon crisis and had no choice but to make quick decisions. Because Carter had no time to develop a coherent policy, his decisions were made in a vacuum. They weren't connected in any way to an overall strategy.

BY FAILING TO TAKE A FIRM POSITION ON AMERICA'S RELATIONSHIP WITH THE SHAH, CARTER LOST THE BATTLE WITH KHOMEINI FROM THE GET-GO.

Reagan exploited this fact beautifully during the campaign, positioning himself as a strong, decisive alternative to the weak-kneed man from Georgia. According to Reagan, the Soviets were banging on the gates of America. It was a theme he returned to again and again. Did Americans want a ruggedly handsome, tough-talking "cold warrior" to keep them at bay or a peanut farmer who had let ignorant ragtag radicals push him around? Carter had a number of problems as he entered the race against Reagan. He had created a dysfunctional relationship with Congress and, therefore, he had few real legislative successes to brag about during his campaign. Gas prices were high, as was inflation. Americans didn't have to think long when Reagan asked them, "Are you better off now than you were four years ago?"

But the hostage situation was the most clear-cut sign of Carter's flaws. The economy and foreign oil prices are exceedingly complex, the control of which does not belong completely to the president. The hostage situation, however, was simple to grasp: It was Jimmy Carter vs. the Ayatollah Khomeini. Carter lost every battle and, in the end, the war. Iran was in the hands of religious fundamentalists, and on election day 444 Americans were still being held captive. How could Reagan lose?

ENERGY CRISIS AND "MALAISE"

JIMMY CARTER

THE POLICE OFFICER TOOK THE STATEMENT FROM CLYDE SLAUGHTER, THE OWNER of a gas station on Sharpe Avenue in Staten Island. Slaughter had called the NYPD with the complaint that he had been threatened by a man holding what appeared to be a handgun concealed by a greasy rag.

It didn't take long for the cops to pick up forty-five-year-old Louis Braddix—a man with a short temper and an empty tank. Braddix was by no means a hardened criminal; he just needed gas. After waiting in line at the gas station for more than an hour, Braddix wanted what was coming to him—his three-dollar quota of leaded gasoline. But when the pump ran dry at just half that amount, he approached Slaughter and said he wanted the rest of his quota's worth from another tank. Slaughter told him to go back to the end of the line. Braddix lost it.

Although such altercations weren't common across the nation, they weren't unheard of, either, and minor squabbles near gas pumps were the order of the day. All a newspaper reporter had to do on a slow day was visit the nearest gas station to pick up a quick human-interest story.

From October 1973 to March 1974, every American with a driver's license felt the squeeze from the Mideast. The Yom Kippur War had begun on October 6, and the Organization of the Petroleum Exporting Countries (OPEC), composed mostly of Arab nations, decided to punish the superpower that had supplied Israel with the tanks and fighter jets that were making short work of the

Egyptian and Syrian armies. OPEC began cutting its output by five percent and pledging to do the same every year until Israel withdrew from Gaza and Jerusalem. As a result, oil and gasoline prices soared. Unable to meet the high cost of fuel, and more important, fearing a greater shortage in the future, factories and other businesses began cutting production, then workers.

America had only recently begun to depend on OPEC for fuel. In 1913, the United States produced two-thirds of the world's oil, and its dominance in World War II was largely due to its vast resources. After the war, the United States was mostly a self-sufficient producer of oil. But during the 1950s and '60s, Americans began dramatically increasing their energy use, and by the 1970s, the country was swallowing a full one-third of the world's energy—giving an excessive amount of power to OPEC. Through World War II and the years beyond, European petroleum companies based in the Middle East got oil for cut rates. But the Arabs had begun to realize how much leverage oil gave them—especially given Europe's and America's increasing demands for fuel. By connecting the embargo to the Yom Kippur War, the oil-producing nations of the Middle East had asserted a new kind of independence from the West, using oil as a "weapon" to shape politics. OPEC became, in essence, as much an instrument of political leverage as a business.

OPEC ended the oil embargo five months later, but it had lasted long enough to make Americans aware—many for the first time—that fuel is not limitless, and that its costs go well beyond the dollars paid at the gas pump. For his part, President Richard Nixon had introduced the Clean Air Act of 1970, created the Natural Resources Department and Environmental Protection Agency, begun looking seriously into building more nuclear energy plants, and attempted to enact a federal speed limit of 50 mph. In order to keep costs down, Nixon also enacted strict price controls on domestic oil. With the gas lines fresh on their minds, legislators began pushing Nixon's proposals through Congress. But when the Watergate scandal hit, the energy issue faded into obscurity.

In August 1974, after Nixon's resignation, President Gerald R. Ford picked up where the disgraced president had left off. When Ford entered office, he introduced the Energy Independence Act, which included proposals to encourage automobile manufacturers to build more fuel-efficient cars and promote energy efficiency in homes and buildings.

What Congress ended up passing was but a fraction of Ford's original plan, but the issue of energy was on the table, for the time being at least. America's increasing use of fuel and other energy was suddenly a major political topic, domestically and globally. By 1977, the country was using 1.85 billion metric tons of oil annually. In comparison, all of western Europe used 1.28 billion. Per capita, the United States burned twice as much fuel as Britain and West Germany. Yet because the United States still supplied some of its own oil, and because Congress had extended the price controls after Nixon's departure, America was still paying much less per gallon than Europeans were.

THE WAR ON ENERGY When Jimmy Carter won the election in 1976, he spoke often about "healing the nation." America, still smarting from Vietnam and Watergate, was a ship without a compass. Carter, a former naval officer, promised to restore economic prosperity and faith in government. "This inauguration ceremony marks a new beginning, a new dedication within our government, and a new spirit among us all," he told the nation on January 1977. A born-again Christian with a strong belief in the power of morale, as well as his own ability to inspire it, Carter spoke mostly about America's important role in human rights and the worldwide spread of democracy. A country's sagging economy and serious energy issues don't make for exciting speeches, but he knew that tackling these practical issues was going to be key to his presidency.

Within two weeks of the beginning of his term, Carter tasked James R. Schlesinger, former secretary of defense under Nixon and Ford and future head of the Energy Department (a cabinet-level department that Carter would soon create), with devising a comprehensive energy plan for the country. Schlesinger was given a deadline of ninety days and instructed to work as secretly as possible in order to prevent the Republicans from building up a comprehensive critique before the plan was announced. Critics would later maintain that the nearly impossible deadline resulted in an unworkable plan, and administration insiders complained that Schlesinger and his team were so clandestine that many key figures were prevented from offering technical and political advice that might have benefited everyone.

Carter's desire to work in secrecy was an early indicator of one of his crippling flaws, which was a general disdain for politics. He believed so strongly in his own ability to enact change that he seemed to take no notice of the realities of Washington. Upon entering office, Carter surrounded himself almost exclusively with friends and cronies from Georgia (later referred to as the "Georgia Mafia" in the newspapers) who weren't just unfamiliar with the ways of Washington but were also clearly uninterested in learning about it. One of Carter's closest advisors and later chief of staff—brash, young Hamilton Jordan—made the president's policy toward Congress clear by refusing to return its members' calls—and later bragged about it! And during a conversation with Speaker of the House Tip O'Neill, Carter once said that if Congress refused to pass legislation he wanted, he would go over their heads to the people—a remarkable statement about a governing body that represents "the people."

Well aware of how plans inevitably get tied up in Congress, Carter wanted action as quickly as possible. He also began receiving diplomatic pressure from his European Cold War allies regarding the subject of energy. Europe, too, was experiencing a serious spate of economic stagnation, and America's exorbitant use of imported oil was considered a large part of the problem. For most of its history, America had been a nearly self-sufficient producer of oil. As a result, fuel prices were relatively low, and Americans had become accustomed to consuming at a higher rate. But by the early 1970s, the known stores of domestic oil were drying up, and although there was plenty of oil in reserve, fears of shortages began taking over. The oil industry argued that because of the price controls keeping profits at a minimum, it couldn't afford to explore for more reserves.

As fear of fuel shortages grew during the Nixon and Ford presidencies, the United States began importing more and more oil from the Middle East. America's unabated consumption (in 1973 it consumed one-third of the world's energy) empowered the OPEC nations, which began raising prices globally. The price controls in the United States kept prices still relatively low, but Europe was suffering. "[E]nergy shortages and price surges were causing widespread unemployment and inflation in all our countries, as well as serious imbalance in world trade," Carter wrote in his memoirs. "Our nation's inability to deal with so crucial a question was becoming an international embarrassment." The Europeans, led by France and Germany, demanded that the United States remove its price controls and allow the global market to dictate prices. In a show of resolve and solidarity, nine European nations placed pressure on the United States by pledging to cut their own consumption in half within seven years.

In July 1978, President Carter met with the leaders of France, West Germany, Great Britain, Japan, and other Western nations, in Bonn, Germany, in an energy summit where he reaffirmed his commitment to curbing Americans' oil use. Carter pledged to lift existing price controls on American oil, which had been designed to ensure a steady but very low rate of price increases. Fuel costs would rise quickly and put America on an equal price footing with the rest of the world. The thinking was that this would both force Americans to conserve energy and promote a boom of investment in oil exploration and alternative supplies. OPEC would then be forced to lower prices. It might have been a persuasive theory, but America also had high inflation to contend with, which an immediate jump in prices of a commodity such as oil certainly wasn't going to help.

The president had publicly launched his National Energy Plan (NEP) in a televised speech on April 18, 1977, famously wearing a sweater instead of a jacket and tie a symbolic gesture implying he had turned down the heat in the White House, and that Americans would have to get used to doing so in their own homes. "Tonight I want to have an unpleasant talk with you about a problem that is unprecedented in our history," he began. "With the exception of preventing war, this is the greatest challenge that our country will face during our lifetime." He told the American public that at the rate at which they were using oil, domestic supplies would quickly dry up. To fix the problem, he contended, was the "moral equivalent to war." This was an echo of President Lyndon B. Johnson's "war on poverty." Many Americans, though, were skeptical that there was actually a fuel shortage; the oil companies, they maintained, were withholding supplies simply to drive up prices. Carter put the nation on notice, warning of a future plagued with unemployment and inflation rates even higher than they already were. Keep consuming oil at the present rate, he implied, and we'll be handing the country over to OPEC—an organization that had proven in 1973 that it was more than willing to wage economic war against America. "If we fail to act soon," the president warned, "we will face an economic, social, and political crisis that will threaten our free institutions."

The speech signaled that Carter was a greater supporter of conservation than increased domestic exploration and production, which he viewed as a short-term solution. To use a term that was then gaining currency among environmentalists, the only *sustainable*, long-term solution was a change in "the American way of life." A main part of reaching Carter's goal would require the placement of taxes on domestic fuel. This, of course, infuriated the oil industry. One of Carter's campaign pledges to his supporters in the oil business was to deregulate prices, which was a promise that the oilmen translated into major profits. Carter's taxing of fuel was viewed as a breach of that promise. Carter's response was that he didn't break the promise, though he may have "bent" it.

Given the fact that Carter was planning to oversee a politically suicidal program ensuring that Americans paid more at the pump, he had little choice but to approach the problem with an attitude of "you can't please all the people all the time." For better or worse, this approach doesn't often work out for presidents in search of a second term. Carter was aware of this, of course. After his election, he commented that he was going to solve the energy problem even if it cost him a second term. For this disregard of politics in the name of what he viewed as the public good, his friends called him brave; his critics called him naïve and stubborn. As a *New York Times* writer put it "It is doubtful that the public will rally quickly to Mr. Carter's trumpet ... [T]o the ordinary householder the problem of how to pay last month's fuel bill looms much larger than whether there'll be enough fuel, at any price, in the winter of 1985."

The week following the speech, Carter outlined the details of his NEP to Congress, and he received his first dose of congressional sloth.

The NEP passed through the House quickly and with almost no changes added to it. In order to prevent serious delays, Democratic Speaker of the House O'Neill had created an ad hoc subcommittee, packed with cronies, that was able to bypass the numerous other committees that would have otherwise been involved. Within three months, the plan moved on to the Senate, which proved to be a much more painful affair. The chairman of the Senate Finance Committee, Russell Long, was a Democrat, as was his father, Louisiana governor and senator Huey P. Long. But his loyalties did not lie with the president—Republican or Democrat. "I'm the president's friend," he once said of Ford, "but I'm not his boy. I don't represent the president in the Senate. I represent the people of Louisiana." And among the Louisianans Long had to please were those who operated the state's extensive oil and natural gas industry. The senator took particular offense to one section of the NEP, the wellhead tax on oil. The tax, which had passed through Congress, was designed to promote conservation. It called for a 63 percent rise in oil prices by the end of Carter's term. (By comparison, oil prices increased about 400 percent between 2000 and 2007.) Consumers would receive a portion of the tax monies as rebates. Long was fine with the taxes, as long as the rebates went to the oil industry, which he

said would be put toward exploration and alternative energy research. Oil industry jobs were more valuable to his constituents than tax rebate checks. Long was known as a master horse trader, but there would be no compromising here. Commenting on his experience, Carter would later say, "The energy legislation was tedious, like chewing on a rock that lasted the whole four years."

PRESIDENT OR PREACHER? On July 15, 1979, Carter addressed the nation once again on the subject of oil and energy consumption. It was considered the most important speech of his presidency. This time Carter wore a suit—more appropriate attire for a serious address—to deliver what has been referred to as his "malaise" speech (although Carter never actually used the word in his remarks). Still considering himself the "people's president," he had canceled an address that had been planned for ten days earlier in order to invite ordinary citizens to Camp David, where he listened to what they had to say about the state of the nation. Carter spoke again, this time in greater detail, about the need to conserve energy, including his plans to conserve five million barrels of oil per day and enact a gasoline rationing program.

What Carter was most remembered for, however, was his tone. During the speech, he read quotations from the people he had met with at Camp David, many of whom were scathingly critical of his leadership. Carter proceeded to speak about America as a nation strong but confused, disjointed, and spiritually adrift—and of the American people as suffering from a "crisis of confidence." Carter was extraordinarily forthright, in terms of both the nation's problems and his own. He came across as a caring, intelligent, passionate, yet vulnerable man. "I realize more than ever that as president I need your help," he said. He readily admitted his faults and failures, and he confessed that in his busyness in the Oval Office and in dealing with foreign policy matters he had lost touch with the American people. The decision to convey such a message was a huge gamble. Did Americans need to hear a confession from the chief executive, the commander in chief? More important, from a political perspective, did they *want* to?

If Carter had been hoping to rally the public to prompt a grassroots, "trickle-up" pressure on their representatives in Congress, which had thus far showed little enthusiasm for enacting new energy legislation, he was to be very disappointed. The safest way for a member of Congress to live to serve another term is to disappear into the crowd. One representative, interviewed before the speech about Carter's chances of getting the public to passionately support his cause, said, "Every time you have to vote on the floor, you displease some of your constituents. The fewer votes, the fewer enemies you make. I don't hear anyone back home shouting for more laws, but I know there are six guys flyspecking my record, just waiting for the 1980 election."

Carter had put himself into the role of easy prey, allowing Republicans to exploit his growing reputation as a weak, vacillating leader halfway through the campaign season. After the speech, soon-to-be-vice-president George H. W. Bush, then in the early stages of his own presidential run (before being picked for vice president by Ronald Reagan), wondered aloud "how much follow-through, courage, and leadership the president will have in standing up to the special interests in his own party and in his own country." And former California governor Reagan commented, "President Carter identified the problems clearly, but he spoke about them as if he and his administration had not been at the center of them for two and a half years."

CARTER HAD PUT HIMSELF INTO THE ROLE OF EASY PREY, ALLOWING REPUBLICANS TO EXPLOIT HIS GROWING REPUTATION AS A WEAK, VACILLATING LEADER HALFWAY THROUGH THE CAMPAIGN SEASON.

After the speech, Carter's approval ratings rose from a dismal 24 percent to a slightly less dismal 37 percent. Most polls showed, too, a boost in the number of Americans who were optimistic that Carter's new proposals were sound. But the gains were short-lived. A president's general image—his "character"—is vastly more important for self-preservation than the details he hammers out on TV. Details don't win elections, as Ronald Reagan well knew. Although Reagan was considered something of a hawk, thanks partly to a Carter campaign strategy that portrayed him as such, Reagan in the 1980 election campaign didn't enjoy quite as much popularity over Carter as his subsequent landslide victory would imply. Two weeks before the election, in fact, Carter's advisors had concluded that Reagan's campaign was stagnating and that their own was gaining momentum, and polls bore them out. However, during a debate just days before the election, Carter lost any momentum he might have made. At one point during the debate, he said, "I had a discussion with my daughter, Amy, the other day, before I came here, to ask her what the most important issue was. She said she thought nuclear weaponry—and the control of nuclear arms." As the audience let out a groan, Carter must have recalled, too late, his aides' advice not to mention the conversation with Amy, who at the time was all of thirteen years old.

And Reagan found ample opportunity to shred Carter's image. As Carter, a detail-oriented micromanager to the core, badgered Reagan about past comments and unsuccessful policy decisions, Reagan remarked: "There you go again." It was a master stroke, a perfect four-word sound bite that summed up the public's diminishing patience with a man who spent too much time on details and too little on solving the problems.

The description Tom Wolfe once offered of Carter as a "matronly-voiced, Sunday-school, soft-shelled, watery-eyed, sponge-backed Millennial lulu" is an exaggeration, to say the least, but standing on stage next to a trained actor keenly honed into his weaknesses and excited to exploit them, Carter came across as anything but a take-charge president.

THE BEST OF PRESIDENTS, THE WORST OF PRESIDENTS Perhaps
Carter was ahead of his time. To a generation beset by rising oil prices and fears of irrevocable climate change from carbon emissions, and a nation wishing "to free ourselves from dependence on foreign oil," as all the candidates say, Carter's policy ideas do seem to have been vindicated. Most now agree that, as President Carter pointed out three decades ago, a change in the nation's approach to fuel consumption is necessary to the future of our economy and national security. Even President George W. Bush warned in a State of the Union address that America is "addicted to oil," surprising words from a former oilman, though not accompanied by any specific plans or actions. Carter's public comments, especially in his "malaise" speech, went where no president had gone before. Holding to his theme of a war on the energy problem, he said, "Every act of energy conservation ... is more than just common sense—I tell you it is an act of patriotism." Carter was certainly the first president to put solar energy panels on the White House roof. (They were later removed by Reagan.) But as Carter so often did, he attacked the country's problems in less than effective ways. In times of peace, a president often finds it difficult to convince the public to sacrifice. It goes against the grain of a consumer society—a national economy driven more by wants than needs—to tell the people that it is time to conserve, to alter their everyday ways of life, to willingly make do with less.

It is important to recognize that Carter inherited the problems he faced. Inflation began rising before he ran for office, and Americans had enjoyed some five or six decades of carefree consumption of gas and oil. But the measure of a president is what he does about the nation's problems during the years of his term. Carter's uneven handling of the Iran hostage crisis, dramatic shake-ups of his staff, and problems dealing with Congress all put on display his managerial shortcomings. When the Iranians cut back on exports to the West as a result of America's support of the shah, American drivers once again found themselves waiting in long gas lines. Many blamed the president, whom they had slowly but surely become accustomed to viewing as weak and indecisive.

In the end, Carter didn't win a second term; he was the first incumbent president to lose an election since Herbert Hoover in 1932. In itself, this is not necessarily a failure, given that he was willing to sacrifice his future as president in order to solve the energy problem. This is a noble idea, to be sure, and one that is rarely seen in politics, especially at the presidential level. Carter did not possess the leadership qualities to make that sacrifice worthwhile, though. The populist Carter said that the "people are looking for honest answers, not easy answers." In this, he showed that he was decidedly out of touch with Americans, and again showed himself as politically naïve because he failed to see that the electorate invariably *does* look for easy answers to such problems as energy. Whereas "we the people" tend to want leaders to solve the problems for us, Carter was asking the public to sacrifice without spelling out how it would pay off. In order to present and oversee a long-term plan regarding energy efficiency, any president would need at least eight years.

But Carter truly believed that "if a decision was correct, it would sell itself," in the words of historian Gary Sick. As a result, he too often refused to use politics as a means to foster change. Vice President Walter Mondale noted, "Carter thought politics was sinful. The worst thing you could say to Carter if you wanted to do something was that it was politically the best thing to do."

Carter's populist approach of "going over the heads of Congressmen" to appeal directly to the people was ill-advised. A man of ideas, he was never an inspiring speaker. He had won the 1976 election based on America's strong desire for change, vague as that desire might have been. Carter's was certainly a brilliantly run campaign, but that was despite the candidate's lack of television presence, so vividly illustrated during his most important speech and, especially, during the debate with "The Great Communicator" on the eve of the 1980 election.

CHAPTER 19

THE IRAN-CONTRA AFFAIR

RONALD REAGAN

IN EARLY NOVEMBER 1986, SECRETARY OF STATE GEORGE P. SHULTZ WAS TRAVELING to a conference in Vienna when reporters' questions alerted him that trouble was breaking out from a certain harebrained scheme he'd thought President Ronald Reagan's cabinet had rejected.

An arms-for-hostages deal that had been proposed by "loose cannons" on the National Security Council (NSC) staff the previous year—which he and Defense Secretary Caspar Weinberger had rejected as illegal and outrageous— not only hadn't gone away, but had metastasized into a full-blown scandal. If the president did not act quickly, acknowledge mistakes, and by all means *not* go into "cover-up mode," Reagan's second term could go down in flames, just as Nixon's had self-destructed when Shultz was Treasury secretary from 1972 to 1974. Shultz cabled National Security Advisor John Poindexter that "the only way to contain the damage is to give the essential facts to the public" as quickly as possible. Poindexter's reply was not cooperative.

As Shultz later recounted in his memoir, "A political tidal wave, I felt sure, was bearing down on President Reagan and would, in my opinion, destroy his presidency unless the arms-for-hostages dealings were stopped immediately."

The secret scheme at the heart of the Iran-Contra affair has been summed up by historian Kevin Phillips this way: "To bribe Iran—still locked in a bloody war with Iraq—into pressuring the Lebanese radicals to release their

VICE PRESIDENT GEORGE H. W. BUSH CONFERS WITH PRESIDENT RONALD REAGAN AT THE WHITE HOUSE. BOTH MEN LATER DENIED KNOWLEDGE OF THE ARMS-FOR-HOSTAGES DEALS, THOUGH ULTIMATELY REAGAN ACCEPTED (SLIGHTLY) MORE RESPONSIBILITY FOR THE MISADVENTURE.

American hostages, a new round of covert U.S. arms sales to Iran was arranged. Then, in order to fund the Contras when Congress would not, some of the profits from the clandestine Iranian deliveries were channeled to Nicaragua." And the political fallout, complete with congressional investigations, an independent counsel, and convictions and presidential pardons, would continue for some six years, up to President George H. W. Bush's final days in office. The legacy and political consequences, however, would remain murky and difficult to pinpoint.

HOW DID IT COME TO THIS?
In the campaign of 1980, then-Republican vice presidential candidate Bush had warned that President Jimmy Carter might pull an "October surprise" to win the fifty-two U.S. embassy hostages' release from Tehran before the election and thereby unfairly tilt the vote his way. Quite to the contrary, said members of the Carter campaign after Reagan won, charging that in fact it was the Reagan-Bush team that had reached a secret deal with Iran. If Reagan were elected, then in exchange for delaying the

INDEPENDENT PROSECUTOR LAWRENCE E. WALSH, CENTER, INVESTIGATED THE IRAN-CONTRA AFFAIR FOR SIX YEARS, SUBMITTING HIS FINAL REPORT IN 1993.

hostages' release, Iran would win a resumption of arms sales from the United States. This allegation has never been proved absolutely, but Carter's CIA director, Admiral Stansfield Turner, believed it was accurate.

A new round of hostage-taking had begun not long after Iran released the embassy captives in January 1981. In retaliation for Israel's 1982 invasion of Lebanon, supported by U.S.-made warplanes and ships from the U.S. Sixth Fleet, the Shi'ite Islamic group Hezbollah and Islamic Jihad in 1984 had taken hostage seventeen Americans and some seventy-five other Westerners.

After Reagan's reelection in 1984, the administration undertook a secret effort to secure the release of seven American hostages held in Lebanon by Hezbollah. In the White House's NSC, Lieutenant Colonel Oliver L. North and associates, with input from contacts in Israel and Iran, were devising a scheme whereby the hostages could be freed and money could be raised for the president's war against the Sandinistas. It was a brilliant combination of two policy objectives. It also happened to be illegal.

On June 17, 1985, National Security Adviser Robert C. "Bud" McFarlane circulated a draft national security directive that proposed a change in the United States' posture toward Iran, allowing "provision of selected military equipment as determined on a case-by-case basis." Secretary of State Shultz immediately opposed the idea as contrary to U.S. interests, and Defense Secretary Weinberger rejected it as "absurd."

Weinberger told the president that such a sale would be illegal: It would violate the 1979 arms embargo against Iran, even if the arms were sold through a third party. In addition, the Arms Export Control Act (1976) prohibited the sale of weapons from the United States to a third party without the express approval of the president and Congress.

According to independent prosecutor Lawrence E. Walsh's account in *Firewall: The Iran-Contra Conspiracy and Cover-Up*, Reagan was not bothered by the illegalities, as long as hostages were freed and the Contras supplied. He said he could deal with charges of illegality, if they arose, but he could not accept the accusation that "big strong President Reagan passed up a chance to free hostages." The president joked that if he went to jail, "visiting hours are on Thursday."

He might not be the only one going to jail, Weinberger warned.

In a cost-benefit analysis, one of the scheme's potential benefits was that it might help in healing the strained relations with Iran. The United States did not want oil-rich Iran ever to become friendly with the Soviet Union— preventing that had been a consistent objective of U.S. Middle East policy since the end of World War II and the 1950s, when the United States helped Mohammad Reza Shah Pahlavi, eldest son of former Iranian ruler Reza Shah Pahlavi (1925–41) and later known as "the shah," replace Mohammad

PRESIDENTIAL BRIEFING
(1911–2004)

• FORTIETH PRESIDENT OF THE UNITED STATES (1981–89) AND GOVERNOR OF CALIFORNIA (1967–75)

• BORN FEBRUARY 6, 1911, IN TAMPICO, ILLINOIS

• DIED JUNE 5, 2004, IN LOS ANGELES

• ELECTED BY A LANDSLIDE OVER JIMMY CARTER IN 1980 IN HIS THIRD RUN FOR THE PRESIDENCY (AFTER 1968 AND 1976); REELECTED BY A LANDSLIDE IN 1984

• INITIATED MASSIVE CUTS IN TAXES AND DOMESTIC, NONDEFENSE SPENDING; PUSHED LARGEST PEACETIME MILITARY SPENDING INCREASE ($2.4 TRILLION) IN U.S. HISTORY

• POPULARITY WEAKENED BY REVELATIONS OF SECRET ARMS-FOR-HOSTAGES DEALS IN THE IRAN-CONTRA AFFAIR (1986–87)

• MET WITH REFORMIST SOVIET LEADER MIKHAIL GORBACHEV FOUR TIMES BETWEEN 1985 AND 1988 AND CONCLUDED INF TREATY THAT SHARPLY REDUCED INTERMEDIATE NUCLEAR FORCES

Mosaddeq, the premier of Iran from 1951 to 1953. In 1979 the shah was over-thrown in an Islamic revolution led by the Ayatollah Khomeini, an eminent and fiery Shi'ite cleric who became Iran's supreme political and religious leader for the next ten years. By the mid-1980s, the Ayatollah was very old, and amid uncertainty about a succession crisis that might follow his death, it was prudent to "keep your friends close, but your enemies closer."

What was in it for Israel? At the same time that it was in Israel's strategic interest to see its two enemies weaken each other in the Iran-Iraq War (1980–88), Israel and Iran had a common enemy in Baghdad, Saddam Hussein; Israel could help Iran with the weapons it needed to fight Hussein, The U.S. embargo had cut off the bounty of weaponry the shah used to buy to his heart's content, but there was still a way Tehran could get good American arms. And how much better it would be if, in the bargain, Israel could dump its outdated stockpiles and get newer, better weapons.

Secretaries Shultz and Weinberger argued against the scheme from many angles besides the U.S. laws that would be broken. Washington had been urging its allies to keep a united front and hold back from dealing with terrorists or shipping supplies to either Iran or Iraq, in hopes that the Iran-Iraq War would die for lack of weapons. Despite official protestations of neutrality, however, the United States was not very secretly backing Iraq in the war Hussein had started against Iran in 1980. In one such overture, Reagan sent former (and future) defense secretary Donald Rumsfeld as a special envoy to meet with Hussein in 1983. The administration's public posture was that Iran was an enemy. About the same time McFarlane was circulating his draft proposal in July 1985, Reagan told the American Bar Association that Iran was part of a "confederation of terrorist states … A new, international version of Murder, Inc." A further contradiction was that the administration had publicly spoken out against dealing with or arming terrorists—and in this case the weapons intended for Iran would, or might, be passed on to Hezbollah in Lebanon. There was no telling where they might end up. In the scheme proposed by the NSC, Washington would be arming terrorists on both ends of the deal, in the Middle East *and* in Central America. Further, the scheme would also break a 1982 law prohibiting the United States from aiding the Contras.

Every time the arms-for-hostages idea was brought up, Secretaries Shultz and Weinberger would argue against it. In his memoir, Shultz recalled, "In four major battles between mid-1985 and fall 1986, I had fought to stop such a deal, and each time I felt—or had been assured—that my view had prevailed. But this snake never died, no matter how many times I hacked at it."

FIDEL CASTRO OF CUBA WITH DANIEL ORTEGA, PRESIDENT OF NICARAGUA. IN THE 1970S ORTEGA WAS EXILED TO CUBA WHERE HE WAS TRAINED IN GUERRILLA TACTICS, THEN RETURNED TO LEAD THE SANDINISTA NATIONAL LIBERATION FRONT IN THE NICARAGUAN CIVIL WAR. IN 1984 HE WAS NAMED PRESIDENT OF NICARAGUA.

THE WILL TO ARM THE CONTRAS

For most of the twentieth century, and especially since the end of World War II, it had been an enduring stance in American foreign policy that the United States would not tolerate a leftward drift by Central American and South American governments. Washington discouraged Latin American nations from even thinking about turning socialist, redistributing land, or nationalizing private corporations' assets, such as the United Fruit Company's in Guatemala. Nothing like the disaster, as Washington saw it, that Fidel Castro had brought upon Cuba in the 1959 revolution could be permitted to happen again. To discourage leftward leanings, the CIA had sponsored coups that overthrew the democratically elected government of Guatemalan agrarian reformer Jacobo Árbenz in 1953–54 and Chilean president Salvador Allende on September 11, 1973, and others before and after.

DEFENSE SECRETARY CASPAR WEINBERGER TESTIFYING BEFORE CONGRESS. WEINBERGER AND SECRETARY OF STATE GEORGE SHULTZ CONSISTENTLY OPPOSED THE ARMS-FOR-HOSTAGES SCHEME, DENOUNCING IT AS ILLEGAL AND "ABSURD." WEINBERGER WAS LATER PARDONED BY PRESIDENT GEORGE H. W. BUSH.

Within days of taking office in January 1981, Reagan administration officials reversed Jimmy Carter's openness to the new revolutionary, Marxist Sandinista government of Nicaragua by cutting off aid. They began working to isolate the Sandinistas (the Sandinista National Liberation Front), led by leftist president and former guerrilla Daniel Ortega. American dollars went instead to the Contra rebel forces in Nicaragua, a CIA-sponsored paramilitary cadre ("Contra" derived from the Spanish *contrarevolucionario*). The soldiers, whom Reagan affectionately regarded as "freedom fighters" and described in 1985 as "the moral equivalent of the Founding Fathers," were mostly disgruntled, displaced former members of the Nicaraguan National Guard who had fled to Honduras after the Nicaraguan dictator Anastazio Somoza Debayle was forced out by the Sandinista guerrilla movement in June 1979.

REAGAN SIGNED THE BILL, BUT HE AND HIS NSC HAD NO INTENTION OF LETTING THE BOLAND AMENDMENT OR ANY OTHER PIECE OF PAPER STOP THE FIGHT AGAINST COMMUNISM.

When evidence surfaced that illegal covert operations in Central America were being funded by American taxpayers, public opinion and Congress turned against support of the Contras. In 1982, followed by revisions in 1983 and 1984, Congress passed a bill, known as the Boland Amendment after sponsoring congressman Edward Patrick Boland of Massachusetts, that banned the CIA and Defense Department from using taxpayers' money to overthrow the Sandinistas and prohibited any U.S. intelligence agency from assisting the Contras. Reagan signed the bill, but he and his NSC had no intention of letting the Boland Amendment or any other piece of paper stop the fight against Communism. This was a personal commitment of Reagan's since his Hollywood days when he cooperated with the House Committee on Un-American Activities in identifying potential or alleged Communists in the film industry.

In 1984, with congressional funds cut off, National Security Adviser McFarlane turned to Saudi Arabia, which agreed to supply about $1 million per month in military aid to the Contras, rising to $2 million per month in 1985. Then, came an opportunity for a new source of funding for the Contras.

TERMS OF THE ARMS-FOR-HOSTAGES DEAL The terms of the multi-party deal, as worked out by McFarlane and his deputy Oliver North through Israeli and Iranian intermediaries, were that Israel would supply weapons to Iran from its own stockpile, and then Israel would buy replacements from the United States. According to the report of the Tower Commission in 1987, McFarlane discussed the matter several times with Reagan. The president said that if Israel sold arms

to Iran, "in modest amounts not enough to change the military balance [of power] and not including major weapons systems," then Israel could buy replacements from the United States. Over the strenuous objections of Secretaries Shultz and Weinberger, and in contradiction of his stated policy of never negotiating with terrorists, Reagan entered an indirect deal with the Hezbollah kidnappers: The United States would sell arms to Iran—a nation then at war with Iraq—and Iran would press the kidnappers to release seven American hostages.

North and retired Air Force major general Richard Secord arranged with Iranian arms dealer Manucher Ghorbanifar the delivery of 1,000 TOW wire-guided antitank missiles to Iran. Deputy National Security Advisor Poindexter (who later succeeded McFarlane as national security advisor in 1985) approved the almost triple markup from $3.7 million to $10 million. North and Secord kept the profit in secret Swiss bank accounts and used it to pay for weapons for the Contras and for other uses not authorized by Congress.

Israel shipped ninety-six TOW missiles to Iran in August 1985 and another 408 in September 1985. In November 1985, McFarlane and Poindexter learned from North that Israel was about to sell as many as 500 large Hawk antiaircraft missiles to Iran, in exchange for which four hostages would be released. The missiles from Israel's arsenal would be replenished by the United States. It was learned in later investigations that not every sale of arms to Iran resulted in a release of hostages.

Reagan authorized Israel's shipment of weapons to Iran, but he deliberately withheld the legally required notification of the transfer from Congress. Reagan noted in his diary for January 17, 1986, "I agreed to sell TOWs to Iran." He authorized the CIA to sell arms directly to Iran, bypassing Israel's role as middleman. North was in charge of these sales.

THE STORY BREAKS

The secret Iran-Contra connection began to be revealed on October 5, 1986, when a military cargo plane was shot down over Nicaragua by the Sandinistas. Three Americans on board died. The lone survivor, Eugene Hasenfus, said he worked for a CIA man named "Max Gomez," which was an alias of a former operative with links to North and Vice President Bush. Then, in early November, after several arms transfers and releases of hostages, the Middle Eastern angle of the scheme was revealed by *Al Shiraa*, a Lebanese periodical. The story was picked up by other news organizations and was confirmed by the speaker of Iran's parliament, Ali Akbar Rafsanjani. It was from these revelations that reporters were quizzing Secretary Shultz on his flight to Vienna.

Soon after the Hasenfus shoot-down, Vice President Bush called a press conference to deny any connection with the plane that had been shot down by the Sandinistas, though he did admit to knowing the man called Max Gomez. This was a curious admission by the usually discreet and secretive Bush, who had been the CIA director from 1976 to 1977. "Max Gomez" was an alias of Felix I. Rodriguez, who was a veteran of the 1961 Bay of Pigs fiasco and the main supply officer for North's Contra pipeline. It was true that Bush and Rodriguez knew each other. In fact, Rodriguez had two autographed photos of himself with the vice president on display at his home.

REAGAN AUTHORIZED ISRAEL'S SHIPMENT OF WEAPONS TO IRAN, BUT HE DELIBERATELY WITHHELD THE LEGALLY REQUIRED NOTIFICATION OF THE TRANSFER FROM CONGRESS.

On November 6, 1986, *Washington Post* reporter Walter Pincus broke a story that linked the release of three hostages over a period of about eighteen months to arms transfers to Iran that had been approved by the Reagan administration. Two days later, the *New York Times* reported with front-page headlines, "Reagan Approved Iranian Contacts, Officials Report; No Mention of Weapons; Secret Approaches Sought to Improve Relations and to Help Free Hostages" and "Shultz Reaffirms His Opposition to Negotiation with Terrorists."

Upon Secretary Shultz's return from Vienna to Washington, he gathered with his staff and reviewed his notes of meetings over the past year and a half to try to piece together the sequence of events and consider how the president might be saved from further damage. According to Shultz's notes from that time:

> Our credibility is shot. We have taken refuge in tricky technicalities of language to avoid confronting the reality that we have lied to the American people and misused our friends abroad. We are revealed to have been dealing with some of the sleaziest international characters around. They have played us for suckers. There is a Watergate-like atmosphere around here as the White House staff has become secretive, self-deluding, and vindictive.

At a November 10 staff meeting, Shultz and Weinberger insisted the arms for-hostages deals must stop. National Security Advisor Poindexter rattled off a list of arms sales and pointed to improved relations with Iran and some releases of hostages, but he insisted the deals were not quid pro quo. "So if the 500 TOWs [anti-tank missiles] plus other items have been supplied to Iran in the context of hostage releases," Shultz asked Poindexter, "how can you say this is not an arms-for-hostages deal?" Reagan insisted, "They're not linked!" but Poindexter undercut the president by demanding, "How else will we get the hostages out?"

As soon as he could, Shultz met privately with the president and urged that the arms transfers cease at once. As Shultz recalled in his memoir, "Clearly this massive, secret White House operation was totally contrary to the long-standing policy that Ronald Reagan and I had constructed to deal with terrorists. The policy could be summed up succinctly by the precept, 'Make sure that terrorism does not pay.' If hostage takers find that they can 'sell' their hostages, their crimes will never cease." Shultz tried to convince the president that he had been misled by subordinates, but Reagan did not see it that way. Reagan believed that the United States was not dealing with terrorists, but with Iranian middlemen with connections to moderates in Tehran. Hostages' lives were at stake.

Shultz walked out of his private meeting with the president thinking that he hadn't gotten through, but Reagan directed Attorney General Edwin Meese to look into Shultz's claims. Meese checked the money trail, and when he told the president that North had funneled some $10 to $30 million to the Contras through Swiss bank accounts, Reagan turned pale. Chief of Staff Donald T. Regan told reporters that the whole mess had been McFarlane's idea, Poindexter resigned as national security advisor, and North was fired. When Reagan dismissed North, he remarked, "One day, this will make a great movie."

INVESTIGATIONS, APOLOGIES, INDICTMENTS, AND PARDONS When news of the arms-for-hostages deal hit the front pages, the public was incredulous. Reagan, bribing terrorists? It couldn't be true. Republicans and Democrats were outraged. Senator Daniel Patrick Moynihan of New York said the secret Iran negotiations were "the worst handling of an intelligence problem in our history." Former president Carter observed, "We've paid ransom, in effect, to the kidnappers of our hostages. The fact is that every terrorist in the world who reads a newspaper or listens to the radio knows that they've taken American hostages, and we've paid them to get the hostages back. This is a very serious mistake in how to handle a kidnapping or hostage-taking."

Reagan's first response to reporters' inquiries was to deny the allegations, but the questions only multiplied. On November 13, 1986, the president appeared on national television and admitted he had authorized the sale of arms to Iran. But Reagan insisted, "We did not, repeat, did not trade weapons or anything else for hostages, nor will we." Only six days later, Reagan had to acknowledge that his repudiation had been based upon an inaccurate chronology assembled by his White House and NSC staff.

The public wasn't buying the president's explanation. Polls showed that 57 percent of Americans believed Reagan had reversed his pledge never to deal with terrorists. It was a rare defeat for the "Great Communicator," who, when problems arose, was usually able to win the public's support by explaining the issue in a nationally televised address. The president's job approval ratings dropped from 67 percent to 46 percent.

Vice President Bush also went on television to defend the administration. He asserted that an arms-for-hostages deal would be "inconceivable." Shultz telephoned Bush the next day and reminded him that he, Bush, had attended the meeting on January 7, 1986, and that he had been in favor of the plan. Shultz recalls that at that meeting "all the key players were present," and Bush's name is first on the list. In July 1986, the vice president had traveled to Israel and, according to arrangements made by North, had met with Israeli counterterrorism deputy Amiram Nir to discuss the arms-for-hostages deal. The officially stated purpose for the meeting was a briefing on counterterrorism.

To assure the public that the White House was taking the matter seriously, Reagan announced on December 1 the formation of a President's Special Review Board, better known as the Tower Commission, after its leader, Texas Republican senator John Tower, a good friend of the vice president. Also on the board were former Democratic senator and secretary of state Edmund Muskie, and General Brent Scowcroft, national security advisor to President Ford and, later, to his friend George H. W. Bush. The commission interviewed some fifty people, including CIA officials. Poindexter and North declined to appear, and the commission lacked subpoena power to compel them to give testimony.

The Tower Commission's report, which was issued in February 1987, was expected to be a whitewash job, but it was surprisingly critical of the president for lack of oversight. The report described Reagan as disengaged, uninformed, and manipulated. Because of Reagan's lax supervision, subordinates had run loose, shaping policy and pursuing initiatives that he was not aware of. More

ADMIRAL JOHN POINDEXTER, MCFARLANE'S SUCCESSOR AS NATIONAL SECURITY ADVISOR AND ANOTHER PRIME INSTIGATOR OF THE WEAPONS-FOR-HOSTAGES SCHEMES. HE LATER RESURFACED IN THE PENTAGON AFTER THE SEPTEMBER II ATTACKS AS DIRECTOR OF TOTAL INFORMATION AWARENESS, A DEFENSE DEPARTMENT THREAT-ASSESSMENT AND PREVENTION PROJECT, BUT THEN WAS DISMISSED.

damaging, the report provided confirmation that there had in fact been an arms-for-hostages deal. The report found no administration official guilty of wrongdoing, however, and its findings presented no particular political obstacle for the presidential aspirations of the vice president.

President Reagan appeared on national television in March and, without explicitly apologizing or taking responsibility, described "activities undertaken without my knowledge" as "a mistake." He added, "As the navy would say, this happened on my watch." The president explained, "A few months ago, I told the American people I did not trade arms for hostages. My heart and best intentions still tell me that is true, but the facts and the evidence tell me it is not."

Former national security advisor Poindexter took some of the blame himself, testifying under oath that he had approved the diversion of funds to the Contras and that he had not told the president. "I made a very deliberate decision not to ask the president so I could insulate him ... and provide future deniability." McFarlane attempted suicide in February 1987, the month the Tower Commission report was released. He survived to plead guilty to four counts of withholding information from Congress.

THE PRESIDENT EXPLAINED, "A FEW MONTHS AGO, I TOLD THE AMERICAN PEOPLE I DID NOT TRADE ARMS FOR HOSTAGES. MY HEART AND BEST INTENTIONS STILL TELL ME THAT IS TRUE, BUT THE FACTS AND THE EVIDENCE TELL ME IT IS NOT."

The Tower Commission is seen by some historians as having done a more thorough job in a shorter time than the subsequent, televised Senate committee hearings that stretched on for four months in the summer of 1987, featuring North winning some public affection by appearing for testimony in his Marines uniform, and his blond secretary, Fawn Hall, describing how she and her boss shredded important, subpoenaed documents.

An investigation begun by the Justice Department led to the appointment in December 1986 of an independent counsel, Republican Lawrence E. Walsh, to investigate possible criminal aspects of the Iran-Contra affair. Walsh pursued the matter for six years, through the entire presidency of George H. W. Bush. Walsh delivered his final report in August 1993.

Criminal indictments were handed down against former national security advisor Poindexter and McFarlane's former deputy in national security, Oliver North. On March 16, 1988, a grand jury handed down a twenty-three-count criminal indictment against Poindexter, North, retired Air Force major general Secord, and arms dealer Albert Hakim. Hakim pleaded guilty on two counts, and Secord on one. North was convicted on three counts, and Poindexter on five, but an appeals panel later dismissed the charges against North and

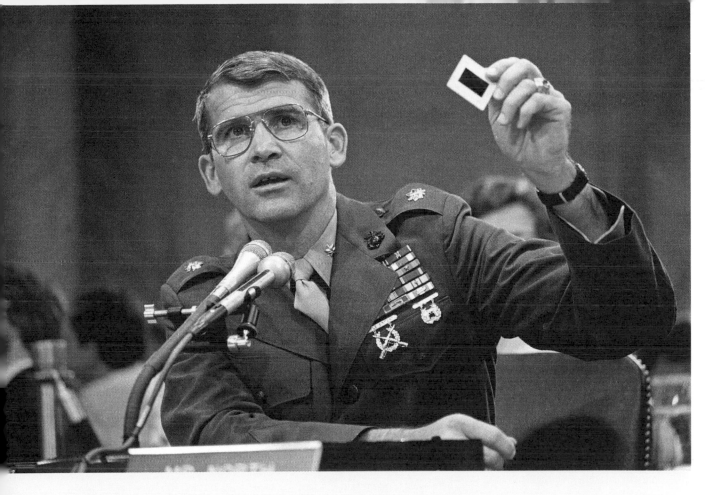

Poindexter on the grounds that an earlier congressional grant of immunity had tainted the trial. On July 5, 1989, Federal District Judge Gerhard A. Gesell sentenced North to a $150,000 fine and probation. Gesell delivered this stinging rebuke: "I do not think in this area you were a leader at all, but really a low-ranking subordinate working to carry out initiatives of a few cynical superiors."

THE MYSTERIOUS ROLE OF VICE PRESIDENT BUSH
From the time the story broke through 1987, the vice president denied any knowledge of the arms-for-hostages swaps or of the illicit aid to the Contras, though in his memoir *Turmoil and Triumph*, Shultz wrote that Bush was present at every meeting where the arms-for-hostages scheme was raised. On March 13, 1987, Bush said, "I wish with clairvoyant hindsight that I had known we were trading arms for hostages." And later, Bush said, "If we erred, the president and I, it was on the side of human life. It was an over concern about freeing Americans."

Bush was also linked to aiding the Contras. The national security advisor to the vice president, veteran CIA agent Donald Gregg, was one of the first people

LT. COL. OLIVER L. NORTH OF THE NATIONAL SECURITY COUNCIL DONNED HIS UNIFORM TO TESTIFY BEFORE CONGRESS IN THE SUMMER OF 1987. HE WAS INSTRUMENTAL IN DIVERTING FUNDS FROM THE SALE OF ARMS TO IRAN THROUGH SWISS BANK ACCOUNTS TO HELP THE NICARAGUAN CONTRAS FIGHT THE LEFTIST SANDINISTAS.

contacted when Hasenfus's plane was shot down by the Sandinistas in October 1986. (The first call was to Gregg's assistant.) As mentioned previously, Hasenfus said he worked for "Max Gomez." Gomez was Felix I. Rodriguez, who drafted a plan for air strikes against leftist guerrilla targets in Central America that Gregg had promoted while a member of Bush's national security staff. (The plan was found in Oliver North's safe.)

Questions about Bush's knowledge and involvement persisted through his presidency from 1989 to 1993, but he, too, was ultimately able to elude prosecution. In late 1992, shortly before Bush left office, he pardoned six men indicted or convicted in the Iran-Contra affair, including Weinberger, McFarlane, and Clair George, former deputy director of operations for the CIA. It was said that Weinberger's diaries would have shown that Bush and Reagan knew about the arms-for-hostages deal at a time when they had claimed they knew nothing.

Further difficulties in substantiating Bush's complicity have arisen because of an executive order signed by his son, George W. Bush, on November 1, 2001, that blocks the release of all presidential documents. Before this executive order, the National Archives had handled the release of White House documents, which automatically became public twelve years after the end of an administration. The new rules, in direct contradiction of the "open government" provisions of the Presidential Records Act of 1978, allow a president to block the National Archives from releasing papers of former presidents from Reagan onward, even long after the former chief executives have died.

Many questions remain. What did the president think they were doing? How did the scheme take form? Did the idea originate in Israel as a way of replenishing weapons and firming up relations with Iran? Who was using whom? What might we have learned from the trials of Weinberger, McFarlane, or George if President Bush had not pardoned them?

Twenty years later, when many of the same people are in power (again) and similar covert dealings with some of the same operators continue to this day, it is difficult to identify precisely what lessons the nation drew from the Iran-Contra affair because despite all the inquiries, not very much was revealed *about* the scheme.

The investigations' scopes were limited, not all witnesses were cooperative—North, for example, was defiantly unapologetic—and presidential pardons forestalled court cases that might have shown in much greater detail the murky connections between hostage-taking, election-year intrigues, the arms-oil-intelligence nexus, and the United States' relations with Iran, Iraq, Israel, and other sometime-friends, sometime-adversaries. One thing that is certain is that a close study of the intrigues and relationships of the Iran-Contra affair gives a clearer understanding of the war on terrorism, which has deeper roots than many people realize.

CHAPTER 20

WAR IN IRAQ

GEORGE W. BUSH

COLIN POWELL LIFTED THE TINY VIAL AND DANGLED IT BETWEEN HIS THUMB AND forefinger. Filled with a white powder, it was perhaps half the diameter of a man's pinkie finger and half the length. The U.S. Secretary of State leaned forward toward the members of the United Nations Security Council.

"Just this amount," Powell told his hushed audience and the millions world-wide watching by television. "Just about the amount of a teaspoon of dry anthrax in an envelope [addressed to Majority Leader Tom Daschle] completely shut down the United States Senate in the fall of 2001. Two postal workers died, and several hundred others were forced to undergo emergency medical treatment."

The Saddam Hussein government in Iraq, Powell went on, had admitted after U.N.–mandated inspections in 1995 to having produced 8,500 liters of anthrax. U.N. inspectors concluded these facilities could have produced 25,000 liters more—"enough to fill tens upon tens upon tens of thousands of teaspoons." Stressing each word, Powell declared, "We have amassed a thick intelligence file indicating that Iraq is continuing to make these weapons."

Ramrod straight with the erect bearing of a career military man, Powell commanded the respect and admiration of much of the diplomatic corps. He was known for his cautious and measured approach even in crises. "The Powell Doctrine," forged after the Vietnam debacle, decreed that diplomacy should always be tried first in international disputes, with military force only a last

MISSION ACCOMPLISHED? UNDER A TRIUMPHANT BANNER, BUSH DECLARED THE END OF COMBAT OPERATIONS IN IRAQ ON MAY I, 2003.

274

PRESIDENTIAL BRIEFING

(1946-)

• FORTY-THIRD PRESIDENT OF
THE UNITED STATES
(ELECTED 2001; RE-ELECTED
2004) AND FIRST GOVERNOR
OF TEXAS TO BE ELECTED TO
CONSECUTIVE FOUR-YEAR
TERMS (ELECTED 1994;
RE-ELECTED 1998)

• BORN JULY 6, 1946, IN
NEW HAVEN, CONNECTICUT

• WON THE 2000 ELECTION
OVER VICE PRESIDENT
AL GORE IN A CLOSE AND
CONTROVERSIAL RACE.
ALTHOUGH GORE WON THE
POPULAR VOTE, BUSH WAS
DECLARED THE WINNER IN
THE ELECTORAL VOTE,
271-266, IN A SUPREME
COURT DECISION

• PASSED THE "NO CHILD
LEFT BEHIND ACT," SETTING
NATIONAL STANDARDS FOR
MEASURING STUDENT
LEARNING AND PENALIZING
SCHOOLS THAT FAILED
TO MEET THEM

• WAS HEAVILY CRITICIZED
FOR POOR GOVERNMENT
RESPONSE TO HURRICANE
KATRINA, WHICH
DEVASTATED NEW ORLEANS

resort. And then America, for all its power, must only go to war with overwhelming force, clear objectives, support at home, and the backing of allies and the international community. That doctrine had guided Powell as chairman of the Joint Chiefs of Staff and as national security adviser to Presidents George H.W. Bush and Bill Clinton.

Now in February 2003, the George W. Bush administration was trading on that sterling reputation in another international crisis, its case against the hated dictator Hussein and the nation of Iraq. After the Gulf War in 1991, Hussein had been forced to give up work on making biological, chemical, and nuclear weapons of mass destruction (WMD) and yield to international inspections, backed up by economic sanctions, to ensure that he complied. The United States suspected that Hussein simply concealed WMD production from inspectors. With Powell's aura of probity, the Security Council wanted to hear what he had to say.

Powell turned to a projector screen. "Look at this," he said. The image showed drawings of an arid landscape with nondescript rectangular buildings and what seemed to be dozens of long trailer trucks and boxcars.

"One of the most worrisome things that emerges from our intelligence is the existence of mobile production facilities to make biological agents," Powell said. "We have firsthand descriptions of these factories on wheels and on rails. The trucks and train cars are easily moved and are designed to evade detection by inspectors. In a matter of months, they can produce a quantity of biological poison equal to the entire amount produced in the years prior to the Gulf War." He leaned forward again. "Ladies and gentlemen, we know Iraq has at least seven of these mobile [bioweapons] factories. They can produce anthrax and botulism toxin, too. They can produce enough lethal biological agent in a single month to kill thousands and thousands of people."

Powell spoke for eighty minutes, enumerating the Iraqi threat. Iraq, he said, had fitted drone aircraft with spray tanks to disburse biological agents from the air or into the water supply. Iraq had never accounted for a four-ton stockpile of the deadly nerve gas VX—"A single drop on the skin will kill in minutes," Powell said.

He showed aerial photographs of what he called a chemical complex for transshipment of poison gases and other chemical weapons. He played intercepted radio conversations between two field commanders said to be discussing the destruction of chemical weapons. And he said, "We have no indication that Saddam Hussein has ever abandoned his nuclear weapons program." In fact Hussein retained two of the three components needed to build a nuclear bomb. "He has a cadre of nuclear scientists with the expertise, and he has a bomb design."

SHOCK AND AWE IN BAGHDAD
Powell thanked the council and sat down. In compliance with his "diplomacy first" doctrine, he had persuaded President Bush to take the case to the United Nations. His speech never mentioned war. But in the Bush White House, that decision had already been made. Six weeks after Powell's speech, President Bush ordered a devastating "shock and awe" aerial bombardment of Baghdad while American armies swept northward across the desert toward the capital.

Five years and more than 4,000 U.S. combat deaths plus countless thousands of Iraqi casualties and varying estimates of costs running up to more than a trillion dollars, the bloody fighting was still going on, amid angry protests at home and in Congress, defections among America's most devoted allies, condemnation of the United States and "Cowboy" Bush across the world, and steadily sinking public support. However, the president who had labeled himself "the Decider" continued to insist that waging war against Iraq was a justified decision.

On September 11, 2001, when two hijacked U.S. airliners crashed into New York's World Trade Center, a third hit the Pentagon, and a fourth was brought down when passengers rose up against the hijackers, Hussein was not the first target in American gun sights. Fifteen of the nineteen hijackers were from Saudi Arabia, two from the United Arab Emirates, and one each from Lebanon and Egypt. A Saudi prince, Osama bin Laden, crowingly claimed responsibility for a shadowy, little-known terrorist group called Al Qaeda. The terrorists had been trained in Afghanistan and mustered support throughout

PRESIDENTIAL BRIEFING (CONT)

· ESTABLISHED THE DEPARTMENT OF HOMELAND SECURITY AFTER 9/11

· ADDED PRESCRIPTION DRUG COVERAGE TO MEDICARE FOR SENIORS

· REDUCED TAXES FOR HIGH-INCOME TAXPAYERS

· APPOINTED TWO CONSERVATIVE JUSTICES TO THE U.S. SUPREME COURT

BRING THE TROOPS HOME! DEMONSTRATIONS ERUPTED ALL OVER THE UNITED STATES AS THE IRAQ WAR CONTINUED.

the Arab world. An international outcry arose to hunt down and punish their supporters and forestall other such attacks.

But retaliation against whom? Centered where? On September 12, according to Richard Clarke, the National Security Council's counterterrorism expert, President Bush pulled him and some aides aside. "See if you can find evidence of an Iraqi connection here," Bush said to Clarke, according to Clarke's version. Clarke was startled. "But Mr. President," responded Clarke, who had warned against the Al Qaeda threat as recently as the previous month, "Iraq didn't do this. Al Qaeda did." "I know, I know," Bush said, according to Clarke. "But see what you can find anyway."

From the first days of the Bush administration, and even before, a tight knot of "neoconservative" thinkers had focused on the threat of Iraq. Encouraged after 9/11 by Vice President Dick Cheney and Defense Secretary Donald Rumsfeld, they included the top civilian brass: Paul Wolfowitz, deputy secretary of defense; Richard Perle, chairman of the Pentagon's Defense Strategy Board; Elliot Abrams, special presidential assistant for Near Eastern and African affairs; and Douglas Feith, undersecretary of defense for policy.

Distrusting the conventional intelligence services of the CIA, the Defense Intelligence Agency, and the intelligence arm of the State Department, they set up the Pentagon Office of Special Plans to operate outside conventional channels and concentrate on intelligence about Iraq. Their major source of information was the Iraq National Congress, anti-Hussein Iraqi exiles led by the shady but charismatic Ahmed Chalabi, whom they subsidized to the tune of $300,000 a year. That these exiles had not set foot in Iraq in a decade and had been dismissed by the other agencies as untrustworthy and unreliable only made them more acceptable to the neocons. Their anti-Hussein messages fit neatly into the neocons' preconceptions.

AFGHANISTAN FIRST

Immediately after 9/11, an American-led international force smashed into Afghanistan, teamed up with local resistance, and quickly routed the Taliban government. The repressive Islamist regime was internationally condemned for oppressing women, committing atrocities, and enforcing a strict code of behavior backed up by beheadings and vigilante groups; moreover, many believed it to be hiding bin Laden in its remote and lawless mountain provinces. A high-tech offensive based on missile attacks failed to capture or dislodge the Al Qaeda leader, however, so Washington shifted its major attention to Iraq.

Secretary Powell had been in Lima, Peru, on September 11 for a meeting of the Organization of American States (OAS). He returned to find his department effectively sidelined in Iraq policy and the Pentagon in charge. Bush had

declared a "War on Terror" and preparations for tracking down and retaliating against Al Qaeda and its supposed supporters were already underway.

A loyal soldier trained to follow orders unquestioningly, Powell dutifully fell into the diplomatic work of forging a global anti-terror alliance. America after 9/11 had the world's sympathy, and Powell at first had little difficulty lining up allies for hunting bin Laden and attacking Afghanistan. More than twenty countries volunteered troops or equipment. Lining up a "coalition of the willing" for the campaign against Iraq proved a tougher sell.

Iraq was a notoriously fragmented country, cobbled together by Britain after World War I from remnants of the Ottoman Empire. The Kurdish tribes in the north were Muslim but not Arab, their territory spilling over into Turkey, Syria, and Iran. Sunni Muslim Arabs clustered around Baghdad and dominated the government. More economically deprived Shiite Muslims populated the

SECRETARY OF STATE COLIN POWELL AND SECRETARY OF DEFENSE DONALD RUMSFELD FOUGHT AN ONGOING AND BITTER WAR OVER IRAQ POLICY. POWELL BELIEVED IN DIPLOMACY FIRST, AND MILITARY ACTION ONLY AS A LAST RESORT.

south and rural areas. Rich oil deposits lay in Kurd and Shiite territory, but little oil wealth reached Kurds or Shiites.

Hussein, a Sunni from the secularist Baathist party, kept all in line with an iron fist, once famously using poison gas to quell a Kurdish uprising and fighting an eight-year war with Shiite Iran. Since 1998, the United States and Britain had enforced no-fly zones to protect Kurds and Shiites against Hussein's attacks, which the allies feared might lead to a wider war. Hussein, a brutal, equal-opportunity dictator, was said to have massacred hundreds of thousands of political enemies from all factions alike.

ANARCHY RULES

"Shock and awe" carried American-led forces into Baghdad in a mere two weeks. Iraq's much vaunted armies simply melted away. The Iraqi National Congress boasted that the "liberators" would be met with flowers, kisses, and dancing in the streets. Shouting crowds did turn out by the thousands, cheering and singing as the giant statue of Hussein in the city's main square was toppled and crumbled into dust.

But then the crowds turned to looting and stripping public buildings and government offices of computers, desks, furniture, even pencils. The city's great museum of antiquities was raided, ransacked, and emptied of centuries-old, irreplaceable treasures. Coalition troops stood idly by, with no orders to interfere. "Stuff happens," Secretary Rumsfeld sniffed dismissively when told of the looting. The troops were there as occupiers, he noted. Their mission was to provide security, not serve as local police.

"SHOCK AND AWE" CARRIED AMERICAN-LED FORCES INTO BAGHDAD IN A MERE TWO WEEKS. IRAQ'S MUCH VAUNTED ARMIES SIMPLY MELTED AWAY. THE IRAQI NATIONAL CONGRESS BOASTED THAT THE "LIBERATORS" WOULD BE MET WITH FLOWERS, KISSES, AND DANCING IN THE STREETS.

Two days before the invasion launch, Powell went to the White House and made a last plea to Bush. The men were closeted for two and a half hours. "I led him through all the consequences of going into an Arab country and becoming an occupier," Powell told his chief of staff, Lawrence Wilkerson. Powell also invoked what *New York Times* columnist Thomas Friedman has coined as the "Pottery Barn Rule": "You break it, you own it." Powell outlined the challenges the United States would have to face in restoring Iraq to some semblance of twenty-first century order. Bush was unmoved. "The express is headed down the tracks," Powell told Wilkerson on return to the State Department. "We can't stop it. The best we can do is try to slow it down."

DOWN WITH A DICTATOR: SOLDIERS WRAPPED A US FLAG AROUND SADDAM'S HEAD BEFORE TOPPLING HIS GIANT STATUE IN BAGHDAD.

A Pentagon choice, Lieutenant General Jay Garner, was installed as Iraq's military governor of the country. L. Paul (Jerry) Bremer, a neocon favorite, soon replaced him as head of a new governing Coalition Provisional Authority (CPA), whose task was to prepare the conquered country for a stable, democratic government. Bremer was given all the powers of viceroy, modeled after General Douglas MacArthur in postwar Japan. Bremer was clear that "my boss is Secretary Rumsfeld," and beyond that the president, not the State Department. The CPA was to rule the country until elections could be held and a new government put into place. It was a plan that was to have serious ramifications for the future.

ACCOMPLISHED? On May 1, President Bush triumphantly proclaimed the end of combat operations, and he did it with a theatrical flourish. Attired in a Navy flight suit, the former Air National Guard trainee (Bush had actually cut short his flight training to participate in a political campaign) landed ceremoniously on the deck of the aircraft carrier *Abraham Lincoln* off San Diego. Bush emerged from the plane under a banner stretched across the carrier's superstructure. "Mission Accomplished," the banner exulted. "We have difficult work to do in Iraq," the president said. "Parts of that country remain dangerous...The War on Terror continues." But, he went on, "In the battle of Iraq, the United States and our allies have prevailed."

But a growing opposition thought otherwise. Rumsfeld had assured Bush that the war could be fought on the cheap. Once the productive Iraqi oil fields were up and running, they would more than defray the costs of the war and the occupation. (As of spring 2008, Iraqi oil production was still below prewar output.) A streamlined military force brandishing high-tech equipment would be all that was needed. American forces could be reduced and hand off the job to Iraqis.

When Lieutenant General Eric Shinseki, the Army chief of staff, told Congress that "something in the order of several hundred thousand" military personnel would be needed, Rumsfeld was outraged. The Army's top officer was hounded into retirement. The Pentagon leadership pointedly refused to attend the customary retirement ceremony.

And Americans were dying. Bremer and the CPA, mostly made up of young and inexperienced recent college graduates but with impeccable political credentials, holed up in the heavily fortified and protected area of Baghdad, the Green Zone.

Beyond, chaos and danger reigned. Snipers picked off individual soldiers. Roads were sown with mines and improvised explosive devices (IEDs), which were designed to blow up and destroy the unprotected undercarriage of military vehicles when they passed over. Personnel carriers were only lightly armored, another money-saving policy. Besides, heavy armor was unnecessary, it was thought, with Iraq conquered and the population friendly. Troops took to fashioning their own armor from scrap metal or persuaded families back home to provide it to them.

THE BOMBING OF A SHRINE

When Baghdad fell, Saddam Hussein was nowhere to be found. As the coalition rounded up other former government leaders on their "Most Wanted" list, the supreme leader's whereabouts remained a mystery. Then, seven months after his statue fell, in December 2003, a disheveled and filthy Hussein was discovered cowering in a tiny subterranean dugout— a "spider hole," his captors called it—near his birthplace of Tikrit. The all-powerful dictator who once had thirty-seven palaces was living in a few cubic feet underneath a mud hut. Bush immediately went on television to trumpet his capture, "I say to the Iraqi people, 'You will not have to live in fear of Saddam ever again.'" But elsewhere, there was little to crow about.

SADDAM'S UNDERGROUND BUNKER: U.S. SOLDIERS EXPLORED THE "SPIDER HOLE" WHERE SADDAM HID AFTER THE FALL OF BAGHDAD.

Even the commander of U.S. ground forces acknowledged that a "low-key, guerrilla-type war" was underway. Suicide bombers blew themselves up in marketplaces, city squares, offices, buses, and crowded streets, often taking as many as 100 fellow Iraqis with them. In one horrifying instance, 140 Shiites enjoying a Shia festival were blown up. Terrorist explosives reduced to rubble one of the most treasured shrines of Shia Islam, the Golden Mosque of Samarra with its gleaming dome, setting off a countrywide wave of violence between Sunnis and Shiites. Trying to quell the rising insurgency that was morphing into a civil war. U.S. troops fought pitched battles with Shiite militia in the teeming Sadr City district of Baghdad. A month later, they were fighting Sunni insurgents for the city of Falluja.

Misled by the Iraq National Congress's belief that Iraqis were united by their hatred of Hussein, American leaders had vastly underestimated the long-standing enmity between the rival Muslim factions. Meanwhile Bremer had undertaken to exterminate root and branch all vestiges of Hussein rule. He outlawed Hussein's Baath party and barred all members from the government payroll, even low-level clerks and drivers who had joined the party simply to protect their jobs. "DeBaathification" eliminated much of the trained bureaucracy and brought normal government function to a standstill, so that even mailing a letter became difficult.

Another Bremer edict disbanded the Iraqi army. Four hundred thousand angry trained soldiers were suddenly turned onto the streets with no jobs or income, to demonstrate or bitterly join the insurgency—where, at least, they would be fed.

The army was the only organization that could bring any kind of order to the country and perhaps stop the widespread looting, Bremer's predecessor, an appalled General Garner noted. "You can get rid of an army in a day, Jerry," he told Bremer. "It takes years to build one." (Bremer was to claim afterward that he didn't disband the army; it had simply "dissolved." And he said he took his action only after consulting the Pentagon.)

Despite these setbacks and growing antiwar sentiment, Bush was elected for a second term in 2004 and promised to prosecute the war until "victory." After the election, Powell went to the White House and submitted his resignation. He had, he insisted, always intended to serve only one term. Bush made no effort to keep him.

"We had a good and fulsome discussion," Powell said in a press briefing afterward. "We came to the mutual agreement that it would be appropriate for me to leave at this time." Washington interpreted that as diplomatic double-speak for "We aired our disagreements in loud and angry voices."

WHERE ARE THOSE WMDS? The bits of broken crockery that the "Pottery Barn Rule" had predicted continued to accumulate. David Kay, named to head a diligent search to find those hidden weapons of mass destruction, failed to turn up a single specimen after two years of looking. Nor could he uncover any evidence of any advanced plans to develop them. The best he could document were a few vials of anthrax powder kept in scientists' home refrigerators as souvenirs after the first Gulf War.

The aluminum tubes said to be designed for enriching and weaponizing uranium were actually for use in unforbidden short-range missiles. The deal to buy yellow-cake uranium from the African nation of Niger, mentioned by Bush in his State of the Union address, was a hoax. No evidence could be found of supposed meetings in Prague between Al Qaeda operatives and Iraqi diplomats.

Then came the revelation—with graphic, almost stomach-turning photos—that American soldiers had mistreated and tortured prisoners in the

notorious Abu Ghraib prison. The Congressional cry to take the troops out grew to a roar. Democratic candidates swept the House and Senate in the 2006 elections. With Bush's popularity sinking to the low 20s in the polls, other Republicans stumbled over each other in haste to distance themselves from the president. Rumsfeld was finally fired, and the Iraq Study Group, an elite panel of Washington wisemen co-chaired by former Secretary of State James Baker, normally a Bush acolyte, deemed the Iraq situation "grave and deteriorating."

Instead of withdrawing troops, however, a defiant Bush increased them. The "surge" of 30,000 reinforcements announced in 2007 was supposedly to allow the shaky, Shiite-controlled Iraqi government time and cover to solve contentious issues—such as sharing oil revenue and regional autonomy—and to train a viable army.

"As they stand up, we will stand down," Bush repeated, almost like a mantra. In the new army's first test of standing up, Prime Minister Nouri Kamal al-Maliki ordered an attack on Shiite militias in the port city of Basra. More than 1,000 recruits deserted or fled the battlefield and had to be rescued by U.S. troops and airpower, with a ceasefire brokered by Iran.

Meanwhile, the country that Bush still insisted was the front line in the "war on terror" lay in shambles, along with the lives of twenty-five million citizens.

SECRETARY OF DEFENSE DONALD RUMSFELD WEATHERED A STORM OF CRITICISM ON IRAQ POLICY, BUT FINALLY RESIGNED IN NOVEMBER 2006.

Except for the Kurdish-held north and the "Green Zone" headquarters of the coalition, no part of the embattled nation could be considered secure. (Later, in the spring of 2008, incessant rocket attacks shattered the supposed safety of the Green Zone.) Cities cleared of resistance by coalition offensives frequently fell back into chaos when the troops moved on. Historic Baghdad, the fabled city of flying carpets and Arabian Nights, was a nightmare of suicide bombing, IEDs, and ruins, with one million impoverished residents in "Sadr City," a Shiite enclave and a law unto itself.

More than one and a half million Iraqis, by official estimate, had fled, most of them huddled in squalid quarters in the unwelcoming cities of neighboring Jordan and Syria. Another estimated two million were displaced within the country, fleeing wrecked homes to crowd in with relatives or live in makeshift tent villages. Much of the educated population of what had once been the most developed country in the Middle East had decamped, including 12,000 of the country's 34,000 physicians. Living conditions for those remaining were abysmal. Whole neighborhoods were without adequate sewage or water.

In July 2007, U.S. Ambassador Ryan Crocker told Congress that most Iraqi cities had electricity only one to two hours a day. On the fifth anniversary of the war, the nation's electric grid was still producing less than 5,000 daily megawatts of power, less than when the war started. Iraqis faced a scorching summer when 11,000 megawatts would be the daily minimum. In oil-rich Iraq, oil to power generating plants was in short supply. The bulk of it was being shipped abroad, the Iraqi government's only source of revenue. And an estimated 35 percent of the population was unemployed.

The repeatedly fought-over city of Falluja, west of Baghdad, was a classic example of the war's devastation. Once a thriving city of 450,000, its surviving population was estimated in 2007 at fewer than 50,000. Eighty percent of the buildings had been damaged in the fighting; half of them were completely destroyed. Half of the homes were gone. Those that remained were largely without water, electricity, or sewage. There were no operating schools. Buildings had been stripped by looters, including floor tiles and window frames. Once Falluja had been known as "the city of mosques," with more than 200 glittering temples of worship. Only 60 remained intact.

The estimates of "collateral damage"—the Pentagon euphemism for civilian and noncombatant casualties—varied wildly. In 2007, the Iraqi Ministry of Health gave a low figure of 151,000 Iraqis killed from war-related causes between February 2003 and June 2006. A survey published in the British medical journal *Lancet* estimated 600,000 "excess" deaths—those above the normal attrition of population—for the period 2003–2006. An Opinion Research Bureau report estimated the war had caused 946,000 to 1,033,000 violent deaths. In one survey, researchers asked individual Iraqis if they had a civilian relative or friend who had been a war casualty. Eighty percent of those interviewed said yes.

One unlamented casualty was Hussein. After a tumultuous trial marked by raucous shouting at the judges of the special tribunal, the onetime strong man was unceremoniously hanged for "crimes against humanity" on December 30, 2006. Reactions predictably ranged from cheering to anger.

And yet the fighting went on. And on.

In December 2005, Bush at last admitted that some intelligence on which the war had been fought was "wrong." But so what? Bush insisted that the war was worthwhile and the decision to bring down Hussein was "the right thing to do." He would have made the same decision even if he had known more. Powell, the obedient soldier, kept silent while writing his memoirs and giving motivational speeches. But in 2007, he finally apologized for the United Nations speech. "The intelligence I was given turned out to be inaccurate," he told Barbara Walters. "That will always remain a blot on my record."

THE HISTORIC RECORD
In 1971, Henry Kissinger asked Chinese foreign minister Zhou En-lai the historical impact of the French Revolution of 1789. "Too soon to tell," En-lai responded.

In the lame duck months of Bush's presidency, in the midst of an election campaign, and with his popularity ratings cratering, by En-lai's reckoning, it is at least 200 years too soon to assess Bush's impact on history, and especially the Iraq invasion.

But writers, historians, politicians, office-seekers, and the world are trying already to size up the eight Bush years. Some contend that Bush is simply "an amiable dunce" (as Clark Clifford dubbed Ronald Reagan), readily manipulated by Vice President Cheney, former Secretary Rumsfeld, and his political Svengali Karl Rove. They say Bush is a president out of the loop, whose priorities were cutting brush on his ranch in Crawford, Texas, and getting a good night's sleep. Many Europeans share that view and believe Bush has destroyed the world's trust in the United States—trust that will take decades to rebuild. Others regard the Bush administration as visionary—the first to recognize an impending "clash of civilizations," and begin to prepare America for it. And meanwhile, to fight a preemptive war before the terrorist enemy got stronger.

How will the decision to invade Iraq be judged 50, 100, 200 years from now? How will Bush's record be written in the twenty-third century? Where is Zhou En-lai when we need him?

★ ★ ★

SUGGESTED READING

The authors recommend the following books and articles for further accounts of the subjects of the chapters.

CHAPTER 1: GEORGE WASHINGTON: THE WHISKEY REBELLION

Hunt, John Gabriel. *The Dissenters: America's Voices of Opposition*. New York: Gramercy, 1993.

Slaughter, Thomas P. *The Whiskey Rebellion: Frontier Epilogue to the American Revolution*.
New York: Oxford University Press, 1983.

CHAPTER 2: JOHN ADAMS: THE ALIEN AND SEDITION ACTS

Miller, John C. *Crisis in Freedom: The Alien and Sedition Acts*. Boston: Little, Brown, 1951.

Stinchcombe, William C. *The XYZ Affair*. Westport, CT: Greenwood Press, 1980.

CHAPTER 3: THOMAS JEFFERSON: THE EMBARGO ACT

Hemenway, Abby Maria. *The Vermont Historical Gazetteer: A Magazine Embracing the History of Each Town*. Volume II. 1871.

Lawson, John D. *American State Trials: A Collection of the Important and Interesting Criminal Trails which have taken place in the United States, from the beginning of our Government to the Present Day*. F. H. Thomas Law Book Co., 1915.

Randall, Willard Sterne. *Thomas Jefferson: A Life*. New York: HarperPerennial, 1994.

Spivak, Burton. *Jefferson's English Crisis: Commerce, Embargo, and the Republican Revolution*. Charlottesville, VA: University Press of Virginia, 1979.

Wolford, Thorp Lanier. "Democratic-Republican Reaction in Massachusetts to the Embargo of 1807." *The New England Quarterly*, March 1942.

CHAPTER 4: JAMES MADISON: THE WAR OF 1812

Hickey, Donald R. *The War of 1812: A Short History*. Urbana, IL: University of Illinois Press, 1995.

Mahon, John K. *The War of 1812*. New York: Da Capo, 1972.

Pickles, Tim. *New Orleans 1815: Andrew Jackson Crushes the British*. Westport, CT: Praeger, 2004.

Pitch, Anthony. *The Burning of Washington: The British Invasion of 1814*. Annapolis, MD: Naval Institute Press, 1998.

CHAPTER 5: ANDREW JACKSON: THE TRAIL OF TEARS

Hill, Sarah H. *Cherokee Removal: Forts Along the Georgia Trail of Tears*. Washington, D.C., and Atlanta: United States National Park Service with the Georgia Department of Natural Resources, Historic Preservation Division, 2005.

Perdue, Theda, and Michael D. Green. *The Cherokee Nation and the Trail of Tears*. New York: Viking, 2007.

Remini, Robert V. *Andrew Jackson and His Indian Wars*. New York: Viking, 2001.

Rozema, Vicki. *Voices from the Trail of Tears*. Winston-Salem, NC: John Blair, 2003.

CHAPTER 6: FRANKLIN PIERCE: REPEAL OF THE MISSOURI COMPROMISE

Freehling, William W. *The Road to Disunion: Secessionists at Bay 1776–1854*. New York: Oxford University Press, 1990.

McPherson, James M. *Battle Cry of Freedom: The Civil War Era*. New York: Ballantine, 1988.

Nichols, Roy Franklin. *Franklin Pierce: Young Hickory of the Granite Hills*. Philadelphia: University of Pennsylvania Press, 1958.

Oates, Stephen B. *To Purge This Land with Blood: A Biography of John Brown*. New York: Harper & Row, 1970.

Rawley, James A. *Race & Politics: "Bleeding Kansas" and the Coming of the Civil War*. Philadelphia: J. B. Lippincott, 1969.

CHAPTER 7: ULYSSES S. GRANT: THE ATTEMPT TO ANNEX SANTO DOMINGO

Foner, Eric. *Reconstruction: America's Unfinished Revolution, 1863–1877.*
New York: Harper & Row, 1988.

McFeely, William S. *Grant: A Biography.* New York: Norton, 1981.

Pham, John-Peter. *Liberia: Portrait of a Failed State.* Reed Press, 2004.

Tansill, Charles Callan. *The United States and Santo Domingo, 1798–1873: A
Chapter in Caribbean Diplomacy.* Baltimore: Johns Hopkins Press, 1938.

CHAPTER 8: GROVER CLEVELAND: THE PULLMAN STRIKE

Andrews, Elisha Benjamin. *The United States in Our Own Time (1870-1903).*
New York: C. Scribner's Sons, 1903, pp. 719–731.

Arlington National Cemetery website. "Nelson Appleton Miles, Lieutenant
General, United States Army" (short essay and photographs).

Bassett, Jonathon. "The Pullman Strike of 1894." *OAH Magazine of History*,
Volume 11, number 2, Winter 1997.

Brendel, Martina. "The Pullman Strike." *Illinois History Magazine*, Northern
Illinois University Libraries, December 1994.

Britannica Concise. "Pullman, George M.," biography.

Cleveland, Grover, and Albert Ellery Bergh. *Addresses, State Papers and Letters.*
New York: The Sundial Classics Co., 1908, pp. 432–436.

Debs, Eugene. *The Federal Government and the Pullman Strike.* Eugene Debs's
reply to Grover Cleveland's *McClure's* magazine July 1904 article, by
Eugene V. Debs, privately published on July 7, 1904, in *Appeal to Reason*
[Girard, KS], whole no. 456 (Aug. 27, 1904), pp. 1–2.

Friedman, Michael Jay. "Labor Day Marks Appreciation of U.S. Workers."
The Washington File, a product of the Bureau of International
Information Programs, U.S. Department of State.

Lloyd, Caro. *Henry Demarest Lloyd, 1847–1903, a Biography.* New York:
Putnam, 1912, pp. 144–147.

Miles, Nelson Appleton. *Serving the Republic: Memoirs of the Civil and
Military Life of Nelson A. Miles, Lieutenant-General, United States Army.*
New York: Harper & Bros, 1911, pp. 251–258.

Muzzey, David Saville. *Readings in American History.* Boston: Ginn and Co,
1921, pp 526–533.

New York Times. "The Secretary of War, Daniel Lamont" (reprinted from the
New-Orleans *Times-Democrat*), September 28, 1895.

Paxson, Frederic L. *Recent History of the United States.* Boston: Houghton
Mifflin Co., 1921, pp. 177–181.

Ridpath, John Clark, Henri F. Klein, Winfred Trexler Root, Harry Elmer
Barnes, and George Morton Churchill. *Ridpath's History of the World;
Being an Account of the Principal Events in the Career of the Human Race
from the Beginnings of Civilization to the Present Time, Comprising the
Development of Social Institutions and the Story of All Nations from Recent
and Authentic Sources.* Cincinnati: Ridpath Historical Society, 1936, pp.
222–224.

Schofield, John McAllister. *Forty-Six Years in the Army.* Norman, ok:
University of Oklahoma Press, 1998, pp. 492–513.

Swinton, John. *Striking for Life: Labor's Side of the Labor Question; the Right of
the Workingman to a Fair Living.* American Manufacturing and Pub. Co,
1894, pp. 80–101.

Weyforth, William O. *The Organizability of Labor.* Baltimore: Johns Hopkins
Press, 1917, pp. 216–218.

Wilson, Frederick T. *Federal Aid in Domestic Disturbances, 1787-1903.* New
York: Arno Press, 1969, pp. 228–238.

CHAPTER 9: WILLIAM MCKINLEY: "A SPLENDID LITTLE WAR" WITH SPAIN

Agoncillo, Teodoro. *A Short History of the Philippines.* New York and Toronto:
New American Library, 1969.

Bain, David Haward. *Sitting in Darkness: Americans in the Philippines.* Boston:
Houghton Mifflin Co., 1984.

Constantino, Renato, and Letizia R. Constantino. *The Philippines: The
Continuing Past.* Quezon City, Philippines: The Foundation for
Nationalist Studies, 1978.

Gleeck Jr., Lewis E. *The American Half-Century (1898–1946).* Quezon City,
Philippines: New Day Press, 1998.

Guerrero, Leon Ma. *The First Filipino: A Biography of Jose Rizal.* Quezon
City, Philippines: New Day Press, 1998.

Karnow, Stanley. *In Our Image: America's Empire in the Philippines.* New York:
Random House, 1989.

Leech, Margaret. *In the Days of McKinley.* New York: Harper and Brothers,
1959.

Linn, Brian McAllister. *The Philippine War, 1899–1902.* Lawrence, Kansas:
The University Press of Kansas, 2000.

Miller, Stuart Creighton. *"Benevolent Assimilation": The American Conquest of
the Philippines.*
New Haven and London: Yale University Press, 1982.

Musicant, Ivan. *Empire by Default.* New York: Henry Holt & Co., 1998.

CHAPTER 10: WOODROW WILSON: THE PUNITIVE EXPEDITION INTO MEXICO

Ambrosius, Lloyd E. "Wilson, Woodrow." *American National Biography*. February 2000.

Blakeslee, George Hubbard, and G. Stanley Hall. *The Journal of Race Development*. Millwood, NY: Kraus Reprint Co., 1910, pp. 1–13.

Brooks, Eugene Clyde, and Woodrow Wilson. *Woodrow Wilson as President*. Chicago: Row, Peterson and Company, 1916, pp. 229–251.

Dodd, William Edward. *Woodrow Wilson and His Work*. New York: P. Smith, 1932, pp. 146–162.

Elser, Frank. "Our Troops Kill Villa's Chief Aide." *New York Times*, May 27, 1916.

Encyclopedia of World History, The. "Relations with Mexico." 2001.

House, Col. E.M. "Is It a Scrap of Paper?" *New York Times*, February 27, 1916.

Information Annual ... A Continuous Cyclopedia and Digest of Current Events. 1915-16. New York: R. R. Bowker Company [etc.], 1916, pp. 382–387.

Lawrence, David. *The Truth About Mexico; Being a Bird's Eye View of Political, Social, and Economic Conditions, Together with an Analysis of Past American Policy and a Suggestion for the Future—Based on a Tour of Observation in Mexico, November–December, 1916*. New York: New York Evening Post Co., 1917, pp. 10–13.

New York Times. "Carranza Government Says It Will Hunt Villa Down," March 10, 1916.

New York Times. "House Debates Villa Raid," Special to the *Times*, March 10, 1916.

New York Times. "Killed 30 Carranzistas," March 10, 1916.

New York Times. "Night Attack on Border," March 10, 1916.

New York Times. "Roosevelt Bitterly Attacks Wilson," November 4, 1916.

New York Times. "Villa Alive or Dead," Special from the *New York World*, March 10, 1916.

New York Times. "Woman Held by Villa Nine Days Tells Story of Mexican Raid." March 10, 1916.

New York Times. "Woodrow Wilson's Administration: Eight Years of the World's Greatest History," February 27, 1921.

New York Times Current History, The. New York: The New York Times Co, 1915, pp. 617–619.

Perkins, George W. "Perkins Arraigns Wilson." *New York Times*, March 10, 1916.

Robinson, Edgar Eugene, and Victor J. West. *The Foreign Policy of Woodrow Wilson, 1913–1917.* New York: Macmillan Co., 1917, pp. 209–211.

Tuck, Jim. "Villa, Pancho." *American National Biography.* February 2000.

Tumulty, Joseph P. *Woodrow Wilson as I Know Him.* Garden City, NY: Doubleday, Page & Co., 1921, pp. 144–161.

United States and Albert Bushnell Hart. *Selected Addresses and Public Papers of Woodrow Wilson.* New York: Boni and Liveright, Inc., 1918, pp. 105–111.

Vandiver, Frank E. "Pershing, John Joseph." In *American National Biography.* February 2000.

CHAPTER 12: HERBERT HOOVER: THE BONUS ARMY

Hoover, Herbert. *The Memoirs of Herbert Hoover: 1929–1941, The Great Depression.* New York: Macmillan, 1952.

Kingseed, Wyatt. "The 'Bonus Amy' War in Washington," *American History* magazine. June 2004.

Manchester, William. *The Glory and the Dream: A Narrative History of America, 1932–1972.* Boston: Little, Brown, 1973.

CHAPTER 12: FRANKLIN D. ROOSEVELT: THE INTERNMENT OF JAPANESE AMERICANS IN WORLD WAR II

Daniels, Roger. *Prisoners Without Trial: Japanese Americans in World War II.* New York: Hill & Wang, 1993.

Harth, Erica, ed. *Last Witnesses: Reflections on the Wartime Internment of Japanese Americans.* New York: Palgrave, 2001. See in particular John Y. Tateishi, "Memories from Behind Barbed Wire," pp. 129–151.

Manchester, William. *The Glory and the Dream: A Narrative History of America, 1932–1972.* Boston: Little, Brown, 1974.

Smith, Jean Edward. *FDR.* New York: Random House, 2007.

CHAPTER 13: JOHN F. KENNEDY: THE BAY OF PIGS INVASION

Johnson, Haynes Bonner. *The Bay of Pigs: The Leaders' Story of Brigade 2506.* New York: Norton, 1964.

Kornbluh, Peter. *Bay of Pigs Declassified: The Secret CIA Report on the Invasion of Cuba.* New York: The New Press, 1998.

CHAPTER 14: LYNDON B. JOHNSON: THE TONKIN GULF RESOLUTION

Barrett, David M, ed. *Lyndon B. Johnson's Vietnam Papers: A Documentary Collection*. College Station, TX: Texas A&M University Press, 1997.

Department of State Bulletin, August 24, 1964. "American Experience, the Presidents." 2002–2003.

Director of National Intelligence. *Special National Intelligence Report*. May 25, 1964 (declassified on June 8, 2004), part of the massive LBJ Library.

Eighty-eighth Congress of the United States of America, 2d session, transcript of Tonkin Gulf Resolution (1964).

Galloway, John. *The Gulf of Tonkin Resolution*. Rutherford: Farleigh Dickinson University Press, 1970.

Herring, George C. *America's Longest War: The United States and Vietnam, 1950–1975*. New York: McGraw-Hill, 1986, pp. 121.

Marolda, Edward J. "Summary of the Tonkin Gulf Crisis, August 1964." July 13, 2005.

McNamara, Robert S., James G. Blight, and Robert K. Brightam. *Argument Without End: In Search of Answers to the Vietnam Tragedy*. New York: Public Affairs, 1999.

McNamara, Robert S., with Brian VanDeMark. *In Retrospect: The Tragedy and Lessons of Vietnam*. New York: Random House, 1995, pp. 127–143.

Public Papers of the Presidents of the United States: Lyndon B. Johnson, Containing the Public Messages, Speeches, and Statements of the President 1963–64. volume 2. Washington, D.C.: United States Government Printing Office, 1965.

Time. "Action in Tonkin Gulf," August 14, 1964.

U.S. Congress, Senate, Committee on Foreign Relations. *Background Information Relating to Southeast Asia and Vietnam*. Fourth rev. ed. 90th Cong., 2d sess., March 1968, pp. 135–141 and 144–145.

U.S. Congress, Senate, Committee on Foreign Relations. *The Gulf of Tonkin, the 1964 Incidents*. Two parts. February 20, 1968, which includes statements by Robert McNamara, Secretary of Defense; General Earle Wheeler, Chairman, Joint Chiefs of Staff; and Captain H. Sweitzer, USN, military assistant to the Chairman, Joint Chiefs of Staff; etc.

CHAPTER 15: RICHARD NIXON: THE BOMBING OF CAMBODIA

Barrett, Nicole. "Holding Individual Leaders Responsible for Violations of Customary International Law: The U.S. Bombardment of Cambodia and Laos." *Columbia Human Rights Law Review*, 2001.

Clymer, Kenton J. *The United States and Cambodia: 1969–2000.* London: Routledge, 2004.

Dobbs, Michael. "Haig Said Nixon Joked of Nuking Hill." *Washington Post*, May 27, 2004, p. A9.

Hersh, Seymour. *The Price of Power: Kissinger in the Nixon White House.* New York: Summit Books, 1984.

Kissinger, Henry. *Ending the Vietnam War: A History of America's Involvement in and Extrication from the Vietnam War.* New York: Simon & Schuster, 2003.

Tucker, Spencer C. *Encyclopedia of the Vietnam War: A Political, Social, and Military History.* Santa Barbara: ABC-CLIO, Inc., 1998.

CHAPTER 16: RICHARD NIXON: WATERGATE

Bernstein, Carl, and Bob Woodward. *All the President's Men.* New York: Simon and Schuster, 1974.

Broder, David. "Nixon Wins with 290 Electoral Votes; Humphrey Joins Him in Call for Unity." *Washington Post*, November 7, 1968.

Caddy, Douglas. "Did Gay Bashing by the Prosecutors Cause the Watergate Cover-Up?" *The Advocate*, August 1, 2005.

Caddy, Douglas. *The Hundred Million Dollar Payoff.* New Rochelle, NY: Arlington House, 1974.

Feldstein, Mark. "Watergate Revisited," *American Journalism Review*, August/September 2004.

Hudson, Mike. "Our 'Deep Throat': Gay Lawyer Douglas Caddy Was the Original Lawyer for the Watergate Burglars …" *The Advocate*, August 16, 2005.

Hunt, E. Howard, and Greg Aunapu. *American Spy: My Secret History in the CIA, Watergate, and Beyond.* Hoboken, NJ: John Wiley & Sons, 2007, pp. 232–251.

Kilpatrick, Carroll. "Nixon Tells Editors, 'I'm Not a Crook,'" *Washington Post*, November 18, 1973.

Lewis, Alfred. "5 Held in Plot to Bug Democrat's Office Here." *Washington Post.* June 18, 1972.

Liddy, G. Gordon. *Will: The Autobiography of G. Gordon Liddy.* New York: St. Martin's Press, 1980, pp. 246–253.

Mitchell, Greg. *Tricky Dick and the Pink Lady: Richard Nixon Vs. Helen Gahagan Douglas—Sexual Politics and the Red Scare, 1950.* New York: Random House, 1998.

Reichard, Gary. "Watergate." In *The Oxford Companion to the United States History.* 2001.

Shepard, Alicia C. *Woodward and Bernstein: Life in the Shadow of Watergate.* Hoboken, NJ: J. Wiley, 2007, pp. 31–48.

U.S. Government Memorandum. "From C.W. Bates to Bolz," June 22, 1972.

U.S. Government Memorandum. "From W. Mark Felt to The Acting Director [FBI]," June 19, 1972.

U.S. Government Memorandum. "From W. Mark Felt to [FBI] Director," June 21, 1972.

Woodward, Bob. *The Secret Man.* New York: Simon & Schuster, 2005, pp. 53–56.

CHAPTER 17: JIMMY CARTER: THE IRANIAN HOSTAGE CRISIS

Bill, James A. "Iran and the Crisis of '78." *Foreign Affairs,* Winter 1978–79.

Bowden, Mark. *Guests of the Ayatollah: The First Battle in America's War with Militant Islam.* New York: Atlantic Monthly Press, 2006.

Carter, Jimmy. *Keeping the Faith.* New York: Bantam Books, 1982.

Gaillard, Frye. *Prophet from Plains: Jimmy Carter and His Legacy.* Athens, GA: University of Georgia Press, 2007.

Graubard, Steven. *Command of Office: How War, Secrecy, and Deception Transformed the Presidency, from Theodore Roosevelt to George W. Bush.* New York: Perseus Books Group, 2006.

Jackson, David. "SAVAK: Like the CIA." *Time,* February 19, 1979.

Jordon, Hamilton. *Crisis: The Last Years of the Carter Presidency.* New York: G. P. Putnam's Sons, 1982.

Ledeen, Michael, and William Lewis. *Debacle: The American Failure in Iran.* New York: Alfred A. Knopf, 1981.

CHAPTER 18: JIMMY CARTER: THE ENERGY CRISIS AND "MALAISE"

Biven, Carl W. *Jimmy Carter's Economy: Policy in an Age of Limits.* Chapel Hill: University of North Carolina Press, 2002.

Clymer, Adam. "Politicians Divided Along Party Lines Over the President's Energy Address." *New York Times,* July 17, 1979.

Clymer, Adam. "Republicans Call Energy Speech Political and Vague."
    New York Times, July 16, 1979.

Gaillard, Frye. *Prophet from Plains: Jimmy Carter and His Legacy.* Athens:
    University of Georgia Press, 2007.

New York Times. "Mr. Carter's Certain Trumpet," April 20, 1977.

Patterson, James T. *Restless Giant: The United States from Watergate to Bush v.
    Gore.* New York: Oxford University Press, 2005.

Perlmutter, Emanuel. "Harried Drivers Lose Tempers." *New York Times,*
    December 30, 1973.

Time. "The Master of the Maze," November, 7, 1977.

Weaver, Warren Jr. "The Turning Point?" *New York Times,* July 15, 1979.

CHAPTER 19: RONALD REAGAN: THE IRAN-CONTRA AFFAIR

"Iran-Contra: White House e-mail." Six White House e-mails from Oliver
    North and Robert McFarlane to John Poindexter, retrieved by FBI and
    Tower Commission investigators. CNN Interactive.
    www.cnn.com/SPECIALS/cold.war/episodes/18/archive

Kelley, Kitty. *The Family: The Real Story of the Bush Dynasty.* New York:
    Doubleday, 2004.

Marshall, Jonathan, Peter Dale Scott, and Jane Hunter. *The Iran-Contra
    Connection: Secret Teams and Covert Operations in the Reagan Era.* Boston:
    South End Press, 1987.

Phillips, Kevin. *American Dynasty: Aristocracy, Fortune, and the Politics of Deceit
    in the House of Bush.* New York: Viking, 2004.

Shultz, George P. *Turmoil and Triumph: My Years as Secretary of State.* New
    York: Charles Scribner's Sons, 1993.

Sick, Gary. *October Surprise: America's Hostages in Iran and the Election of
    Ronald Reagan.* New York: Times Books, 1991.

Stiglitz, Joseph E. and Linda J. Bilmes. *The Three Trillion Dollar War: The
    True Cost of the Iraq Conflict.* New York: W. W. Norton, 2008.

Tower, John. *The Tower Commission Report: The Full Text of the President's
    Special Review Board.* New York: Bantam, 1987.

Walsh, Lawrence E. *Firewall: The Iran-Contra Conspiracy and Cover-Up.* New
    York: W. W. Norton, 1997.

Walsh, Lawrence E., Independent Counsel. *Final Report of the Independent
    Counsel for Iran/Contra Matters.* Washington, D.C. 1993.

CHAPTER 20: GEORGE W. BUSH: THE IRAQ WAR

Berman, Paul, *Terror and Liberalism*. New York: W.W. Norton, 2005.

Chandrasekaran, Rajiv. *Imperial Life in the Emerald City*. New York: Alfred Knopf, 2006.

Cockbrun, Andrew. *Rumsfeld: His Rise, Fall, and Catastrophic Legacy*. New York: Scribner, 2008.

DeYoung, Karen. *Soldier: The Life of Colin Powell*. New York: Alfred Knopf, 2006.

Draper, Robert W., Dead Certain. New York: Free Press, 2007.

Hare, David, Stuff Happens. New York: Faber & Faber, 2005.

Isikoff, Michael and David Corn. *Hubris: The Inside Story of Spin, Scandal and Selling of the Iraq War*. New York: Crown, 2006.

Woodward, Bob, *State of Denial*. New York: Simon & Schuster, 2006.

Wilson, Valerie Plame. *Fair Game*. New York: Simon & Schuster, 2006.

ACKNOWLEDGMENTS

My sincere thanks to my coauthors, Robert Schnakenberg, Matthew Phelps, Mark LaFlaur, and Edwin Kiester. Mark also doubled as the editor: His critiques were unfailing fair, and his suggestions improved the final product. Some of the episodes recounted here will come as a surprise to readers—for that I have to thank Ed Kiester, a walking encyclopedia of presidential history. Jennifer Reich was a wonderful copyeditor who watched for any inconsistencies in the narrative while keeping an eye on the nitty-gritty details of grammar and punctuation. And finally, my thanks to Will Kiester—a great friend and an inspired publisher.

★ ★ ★

ABOUT THE AUTHORS

THOMAS J. CRAUGHWELL is the author of more than a dozen books, most recently *How the Barbarian Invasion Shaped the Modern World*, *Stealing Lincoln's Body*, and *Saints Behaving Badly*. He has written articles on history, religion, politics, and popular culture for the *Wall Street Journal*, the *American Spectator*, and *U.S. News & World Report*. He lives in Bethel, Connecticut.

Journalist, lecturer and young historian M. WILLIAM PHELPS is the author of eleven books, including his most recent *Nathan Hale: The Life and Death of America's First Spy* (Thomas Dunne Books, 2008). He lives in a small Connecticut farming community with his wife, three children, and Labrador.

★ ★ ★

PHOTO CREDITS

★ ★ ★

INDEX